Shorter Philosophical Poems of
Narayana Guru

Shorter Philosophical Poems of

NARAYANA GURU

•Brahmavidyā Pañcakam •Advaita Dīpikā
•Aṛivu •Homa Mantram •Daiva Daśakam

Translation with Extensive Commentary

by

Swami Muni Narayana Prasad

D.K. Printworld (P) Ltd.
New Delhi

Cataloging in Publication Data — DK
[Courtesy: D.K. Agencies (P) Ltd. <docinfo@dkagencies.com>]

Narayana Prasad, *Muni,* 1938-
Shorter philosophical poems of Narayana Guru : Brahmavidyā pañcakam, Advaita dīpikā, Aṛivu, Homa Mantram, Daiva daśakam / translation with extensive commentary by Swami Muni Narayana Prasad.
p. cm.
Text in Sanskrit (Devanagari and roman); translation, commentary and introductory matter in English.
Includes index.
ISBN 13: 9788124605158 (PB) ISBN 10: 8124605157

1. Narayana Guru, 1856-1928. 2. Advaita. 3. Philosophy, Hindu. I. Narayana Guru, 1856-1928. Selections. English & Sanskrit. II. Title.

DDC 181.4 22

First published in India, 2010

ISBN 13: 978-81-246-0515-8 (PB) ISBN 10: 81-246-0515-7

Published and printed by:
D.K. Printworld (P) Ltd.
Regd. office : *'Srikunj'*, F-52, Bali Nagar
Ramesh Nagar Metro Station
New Delhi – 110 015
Phones : (011) 2545 3975; 2546 6019; *Fax* : (011) 2546 5926
E-mail: indology@dkprintworld.com
Web: www.dkprintworld.com

Preface

NARAYANA GURU is mostly known in India for his activities for the upliftment of the socially downtrodden, especially the oppressed class. In truth, his concern was not merely for the downtrodden, but for the human race as a whole. This concern of his was not as an active humanist, but as an enlightened seer who was the embodiment of the Upaniṣadic wisdom. The clarity of his vision of Reality was such that he could revalue and restate that wisdom making it comprehensible to the mindset of the Age of Science. The oneness of Reality is what this wisdom reveals. A seer of this Reality cannot but perceive the human race as of one species, and all humans as equals. Any inequality among humans, then, based on caste, social status or other prejudices, is unjustifiable. He therefore stood against all such discriminations, and thus could be seen as working for the cause of the downtrodden. Of course, the people belonging to the lowest stratum of the society benefited much from the Guru. This should not belittle the sublimity of the wisdom he taught directly to his closest disciples, and put on record in his sixty philosophical poems.

An English translation of the complete works of Narayana Guru was recently published by the National Book Trust, India. He gives precise expression to his philosophical vision in his major works *Ātmopadeśa Śatakam* (One Hundred Verses of Self-Instruction), *Darśanamālā* (Garland of Visions), *Vedānta-Sūtras* and in the five shorter works commented on in this volume. The commentaries on these major works have already been published by Messrs D.K. Printworld, New Delhi. Another book, summarizing the Guru's philosophy entitled *The Philosophy of*

Narayana Guru, has also been brought out by them. With the publication of the present volume, commentaries on all the philosophical works of Narayana Guru have now become available in English. What remains to be published are the same kind of commentaries on his highly poetical hymns that also contain sublime philosophical insight. Though the commentaries on these works are already available in the Malayalam language, I feel doubtful how far I'll be able to render all of these into English. It seems therefore better for me to leave it for others to do. Having been able to translate and publish all the original works into English makes me fully satisfied.

As a long time friend of the Gurukula, Dr Peter Oppenheimer took much pain to go through these commentaries, carefully editing them.

Messrs D.K. Printworld have shown much interest in bringing out these commentaries, along with ones on the Upaniṣads and the *Bhagavad-Gītā*, and some other important works. I appreciate their sticking to the idea of publishing scholarly works alone. I wish their endeavour the best.

It is the philosophical insight given by Nataraja Guru, the wisdom-successor of Narayana Guru, and also by his successor and my predecessor in the Narayana Gurukula heirarchy, Guru Nitya Chaitanya Yati, that helped me muster the courage to write these commentaries. By prostrating at the feet of these direct *gurus* and above all of Narayana Guru, I offer these commentaries as my flowers of worship.

Varkala **Swami Muni Narayana Prasad**
13 January 2010

Contents

Introduction

Narayana Guru was a philosopher-saint who lived in the modern State of Kerala in South India. He was also a formidable inspiration behind the social revolution that Kerala underwent in the first half of the twentieth century.

After his higher education in Sanskrit, he left home and walked all over South India as a seeker, leading the pattern of life of a wandering mendicant. This stage of life came to an end as he began his intense process of seeking the Self, undergoing intense disciplines of meditative austerity (*tapas*), in a cave at the top of a hill called Maruttvāmala near Kanyākumārī at the tail-end of the Western Ghats. Later he moved to a cave at Aruvippuṛam on the banks of the river Neyyār, about 70 km north of Maruttvāmala. He attained enlightenment, as is presumed, when he was at Aruvippuṛam. Even though he began his literary career as early as his studenthood days, his most important philosophical work *Ātmopadeśa Śatakam* (One Hundred Verses of Self-Instruction) was composed at Aruvippuṛam. A description of enlightenment in the above work and quoted below must be considered as an exposition of his own mystical experience:

> Like ten thousand suns rising all at once
> Dawns the discriminative enlightenment.
> That really is the original sun that cuts through
> The ephemeral *māyā*-darkness that puts a veil
> Over the pure and unconditioned Consciousness.
>
> — v. 35

He founded an *āśrama* at Aruvippuṛam and installed a Śiva temple there in total disregard of the prevailing religious custom that brāhmaṇas alone were entitled to perform such a rite. It was the strength of his wisdom that made him bold enough to do so. Later he established *āśrama*s at Varkala and Aluva also. Varkala, in course of time, became the centre of the spiritual movement initiated by him.

Inspired by his daringness to install a temple-deity, people all over South India approached him with demands for more such temples at numerous places. He readily complied with their wishes and the outcome was the coming into being of nearly eighty temples, all allowing everyone to enter. The existing orthodox temples allowed only caste-Hindus to enter the temple and offer worship. In some cases he wrote hymns praising the deity of the temple, as a method of instruction on how people should understand that particular deity, and idol-worship in general.

His uncompromising stand against casteism, and the bold messages he gave to his followers, resulted in a social transformation of long-standing effect, particularly in the state of Kerala. He also influenced the National Freedom Movement that was at its peak at that time, through the correction he gave to the caste-concepts of Mahatma Gandhi during one of the Mahatma's visits to the Guru.

All these social transformations were a sort of applied aspect or rather a reflection of his philosophy of oneness, in human affairs. He thought that philosophy must ensure happiness to a person in his/her personal and social life, and must be made use of to do away with all that is wrong in life.

Though avowedly a follower of Śaṅkara's Advaita philosophy, he was not simply restating what Śaṅkara and his followers said on Vedānta. He did not write any commentary on the canonical texts of Vedānta — the Upaniṣads, *Bhagavad-Gītā* and *Brahma-Sūtras*, — as Śaṅkara did. Instead, he wrote original works on Vedānta as profound as the Upaniṣads and as precise as modern textbooks on sciences. He wrote even a new text named the *Vedānta-Sūtras*. Narayana Guru's contribution, thus, was a revalued restatement of non-dualism.

The Guru, in re-presenting Vedānta with such a new tone, instead of resorting to traditional methods, adopted his own new ones that could accommodate the modern minds of the Age of Science, while not compromising the originality and purity of the mystical content of the philosophical visions the Upaniṣads portray. The strictness of philosophical speculation, the precision natural to the Age of Science, and the sublimity of mystical vision — all these could be seen in harmony in the Guru's philosophy, each forming a formidable prop for the others. Here and there we come across certain corrective touches given to Vedānta, and also the avoidance of many subtle epistemological problems arising from cumbersome methods.

His literary works can be classified into five as hymns, philosophical works, works of moral import, translations and prose works. Spread out in three languages — Malayalam, Sanskrit and Tamil — his hymns are thirty-one in number. They praise the deities Vināyaka, Viṣṇu, Śiva, Devī and Subrahmaṇya, all with a poetically sublime touch of non-dualism.

Ātmopadeśa Śatakam (One Hundred Verses of Self-Instruction), *Darśana Mālā* (Garland of Visions), *Brahmavidyā Pañcakam* (The Science of the Absolute in Five Verses), *Advaita Dīpikā* (Lamp of Non-Duality), *Aṛivu* (Consciousness), and *Daiva Daśakam* (Ten Verses Addressed to God — A Universal Prayer) are his philosophical works. His translations are from Sanskrit or Tamil originals to Malayalam — e.g. *Īśa Upaniṣad*, part of *Tirukkuṛal* — and one single verse from Sanskrit to Tamil. All prose works were written in an earlier stage of his life and are reflective of a meditative mood in the Guru.

Of the two major philosophical works, *Ātmopadeśa Śatakam,* originally in Malayalam, was commented on both by Nataraja Guru and his disciple Nitya Chaitanya Yati. The latter actually wrote two commentaries — an extensive one entitled *That Alone — The Core of Wisdom* and the other, a series of meditations on its one hundred verses, under the title *Neither This Nor That . . . But Auṁ,* both published by Messrs D.K. Printworld. The essentials of its philosophy was codified and brought out by the present commentator in the format of a textbook entitled *The Philosophy of Narayana Guru,* published again by D.K. Printworld.

Darśana Mālā, in the Sanskrit language, is written in an idiom familiar to traditional Vedāntins. Yet it adopts a novel method of presentation hitherto uncharted by any philosopher anywhere in the world. This method is that of perceiving and examining the one non-dual Reality from different perspectives in such a way that from each vision the contemplative eye of the seeker could intuitively perceive what the Guru intended to communicate. *Adhyāropa* (Superimposition), *Apavāda* (Methodic Refutation), *Asatya* (Non-existence), *Māyā, Bhāna* (Manifestation of Consciousness), *Karma* (Actions), *Jñāna* (Knowledge), *Bhakti, Yoga* and *Nirvāṇa* are the ten vantage points from which the non-dual Reality is viewed in the ten chapters of this composition.

Nataraja Guru, the wisdom-successor of Narayana Guru, interpreted this work showing it could serve as a firm foundation for formulating a Science of sciences or the Science of the Absolute, in a *magnum opus* which was published in two volumes. Nitya Chaitanya Yati, Nataraja Guru's successor, wrote yet another commentary on it revealing the psychological implications of this work, under the title *Psychology of Darśana Mālā.* The present commentator also wrotea commentary, named *Garland of Visions,* expounding how the Vedāntic non-dual vision becomes revealed in this text. All these commentaries are published by Messrs D.K. Printworld.

The *Vedānta-Sūtras* is the first *sūtra*-text on Vedānta written since the unknown time of the ancient Bādarāyaṇa who wrote the first *Vedānta-Sūtras* or *Brahma-Sūtras*. A major part of this ancient text is set aside to refute other schools of thought and to establish that Advaita (non-dualism) is the philosophy expounded in the Upaniṣads. Narayana Guru, on the other hand, in his modern *sūtra*-text on Vedānta, clearly expounds in 24 simple *sūtra*s (aphorisms) what the essential content of Vedāntic teaching is. Perceiving *Brahman* from the *sat* point of view and the *asat* point of view and showing how both lead us to one and the same conclusion, is the method adopted in this work. A commentary on it written by the present commentator has been published again by Messrs D.K. Printworld.

The present volume is a compilation of commentaries on the five shorter philosophical poems of the Guru, namely *Brahmavidyā Pañcakam* (The Science of the Absolute in Five Verses), *Advaita Dīpikā* (Lamp of Non-duality), *Aṛivu* (Consciousness Examined), *Homa Mantram* (Chants for Oblation in Fire), and *Daiva Daśakam* (Ten Verses Addressed to God — A Universal Prayer).

Brahmavīdyā Pañcakam is a short composition of five verses in the *Śārdūla-vikrīḍitam* metre, written in the traditional style, but with the Guru's new touches of revision. The first verse states the prerequisite qualities of a true seeker, who is a true *guru*, the importance of the rapport between the *guru* and the disciple, and what are the philosophical questions a disciple supposedly asks. The second verse gives the most direct answer to the question in the words, "You are *Brahman* indeed," and how you are not anything else. The next three verses expound in the *guru*'s own way how *Brahman* or oneself is *sat* (Existence) in essence, *cit* or *pratipat* (both meaning "Consciousness") in essence, and *ānanda* (Value experience) in essence repectively.

Advaita Dīpikā is a Malayalam poem in the *Vasantatilakam* metre. In the beginning of its nineteen verses, the Vedāntic doctrine is elucidated in terms of causality, that is to say, that cause alone has real existence and the apparent existence of effects is illusory. Then a question arises: why does the apparent world continue to appear to be real even after one becomes fully convinced of its illusoriness? This problem, raised at the very middle of the composition, is answered in the rest of the poem. It seems, this problem has never been raised by Vedāntins before nor answered tellingly as the Guru does here, shedding more light on the finality of Vedānta.

Aṛivu, a unique composition, is an original contribution of Narayana Guru to world philosophy. The word *aṛivu* means consciousness or knowledge. An important element in the philosophy of Narayana Guru is the special emphasis he gives to the Reality or *Ātmā* being Consciousness in essential content. This peculiarity helps avoid many of the epistemological problems Śaṅkara tries to wade through in various contexts of his commentaries. We have tried to clarify this point in our *The Philosophy of Narayana Guru*.

Written in the *Gīti* metre, its fifteen verses elucidate how everything is but one Consciousness in essence, how you are also the very same Consciousness, and how one unconditioned Consciousness, in its conditioned states, assumes the subjective and objective aspects of appearance, with a strict parity between the two. It could also be said, this work is an exposition of Vedānta as pure epistemology in the strict sense of the term, i.e., the science of consciousness. Nataraja Guru evaluates this work as "a masterpiece of contemplative workmanship unrivalled in literature anywhere."

The Guru composed the *Homa Mantram* on an occasion in which he was visited by Swami Śraddhānanda, then a senior saṁnāysin of the Ārya Samāj. During the visit the Guru and the Swami came to discuss at length the greatness of Vedic fire-sacrifices. In the course of their conversation, the Guru asked, "Why shouldn't we perform such a fire-sacrifice here?" The Swami liked the idea, and so the following morning everything was prepared for the event. But just before the fire-sacrifice was ready to commence, Guru handed the Swami a piece of paper while asking, "Couldn't we perform the *homa* by chanting this *mantra*?" Upon examining the contents scrawled upon the paper, the Swami, to his surprise, found a *mantra* nowhere to be found in the Vedas. That is because it was in fact a new *homa mantra*, composed by the Guru himself. This new *mantra* revealed how the fire-sacrifice itself could be utilized to teach the non-dual Wisdom. By using such an ancient ritual, so deeply imbedded in Indian culture, the Guru showed his talent for wasting no opportunity to teach the Wisdom secret.

Daiva Daśakam, in the *Anuṣṭubh* metre, though in the format of a prayer, contains the entire philosophy of the Guru represented in a poetical idiom. Prayer, in the usual course, is a religious practice; this is no exception. Still it is not possible to limit it to the confines of any particular religion. Rather it is a universal prayer. How it is so, is made amply clear in our commentary. Though not strictly a philosophical work, it is also included in this volume, as it helps the reader form a clear picture of the Guru's philosophy and how he perceives life.

India's wisdom tradition is a hoary one, and time and again it has been restated by various masters of many epochs, systematizing it in different ways, but all clinging to a traditional Indian way of presentation. Restating the same wisdom in modern terms, imbibing fully the spirit of the mindset of the modern Age of Science, is a need of the day. This, to a great extent, we feel, has been accomplished by Narayana Guru. Such a revised restatement of India's wisdom elevates itself to the status of a formidable world philosophy, or a Science of sciences in which physical science and metaphysical science find a common ground. The emergence of such a Science, or rather philosophy, is the need of the age, especially when mankind tends to be strife-ridden either in the name of religion or politics instead of finding their unity. Only the wisdom of the masters of the cadre of Narayana Guru can lend at least a straw of hope to mankind in the days to come. Such resurrection for the world would be possible only if we could reinterpret the hoary wisdom-traditions of mankind in terms comprehensible to the modern Age of Science, cutting across the barriers of nations and religions. Such a restated philosophy would be a science as well. It is with such an aspiration that we present the philosophy of Narayana Guru through our commentaries.

Part I

Brahmavidyā Pañcakam

(The Science of the Absolute in Five Verses)

Introduction

NARAYANA Guru in the present work *Brahmavidyā Pañcakam* (*Brahmavidyā* in Five Verses) condenses the essential content of Vedānta in five verses, originally composed in the *Śārdūlavikrīḍitam* metre. Vedānta as introduced by the Guru here, is not merely meant for a doctrinal understanding. On the other hand, it is about how one can visualize for oneself the Reality that manifests as oneself, how one becomes fully convinced that that Reality in essence is but unconditioned Consciousness, and how the seer of that Reality perceives himself as a functional modulation of It. Seeing this Reality alone as functionally existing even in the minutest of all aspects of life makes one's own life an unbroken stream of Happiness.

This Sanskrit work is named *Brahmavidyā Pañcakam. Pañcakam* means "that which consists of five," and what these verses deal with is *Brahmavidyā* (the science of *Brahman*). The word *Brahman*, translatable as "the Absolute" is derived from the verb root *bṛh* meaning "to grow" (*bṛhi vṛddhau*). The word thus signifies the inconceivable, unconditioned Reality that unfolds Itself incessantly as all the conditioned, conceivable and perceivable forms in all the worlds. The one invisible Reality is poetically imagined as growing into all the multitudinous visible forms. Whatever be the extensiveness we can conceive, it transcends the bounds of all such conceptualizations. That Reality, in essence, is pure Consciousness (*cit*). The nature of this Consciousness-Reality is pictured by Guru in the work called *Aṛivu* (Consciousness) thus:

The being of Consciousness
Is all-inclusive plenitude.
Then, where else can exist
Anything that is not Consciousness?
— v. 4

That is to say, what is supposed to be non-Consciousness also has its being necessarily in Consciousness. Thus nothing outside the plenitude of Consciousness has a being of its own. (See Part III of this volume.) Guru indicates also in this short composition, *Brahmavidyā Pañcakam,* the vastness of this theme, the problems to be solved that arise in it, the method adopted to resolve them, and the validity of such a method, and the like.

Following the traditional manner of the Upaniṣads, this work adopts the format of a dialogue between a *guru* and a *śiṣya*. The method of such an enquiry into Reality is that of the interiorized search for the self, for the being of oneself is the surest of all existent realities. The Reality thus visualized is certain and precise, giving room for no doubt at all. The work thus validates scientific enquiry by the Blissfulness of the philosophical vision of Reality, while revealing the scientific validity of belief in the one Reality or God thus realized.

In this work Guru does not leave unnoticed the problems of ethics, or the natural human curiosity about the state after death. At the same time, he makes quite clear, to what context of thinking or frame of reference *Brahmavidyā* as a science pertains. One of the beliefs well-rooted in the Indian psyche is the theory of *karma*. How far this is acceptable to the Vedāntic perception of life is also clarified by the Guru here.

Text, Translation and Commentary

Verse 1

नित्यानित्यविवेकतो हि नितरां निर्वेदमापद्य सद्-
विद्वानत्र शमादिषट्कलसितः स्यान्मुक्तिकामो भुवि ।
पश्चाद् ब्रह्मविदुत्तमं प्रणतिसेवाद्यैः प्रसन्नं गुरुं
पृच्छेत् कोऽहमिदं कुतो जगदिति स्वामिन् वद त्वं प्रभो ॥

nityānitya-vivekato hi nitarāṁ
nirvedam āpadya sad-
vidvān atra śamādi-ṣaṭka-lasitaḥ
syān-mukti-kāmo bhuvi ।
paścād brahmavid-uttamaṁ praṇati-se-
vādyaiḥ prasannaṁ guruṁ
pṛcchet ko 'ham idaṁ kuto jagad iti
svāmin vada tvaṁ prabho ॥

A well-learned one, because of being naturally
Endowed with the ability to discriminate
The eternal from the transient (aspects of life),
Becomes completely uninterested in the transient.
He, then, having become luminous
By undergoing the six self-imposed disciplines
That begin with *śama*,
Develops the intense desire to attain liberation
While being in this world.
He, then, should properly approach
A best *Brahman*-knowing-*guru*,
And after pleasing him with prostrations and services,

Should ask him, "O Master, who am I?
How was this phenomenal world originated?
Please teach me, O Lord !"

Guru in this first verse makes clear, who is qualified to attain the secret teaching of *Brahmavidyā*, what the vital role of the bipolarity between *guru* and disciple is in the imparting of this wisdom, and what are the fundamental problems *Brahmavidyā* deals with.

While Being in This World (*atra bhuvi*)

Both gaining the wisdom of *Brahmavidyā* and experiencing its ultimate benefit as liberation (*mukti*) are together to be actualized while living in this world. That *mukti* or *mokṣa* is not a state to be experienced hereafter, are indicated by the words *atra bhuvi* (while being in this world) by Guru. The Reality that transcends the realm of apparent becoming, in other words, is to be intuitively perceived as inseparably underlying all phenomenal appearances, and not somewhere else.

A Well-Learned One (*sad-vidvān*)

A well-learned one alone seeks to know *Brahman*. The word *vidvān* means "one who knows everything" (*vetti sarvam iti vidvān*). No dullard usually yearns to know what is ultimately Real in all the fleeting appearances. The urge for perfecting one's own knowledge arises only in someone who already knows something. *Brahmavidyā* is the one science that gives perfection to all the sciences or disciplines of knowledge. Therefore, the well-learned one referred to here has to be a person who knows all that is to be known in this world, but has not yet reached where knowledge attains perfection. Śaṅkara in his *Vivekacūḍāmaṇi* (Crest-jewel of Discrimination) says, a man highly intelligent with a good memory (*medhāvin*), well-learned (*vidvān*), and expert in reflections on the pros and cons (*ūhāpoha-vicakṣaṇaḥ*) is fit to attain wisdom. This learnedness does not necessarily imply acquiring a formal education. Many are those who have become enlightened even while having had no formal education at all.

Discriminating the Eternal from the Transient (*nitya-anitya-viveka*)

The highly intelligent one who is also an expert in reflecting on the pros and cons of the problem concerned, when having an insatiable urge to perfect his knowledge, naturally discriminates what eternally exists from that which is momentary in nature, and what is of eternal value from fleeting values. The word *nitya* means "that which exists always, that which is incessant, and that which is invariable" (*niyatam bhavati iti nityam*). That Reality or Substance which incessantly and invariably manifests Itself as all that is apparent, is what always exists. A *vidvān*, thus, is the one who is capable of discriminating the transient manifest forms from the causal Substance eternally underlying all such forms.

It may be asked, "Is it not knowing the eternal *Brahman* as distinct from the transient appearances that constitutes the essence of this wisdom? Then, is attaining the ultimate aim of *Brahmavidyā* itself the prerequisite for knowing that science?" This discrimination need not necessarily be understood as attaining the perfect knowledge of the eternal Reality or *Brahman*. It signifies rather that the seeker, in the beginning, perceives instinctively the unavoidability that there is an eternal Reality underlying and distinct from all appearances; but becoming convinced of the nature of that Reality, and how It is related to appearences, becomes transparent only at the final stage of his search. *Viveka* means "differentiated knowledge" (*vivicyate iti vivekaḥ*), and *vic*, meaning "to separate," is the verb root from which it is derived (*vicir pṛthag-bhāve*). In fact, discriminating the eternal Reality from transient appearances is not the ultimate goal of *Brahmavidyā*; it rather is realizing the inseparable oneness of eternal *Brahman* and the transient flow of appearances. This realization initially requires discriminating between the two.

This kind of discrimination arises in one naturally, mostly when facing some unexpected crisis in life. It may happen in the case of the learned, as they perceive such crises being faced by others. They ask themselves, "Is there anything of eternal meaning behind all that comes and goes?" Determining that there should be some such Reality and that It should necessarily be beyond all that is ephemeral, is termed *nitya-anitya-viveka*. Śaṅkara defines it as follows in his *Vivekacūḍāmaṇi*:

> The certainty that *Brahman* alone is Real and the changing world is mere appearance, is termed *nitya-anitya-vastu-viveka*.— v. 20

This discrimination, in the case of the one who is capable of reflecting on the pros and cons, happens as a natural course with no incidental cause, and is not something to be accomplished through some spiritual practice. To become endowed with such a nature is beyond the control of anyone, which is why it is often thought that becoming a seeker happens by the will of God.

Becomes Completely Uninterested in the Transient (*nirvedam āpadya*)

What is of lasting interest in life? And what are the fleeting interests that appear and disappear? This discrimination makes one naturally aspire more and more for that which is of lasting interest and become uninterested in anything otherwise. In life, most people value securing physical comforts, establishing respect and position, accumulating money, and the like. But these pursuits do not bring lasting happiness. It is not only that such are fleeting in nature, but very often they eventually end up in suffering. Such an understanding makes you keep your attention withdrawn from such, and aroused to that of lasting value. Of these two aspects, the former is known as *vairāgya* or *virāgatā*. *Rāga* is the passion you feel for pleasurable objects, and the lack of such passion is called *vairāgya*. Śaṅkara defines it as follows in the *Vivekacūḍāmaṇi*:

> *Vairāgya* is the yearning to give up all transient enjoyables ranging from one's own physical body to *Brahman* (as thought of as an object) with the sense organs and faculties as means.
> — v. 21

This habit, also known as *iha-amutra-phala-bhoga-virāga* (having no passionate desire for enjoying pleasures here and the hereafter), can be developed through deliberate practice, but only when endowed with *nitya-anitya-viveka*. One endowed with *vairāgya* is called a *vairāgin* or *virakta*.

Narayana Guru calls it *nirveda* here, meaning both "having no passionate desire for pleasures" and "not acknowledging the Vedas." Vedism in general makes you hedonistic, and thus the latter sense is also relevant here.

Śaṅkara, in the *Vivekacūḍāmaṇi*, simply enumerates the prerequisite qualities of a seeker of *Brahmavidyā*, calling them together *sādhana-catuṣṭaya-sampatti* (being endowed with four expedients). Here Guru also follows the same order, but with the difference that instead of merely enumerating and defining the four prerequisites, Guru presents the four as pertaining to an organic process, i.e., *nitya-anitya-viveka* has to happen naturally; it leads to *vairāgya* or *nirveda;* a *vairāgin* then has deliberately to practise certain self-imposed disciplines known as *śamādi-ṣaḍka* (six disciplines beginning with *śama*). These six are *śama, dama, uparati, titikṣā, śraddhā* and *samādhāna.* The final prerequisite is *mumukṣutva or mumukṣutā* (yearning for liberation), which becomes well-rooted in one as a result of practising the six disciplines. Now let us see what the six disciplines are:

RESTRAINING THE MIND (*ŚAMA*)

Becoming certain that there must be an eternal Reality that transcends all that is visible, and thus developing a sense of detachment towards all that is fleeting, make it essential to keep a sort of steadfastness with respect to aiming at that one eternal Reality alone. A seeker of such a steadfastness, though fully conscious of the relevance of interiorizing one's perception and sense of detachment towards the pleasurables, may still instinctively think of pleasures and pleasurable objects. This trend of mind will naturally be followed by the senses searching for those pleasures. Eventually such a one will cease becoming immersed in sense pleasures. Being conscious of the original goal in life, one regrets what happened to oneself, and thus loses one's peace of mind. In order to save oneself from this eventuality, it has to become a habit to remain always watchful of the movement of one's own mind. Whenever it begins to lead one astray, one must restrain it and keep it oriented towards the originally conceived goal, with all firmness. This habit of restraining the mind is called *śama* or tranquility. Śaṅkara defines it as follows:

> Keeping the mind steadfast in its goal after having detached itself from manifold sense objects, by observing again and again their inherent defects, is known as *śama*.
>
> — *Vivekacūḍāmaṇi*, v. 22

One who has this habit is called *śānta*.

RESTRAINING THE SENSES (*DAMA*)

Mind alone is not what makes us enraptured in worldly pleasures. Even when remaining with no thought of such pleasures, our senses may by chance get into contact with such objects, which arouse a desire for them in the mind, resulting again in the same danger. To keep ourselves away from such a plight requires restraining our sense organs and organs of action from wandering aimlessly, and, instead, interiorizing their perceptive faculty. This discipline is known as *dama*. Its important role is also underscored in the *Kaṭha Upaniṣad* (II.i.1) when it says, "Brahmā the Creator devised the sense organs and thus punished us by orienting them towards outside, and therefore they perceive only what is outside, never the interior Self. The one of steadfast mind, desirous of immortality, interiorizes one's perception and visualizes the Self (*Ātmā*) that is behind everything." Śaṅkara's definition of *dama* is as follows:

> Turning both sets of senses (sense organs and organs of action) from their respective objects and fixing them firmly in their one centre, is well known as *dama*. — v. 23 Ibid.

An adept in this discipline is known as *dānta*.

NON-DEPENDENCE ON THE OTHER (*UPARATI*)

We, in the usual course, decide what to do, what to say, and what to think by taking into account what others will say or think of such things. This tendency escalates the worldly instinct (*loka-vāsanā*) in us. Only in one who bases his thoughts not on others but on oneself, who tells freely and frankly what one knows, and who boldly engages oneself in activities as one's own thought dictates, does the habit of interiorized perception that enables one to visualize the Self (*Ātmā*) and thus liberate oneself in life, become well-stablized. A seeker therefore has particularly to keep to this discipline of non-dependence on others and the external world in one's activities whether mental, verbal, or physical. This is the best form of *uparati* according to Śaṅkara (Ibid. v. 23)

ENDURANCE (*TITIKṢĀ*)

One who thus does not care for the opinions of the world, but relies on one's own convictions in his words and deeds, may have to encounter much abuse, malice and maltreatment, sometimes even including physical assaults, from others. Unless one has the neutrality and stability of mind to face all such circumstances with equanimity, provoked to react one will be towards each such situation with an emotional fervour, and thus become all the more bound, instead of attaining wisdom and liberation in life. Therefore, a seeker necessarily has to have a firmness to endure all sufferings and face every moment of the present with an unmoved mind, having no complaint or regret about what happened in the past, and no anxiety about what will happen in the future. This capability is called *titikṣā* (endurance). Śaṅkara's definition of it is as follows:

> Enduring all afflictions with no mind to redress them, with no anxiety or regret, is termed *titikṣā* (endurance).
>
> — Ibid., v. 24.

FAITH (*ŚRADDHĀ*)

First a disciple hears the words of wisdom from his *guru*; then he cogitates on what he heard thus, and finally realizes the real intention of the *guru* and thus the truthfulness of what he heard first. This first stage of hearing is known as *śravaṇa*, the second stage, the cogitation on it, as *manana*, and the last stage, realization, as *nididhyāsana*. In order to cogitate on what he heard, aimed at realizing the Reality, one has to have full faith in the existence of the Reality that one has yet to know and in the *guru*'s words of instruction on It. Otherwise, one will have nothing to cogitate and meditate on. One thus first believes in the veracity of the teaching of the *guru*, and then proceeds to ponder on it by relying on one's reasoning faculties (*yukti*) as well as direct experiences (*anubhava*). The final realization makes one fully convinced of the truthfulness of what one simply believed in, in the beginning. One then realizes that what the *guru* taught was not based on blind belief, but on the realization of the all-underlying ultimate Reality — the Self (*Ātmā*). The seeker reaching this final realization occurs only because of first believing in it. Had one doubted it, one would have reached nowhere in one's search for Reality, because one would have nothing to contemplatively search for. Such a search, in other words, would have been for a reality that he/she did not believe in. One is saved from such a predicament by one's faith in the *guru* and the *guru*'s words. Equally valid as the words directly heard from a *guru*, are the words of the *guru*s of the past, recorded in all the scriptures. Therefore, reading and understanding such scriptures is also considered as equally valid as directly hearing a *guru*. Both are really signified by the word *śravaṇa* (hearing). Having this full faith in the words of the scriptures and in one's own *guru*, accompanied by a willingness to contemplate on them with all attention, is known as *śraddhā*, translatable as "faith" or "reverence." Śaṅkara's definition of it is as follows:

> Accepting as true with definite understanding, what the scriptures and the *guru* teach, is called *śraddhā* by the virtuous,

> and with it as a means the ultimate Reality is attained.
>
> — Ibid., v. 25.

The most important of all qualities in a seeker who approaches a *guru*, it could thus be seen, is *śraddhā* or faith. One who lacks this factor is called *saṁśayātmā* (a doubting person) by the *Bhagavad-Gītā*. The *Gītā* says also *śraddhāvān labhate jñānam* (one endowed with *śraddhā* attains wisdom), and *saṁśayātmā vinaśyati* (a doubting person perishes).

AWARENESS DWELLING IN THE ONE GOAL (*SAMĀDHĀNA*)

Our inner faculties, in the ordinary course of life, are not guided by our ultimate goal. They merely remain an incessant flow of reactions to the objects we get into contact with, and also to the people we meet with and their thoughts. In such cases no guiding principle exists to lead us forward. Therefore, as far as a *brahmacārin*-seeker is concerned, an ultimate value notion and way of life fully in line with it, are essential. One should have the expertise to transform all one's voluntary and involuntary actions to become guided by and conducive to the achievement of the final goal, i.e., realizing *Brahman* in oneself. Otherwise, one's reasoning faculties will follow the dictates of the fantasies of the mind, and thus will aimlessly wander around. This discipline of keeping the awareness always dwelling in the one goal of life is known as *samādhāna*. Śaṅkara defines it as follows:

> Constantly making the awareness dwell on the ever-pure *Brahman* is what is termed *samādhāna*; it never is the pampering of the mind.
>
> — Ibid., v. 26.

Quest for Liberation (*mumukṣutā*)

That life is bound in various ways, is felt by everyone who begins to ponder on its meaning. Our relationship with our families, with our own native place, with our nation, with our religion, with our ideology and many such are the factors that keep us bound. Such obligations, many feel, restrict our freedom in various respects.

Eventually one feels within the necessity of liberating oneself from all such bondages; and then one begins to yearn for a means to achieve it.

How is it that our identity with family, friends, local people, nation, religion, ideology and the like, becomes factors that bind us? The root cause of the feeling, "I am bound" is the idea that "I," as an individual, is distinct from all else. The origin of this idea comes from our ignorance of what this "I" really is. Thus it becomes clear that the one means to liberate us from all bondages is the knowledge of the real nature and content of one's own being, called self-knowledge or *ātma-jñāna*.

The consciousness I have of myself as the knowing subject is called *ahaṁkāra* or 'I'-sense. Such a separateness of myself from all else happens when I limit my being within the boundary of the physical body. This *ahaṁkāra* has two extremes — one, my own consciousness, and two, the exterior gross body. In between these two extremes are to be seen other factors like inner faculties, vital breaths (*prāṇaṣ*), sense organs, organs of action, all of which give shape to me as an individual. All these limiting adjuncts are known in Vedānta, as *upādhi*s. The role of *upādhi*s (limiting adjuncts) is understood as follows: space (*ākāśa*) is one and all-pervading (*mahākāśa*). But when it is thought of as being within the limits of a building it is called *maḍhākāśa*; the same space confined within a pot is called *ghaṭākāśa*. The building (*maḍha*) and pot (*ghaṭa*) are *upādhi*s that condition the one space and make it appear as many. Eliminating such conditioning factors makes the space remain one and all-pervading as before. Similarly, eliminating all the *upādhi*s ranging from the I-sense to the gross body, makes the real essential content of myself remain pure and unconditioned. This results in realizing that the self-reality or the reality in myself is not subject to any bondage which really was caused by the above-said conditioning factors (*upādhi*s). The intense desire one has to liberate oneself from all such conditioning factors and the bondage they cause, is called *mumukṣutā* or *mumukṣutva.* A person having such a yearning is called *mukti-kāma* by Guru. This quest for liberation becomes well-rooted only in one endowed with the previous three qualities, namely, *nitya-anitya-viveka, vairāgya* or *nirveda* and the six disciplines, *śama, dama, uparati, titikṣā, śraddhā* and *samādhāna.* Śaṅkara defines *mumukṣutā* as follows:

> *Mumukṣutā* is the quest to liberate oneself from all bondages formed of factors ranging from I-sense to the gross body — all superimposed on oneself because of ignorance. This is accomplished by realizing one's own true nature and content.
>
> — Ibid., v. 27.

The Role of Guru-Disciple Bipolarity (*guru-śiṣya-pārasparya*)

Rarely one among such *mukti-kāmas*, by the Grace of God, realizes the Self-Reality on one's own, and thus becomes a *mukta* (liberated person). Narayana Guru, Ramaṇa Maharṣi, Śrī Rāmakṛṣṇa Paramahaṁsa of India were such in modern times. All the other *mukti-kāmas* need the guidance of a *guru.* Narayana Guru clarifies this point as follows:

> One ought to remain unconditioned pure Consciousness
> Without waking up and without sleep.
> If found unfit for this state of *yoga,*
> One should lend oneself to
> The devout service of a silent recluse-master
> Living enlightened as to the mystery of *praṇava,*
> And freed from repeated births. — *Atmopadeśa Śatakam,* v. 7.

Who is a real *guru*? One must be the best of all *Brahman*-knowers (*brahmavit* and *uttama*) and who has thus liberated oneself from the worldly life that is a never ending process of birth and death, of phenomenal becoming. By merely being a person who knows the ultimate Reality as oneself and lives as that Reality, does not make of one a *guru.* Such enlightened ones could be called *jñānins.* A *jñānin* who is also willing to impart his wisdom to others with all kindness, alone is a *guru*. Replete with the urge to help seekers fill their being with the enlightenment one feels oneself filled with, a *guru* always eagerly waits for a real seeker to approach. Śaṅkara describes a real *guru* as follows:

> He is well-versed in the scriptures, is staightforward, is unsmitten by desires, has withdrawn himself to *Brahman*, is tranquil, is like fire that flames with no fuel, an ocean of mercy for no reason, and is the friend of the virtuous prostrating themselves before him. — op. cit., v. 33

Such a *guru* is to be approached by a seeker for the solution to the fundamental problems concerning life.

Why can't one attain wisdom and become liberated simply by learning the basic scriptures that reveal the secret of Self-knowledge, the knowledge of the Absolute Reality? Here we notice the uniqueness that differentiates Self-knowledge from all other kinds of knowledge. In the latter kind of knowledge, a subject knows an object, and its goal is knowing that object, and sometimes to make use of it. The ultimate goal of a seeker, on the other hand, is liberating oneself from all bondages, and the means for this attainment is becoming a *jñānin*, one who finds oneself merged in the being of the Total, in the Supreme Self, in *Brahman*. On attaining this goal one realizes that, in the case of Self-knowledge, the means resorted to turns out itself to be nothing other than the Self, the final goal. Only then one also realizes that the apparent difference between "I" the individual in bondage and the objects "I" encounter that cause "my" bondage, is simply unreal and imaginary. Really, mistaking the unreal for the real because of "my" ignorance, was the root cause of "my" bondage.

Uprooting this cause is the solution to the problem. Ignorance, in fact, is a negative functional aspect of consciousness, and uprooting it also is a negative process. This double negation thus results in the positive knowing function, i.e., true understanding. A dialectical secret beyond the bounds of logical thinking, is implicit in this. What the scriptures do is to proceed to the ultimate limit of logical thinking, and then to point to that which is beyond, directing us towards That, so that we could experience It directly ourselves through our own dialectical intuition. A *guru*, on the other hand, is a person who has realized the Reality indicated by scriptures, and who lives as the embodiment of that Reality.

What the *guru* directly experiences is, who he/she really is. What the disciple aims at is directly experiencing, who he/she really is. A *guru* can teach only what the *guru* knows. What the *guru* knows is himself/herself. This self-knowledge, when revealed through words, sometimes even by means of mere silence, has to become transformed as the self-knowledge of the disciple. This transformation of one's experiential self-knowledge as the other's experiential self-knowledge, becomes effective when the rapport between the two reaches its zenith of the two becoming one. This, in actual life, is accomplished by the bipolarity the two establish between them in day-to-day affairs. Such is the important role of *guru-śiṣya pārasparya* (rapport between *guru* and disciple). The need of this rapport is suggested by Narayana Guru in his words, *praṇati-sevādyaiḥ prasannam gurum* (after pleasing the *guru* with prostrations and services).

A *guru* does not teach everyone who approaches as a seeker, nor immediately upon a seeker's arrival. The *guru*, first of all, has to make sure of the seeker's competence for wisdom. If competent at all, whether the seeker is of the best type (*uttama-adhikārī*), of the mediocre type (*madhyama-adhikārī*), or of the lowest order (*manda-adhikārī*) also has to be determined. Only after making sure of all such things does a *guru* begin serious teaching. The way the *guru* teaches and the time taken to begin and end the teaching, depend on the nature of competence of the disciple. In the course of all this, a disciple may have to live with the *guru* for many years performing all the services he may need. The *Chāndogya Upaniṣad* tells the story of Indra having to live with Prajāpati for 101 years to get into the final secret concerning *Ātmā*. The *guru*, in the meanwhile, may subject the seeker to severe tests to check the competence and perseverence of the disciple. Stories of many such ancient disciples as well as those in the modern age are numerous. Disciples doing services to a *guru* is known as *guru-śuśrūṣā*, which literally means "the earnest desire for hearing a *guru*" (*śrotum icchā śuśrūṣā*). It is not as a servant that a disciple does these services, but as part of his physically being near a *guru* to listen. A disciple who is perfectly devoted to a *guru* with full faith, when adequately ripe in competence, is allowed to ask the proper question, or is taught by the *guru* without any question being asked.

The Problems

An intense quest for liberation from all bondage was what led you to a *guru*. Becoming a *mukta* or a liberated one needs a knowledge of "who you really are" who desires to be liberated, and also a knowledge of the world around you that causes your bondage. Thus, there are two major problems before you: "Who am I?" and "From where did this world originate?" The disciple, therefore, asks these two questions to the *guru*. These two are the fundamental problems all philosophy has to find an answer to. Though imagined to be asked here, it is not necessary that you should formally ask so. Whatever a *guru* teaches, in essence, answers these two questions. It is asked here simply to make clear what are the problems any disciple has to resolve.

Verse 2

त्वं हि ब्रह्म न चेन्द्रियाणि न मनो बुद्धिर्न चित्तं वपुः
प्राणाहङ्कृतयोऽन्यदप्यसदविद्याकल्पितं स्वात्मनि ।
सर्वं दृश्यतया जडं जगदिदं त्वत्त्वः परं नान्यतो
जातं न स्वत एव भाति मृगतृष्णाभं दरीदृश्यताम् ॥

tvaṁ hi brahma na cendriyāṇi na mano
buddhir na cittaṁ vapuḥ
prāṇāhaṁkṛtayo 'nyad apy asad avi-
dyā-kalpitaṁ svātmani ।

sarvaṁ dṛśyatayā jaḍaṁ jagad idaṁ
tvattaḥ paraṁ nānyato
jātaṁ na svata eva bhāti mṛgatṛ-
ṣṇābhaṁ darī dṛśyatāṁ ||

(The Guru replies):

You are *Brahman* indeed.
You are not the senses.
You are not the mind.
You are not the intellect.
You are not the store-house of knowledge (*citta*).
You are not the physical body.
You are not the functional vitality (*prāṇa*).
You are not the I-sense.
You are not anything else.
All these are just superimposed on *Ātmā*,
(On the Self or on yourself),
Because of ignorance,
And thus are all unreal.
All these being objects of knowledge,
The world (constituted of these) is inert non-Self.
Nothing was born other than of you.
This world does not and cannot have existence on its own.
Its appearance is like that of water in a mirage.
This truth is to be properly and
Intuitively perceived by you.

You are *Brahman* Indeed (*tvam hi brahma*)

The disciple, as we know, approaches a *guru* with the questions, "Who am I?" and "From where did this world originate?" The *guru*'s teaching is initiated by saying, "You are *Brahman* indeed." While being the direct answer to the first question, what this sentence signifies is itself the final certitude we arrive at by the Vedāntic search for Reality. Stating the final teaching at the very beginning is advantageous in more than one way. The most important is that the disciple immediately becomes free of all fears he/she had so far concerning life and its problems. No one in fear can ever be taught properly. One's fear should first be allayed if one has to understand anything taught to one. A *guru* therefore should first of all pacify the disciple's fear.

Fear arises always from the notion that "I," the person who fears, is different from the world that makes "me" frightened. This notion is rooted out by the assuring words, "You are *Brahman* indeed" (*tvam hi brahma*). The word "you" (*tvam*) signifies the disciple's own being that is thought of as separate from all else. Really, that individual being does not exist separate from the Total Being signified by *Brahman*. One who perceives this Reality sees oneself in all the beings and all beings in oneself, as the *Īśa Upaniṣad* puts it (verse 6). On seeing oneself in everything, one no longer fears anything. With this assurance gained, one's inner agony as well as one's confused state of mind is calmed. Just on hearing this word of the teaching, one does not become fully aware of its philosophical implications. Still, a full faith in the veracity of the *guru*'s word frees one from worries and fears. Being thus settled allows one to further listen to the *guru*'s instruction. The indeclinable '*hi*' (indeed) in the words (*tvam hi brahma*), has implicit in it the suggestion, "Why are you afraid? Are you not *Brahman* itself?"

The word *Brahman* signifies the one all-pervading Reality that assumes the form of everything, both physical and mental, in all the worlds. Derived from the verb root *bṛh*, meaning "to grow" (*bṛhi vṛddhau*), it literally means "that which is always in the growing process." As the birth of a chick involves destruction of an egg, a new growth always involves the destruction of something previsously existed. *Brahman*, thus, is the one Substance that ceaselessly is in the process of assuming new forms involving the destruction of old forms, in all the worlds. As Substance, *Brahman* is understood as *sat* (Existence). This aspect will be dealt with in the third verse of the present work. This Substance being Consciousness in essence, It is thought of as *cit* (Consciousness). Verse 4 elaborates on this aspect. The ultimate benefit of realizing this Reality is one's supreme Happiness (*ānanda*) and absolute Freedom, experienced in consciousness (*cit*) as existing (*sat*). This aspect will be dealt with in verse 5.

Vedānta's Method of Approach

Another benefit of the cryptic teaching *tvam hi brahma* (you are *Brahman* indeed) is that it provides the seeker with a firm basis from which one should start one's thinking, and in which direction one's thinking is to be guided. A disciple, on hearing these words, does not at once comprehend the real significance of that teaching. But, believing in its truthfulness, because it came from a *guru,* one should proceed to cogitate on it using one's own thinking faculties and direct experiences. The aim is to realize the real meaning content of the teaching as one's own experience. All this begins from the assumed veracity of the teaching *tvam hi brahma,* and is possible only because of this teaching. We could in one sense say that the rest of the work is a sort of expansion of these cryptic words.

As we know, there are two problems the disciple has to resolve. Closely looked at, the questions are found to be merely two facets of the one and only problem that arises about ultimate Reality. Therefore, instead of giving two different answers to these questions, the *guru* gives a single answer that unitively resolves both questions fully in accordance with their dialectical nature. The first question arose when looking at the Reality from the individual perspective, or the knower-perspective. On the other hand, the second question arises from the universal perspective or the perspective of the known. Whether seen as the known or the knower, what is Real is one alone. The answer given by the *guru*, therefore, unifies the knower and the known, the particular and the universal, into the non-dual Reality, and thus cancels out these dualities.

The Reality that is neither subject nor object, neither universal nor particular, is to be understood or rather realized, not as an object known. All objective knowledges have implied in them the subject-object duality. But realizing *Brahman* is not a knowledge of *Brahman* as an object we can know of. This realization, on the other hand, is the experiential awareness of the subject becoming fully merged in the Reality of *Brahman*, of realizing *Brahman* as the being of oneself or the self (*ātmā*). *Brahman* then is *ātmā*, and *ātmā* is *Brahman*. It is this dialectical unity that the sentence *tvam hi brahma* has implicit in it.

Because *Brahman* is realized as *ātmā* or one's own self-content, the teaching concerning *Brahman* has to be in the form of self-instruction. *Brahmavidyā* thus becomes *Ātma-vidyā* (Self-knowledge). Hence the teaching answers the questions, "Who you are?" and "Who you are not?"

The Self and the Non-Self

We perceive external objects with our sense organs and mind together, and this creates an unconscious impression in us that our own being exists apart from the existence of all that we perceive. Similarly, our mind (*manas*) imagines and asks questions about what we perceive, our intellect (*buddhi*) thinks about it and conceives ideas, our memorizing mind (*citta*) keeps in store all such ideas and experiences in the form of memories, and *ahaṁkāra* (I-sense) evaluates the perceived object in terms of our happiness or suffering. All these internal and subtle functions have one abode only — our gross body. Each of us therefore has a preconceived notion that "I" is an entity made up of all such factors both gross and subtle. No one questions the correctness of this notion. Along with this superfluous idea about ourselves, we are also used to saying "my body," "my senses," "my *manas*," "my *buddhi*," "my *ahaṁkāra,*" "my *prāṇa,*" "my knowledge," and the like. When we say, for example, "my senses," though unconsciously, we are admitting "my" existence as different from the senses. So with other factors as well. Let us ask ourselves, "Who is this 'I' that owns everything that could be considered as 'mine'?" Then we realize, the "I" is something different from body, senses, *prāṇa, manas, buddhi, ahaṁkāra* or any other factor that could be counted as "mine." Sometimes we even say "my self," where we are separating the self from "I."

We thus become fully convinced that this "I" is something imperceptible, something that cannot be made the object of our knowledge, something ineffable. That is the reason why most of the *gurus*, instead of teaching directly what *Ātmā* is, adopt the negative method of first detailing what the non-Self (*anātmā*) is, and then proceeding to say that that which is beyond this *anātmā* is *Ātmā*. Narayana Guru also follows this line of thought here. He, in effect, says, "While you are neither the body, *prāṇa, manas, buddhi, citta, ahaṁkāra,* nor anything that can be considered "yours," you are used to the idea that you are all these, and that is what is wrong with you. You remain ignorant of who you really are, and you think of yourself as what you really are not. That means, you remain ignorant of the Self and consider the non-Self as the Self, and this causes confusion in you." Such a state is called *avidyā* (ignorance). Narayana Guru defines *avidyā* as follows :

> That because of which
> The Self (*Ātmā*) is understood as the unreal,
> And the non-Self (*anātmā*) as the real,
> Is what this *avidyā* is.
> As in the case of wrongly seeing
> The rope as unreal and a snake as real.
>
> — *Darśana Mālā* IV.4

Avidyā is defined here not as our wrong knowledge that *Ātmā* is unreal and *anātmā* is real, but as the function of consciousness because of which this mistaken notion arises in us. What happens in the state of *avidyā* is to not know *Ātmā*, to ignore it as unreal, and to think of *anātmā* as the real. On the other hand, because of not knowing *Ātmā* at all, one considers what is *anātmā* as the real, as *Ātmā*. The possibility of this mistaken notion exists in everyone. This possibility of error concerning oneself, in each individual, is called *avidyā*. The very same possibility in its universal dimension is called *māyā*, defined by Narayana Guru as *na vidyate yā sā māyā* (that which does not exist is *māyā*) (*Darśana Mālā*, IV.1). Śaṅkara gives a somewhat lengthy description of it in the *Vivekacūḍāmaṇi* as follows:

> *Māyā*, also named the indistinct (*avyakta*), because of which the entire universe is given birth, is the power of the supreme Lord. It is beginningless *avidyā*, is of the essence of three *guṇa*s (nature-modalities), and is beyond all comprehension. Its being is inferable from its effects to those of clear intellect.
>
> It is neither existent nor non-existent, nor of the essential content of both; neither divided nor undivided nor both; neither having body nor bodyless nor both; it is the most mysterious and of indescribale nature. — vv. 108, 109.

This potential in the Lord or *Brahman* to cause the error universally (*māyā*) and individually (*avidyā*) is beginningless (*anādi*), but is not endless (*ananta*), because it vanishes just when one becomes enlightened. Everything is an illusory appearance caused by this *māyā* or *avidyā*, and so are our wrong understandings, "I am this body," "I am the senses," "I am the *prāṇa*," "I am the mind," "I am knowledge," and the like. All such appearances and notions are unreal (*asat*) and thus are to be understood as *anātmā* (non-Self). *Anātmā*, thus, is the dialectical counterpart of *Ātmā*. Śaṅkara defines *anātmā* (non-Self) as follows:

> All the modes of appearance like body, sense organs, *prāṇa*s, *manas*, I-sense, the objects of knowledge, pleasures and pains, all the five physical elements such as space (*ākāśa*), the entire universe inclusive of the indistinct (*avyakta*) — all these are non-Self (*anātmā*).

> *Māyā* and all the effects of *māyā*, from *mahat* (the Great) down to the gross body, you must understand, are all unreal and thus *anātmā*. All these are just like a mirage seen in the desert.
>
> — vv. 122, 123.

After defining *anātmā* thus, Śaṅkara goes on to say,

> When all the five sheaths have been eliminated by reasoning on the passages of the scriptures, what remains at last is the witness in the form of consciousness.
>
> This self-effulgent *ātmā* that is distinct from the five sheaths, the witness of these states, the Real, the changeless, the untainted, the everlasting Happiness, is to be understood as his self by the wise one. — vv. 210, 211.

The word *ātmā* is derived from the verb root *āt* meaning, "to pervade" (*ād vyāpane*), which again is subsidiary to another root *at* "to be constantly on the move" (*ata sātatya-gamane*). The substance that pervades the being of something, and that appears as the thing, is called its *ātmā*. Gold, thus, is the *ātmā* in the being of a bangle. In the same way, *ātmā* is the substance that pervades one's own being, extending from the most subtle mind or soul to the most gross physical body, and that assumes the forms of all such. This substance finally is understood by us or rather experienced by us in essence as of pure and unconditioned Consciousness (*cit*). The same *Ātmā*, as understood as pervading the being of everything in all the worlds, is sometimes understood as *paramātmā* (the Supreme Self), also designated as *Brahman*.

Mind and Matter (*cit and jaḍa*)

We are somehow taught to think of our being as comprised of our body and soul or matter and mind. For the same reason we believe, the world also is of the same nature. Another reason for such a concept is that, not only our being but the universe as a whole also seems to be controlled by a thinking mind. Even Quantum Mechanics demonstrates the connection between mind and matter; the nature of matter observed depends upon the chosen position of the observer functioning in it. But how mind and matter, two phenomena diametrically opposite in nature, do exist inseparably as one, is a question that has ever been tormenting logically-minded thinkers all over the world. Vedāntins think of the world as well as the individual being in a different way — either as divisible as gross body (*sthūla-śarīra*), subtle body (*sūkṣma-śarīra*), and causal body (*kāraṇa-śarīra*) or as ranging from the most subtle aspect, consciousness (*cetanā*) or soul, to the most gross aspect, the physical body extending to the ever-expanding universe. A witnessing consciousness, I-sense (*ahaṁkāra*), memorizing mind (*citta*), intellect (*buddhi*), mind (*manas*), senses (*indriyas*), and physical body (*śarīra*) are the graded constituents that form the three bodies according to the former concept. Of these, the inert physical body could be thought of as "matter" and all the rest together as forming the "mind." This mind-matter duality, in our experience, consists of the knower and the known (*dṛk* and *dṛśya*). The latter two could as well be seen as the two extremes or poles of what we call world-experience. What we mean by *dṛśya,* literally, "the seen," in the ordinary sense of the word, consists of everything we see with our eyes. But in the philosophical context, *dṛśya* means "that which could become an object of knowledge." Everything ranging from the most subtle I-sense to the gross body is an object of our knowledge, and hence are all parts of *dṛśya.*

In fact, our own individual existence or the existence of the world, when directly experienced by us, is not at all divided into mind and matter or subject and object. These dual notions arise only when we *think* about what we *experience* and try to understand what are the constituent factors involved in that experience. That means, these dualities are mere constructs of our intellect. Though such faulty thinking is natural with the intellect, understanding something without intellect is not possible either. This intellect, in the context of the search for Reality, is merely a minute functional mode of what we search for. Therefore, understanding Reality as it is would be possible only when we transcend this division by some means. This is why the seers repeatedly remind us that the ultimate Reality is incomprehensible to the intellect. How this duality could be transcended by resorting to the dialectical method that transcends logical reasoning, is portrayed by Narayana Guru thus:

> Countless are the particles of dust
> That constitute the earth;
> And the earth that exists in and through the particles
> Has no different being either.
> Likewise, matter merges in the being of mind,
> And mind in the material bodies.
> The two thus become revealed to be
> One in essence when contemplatively perceived.
>
> — *Ātmopadeśa Śatakam*, v. 74

The *guru* teaches the disciple, "You are the Reality beyond the duality of mind and matter." This intuitive perception of the living Reality as one's own being makes clear that what we saw divided as mind and matter, as the knower and the known, is not the Reality in its living state, but was only an inert aspect of It. When the *guru* says, "All these being objects of knowledge, the world (constituted of these) is inert non-Self," the "inert non-Self" consists not only of the external world but the subject that knows it as well.

False Attribution (*adhyāsa*)

"Where did this world originate from?" is one facet of the basic philosophical question we are dealing with. The *guru*, having given the direct answer to the question, "Who am I?," now says, "The world did not emerge from anywhere else than yourself." The disciple has not yet thought of the world as having emerged from his/herself. But the *guru* categorically says, "If you think this world was created at all, it was out of yourself." This does not mean that the world really was created; if it is imagined that it was created, then you have to understand that it was of yourself. The real sense, therefore, is that the world really is not a created one, but, seen from the view of the ultimate Reality, an imagined one.

The *Ātmā* we have examined earlier, is defined by Narayana Guru thus:

> That which is conscious of itself
> Even when in darkness, is that *Ātmā*.
> It is pure, unconditioned Consciousness.
> And it manifests as all names and forms,
> As all mental faculties and senses,
> As all *karma*s and their doers.
> Lo and behold ! what a Great Magic all this is !
> — *Ātmopadeśa Śatakam*, v. 27

Guru here teaches, fully in line with the Upaniṣads, that the external worlds of forms and names, all the internal faculties like senses and mind, the sense of being the doer of actions, one's own actions — all these are nothing but various manifest aspects of the one unmanifest *Ātmā*, or of the essential content of one's own being. This could easily be construed as idealism. Idea alone is real; what is seen externally is unreal; if a knowing mind does not exist, no world would be seen; the world seems to exist because it is seen; therefore the knower and the knowing mind alone is real — this is the basic stand of idealism. A stand diametrically opposite to this is that of materialism. The materialists' stand is that matter alone is real; mind is simply a biproduct of some peculiar mix of matter.

When the verse says, "Nothing was born other than of you," it signifies, in the light of Guru's definition of *Ātmā*, that the knowledge that I am the knower, and my own knowledge of the world, are simply illusorily attributed on the one Consciousness. On negating these attributes with the awareness that both are unreal, what becomes revealed is the Self or Consciousness pure and simple. These illusory attributes, in Vedānta, are called *adhyāsa*. Not seeing what really exists and seeing something unreal attributed as the real, is what this word signifies. The nature of this *adhyāsa* is depicted with the help of the analogy of the mother-of-pearl and silver. Upon seeing a mother-of-pearl, we may wrongly see it as silver. The real mother-of-pearl here remains unseen, and the unreal silver illusorily attributed to it is seen. Similarly, the world-experience, having "I the knower" and "the world I see" for its two facets, is superimposed illusorily on the Self. In other words, one Consciousness itself manifests both as the knower and the known. Narayana Guru thinks of "the Knower" aspect as *sūkṣma-bhāna* (subtle manifest expression) and "the knower" aspect, the *sthūla-bhāna* (the gross manifest expression) of the unmanifest Consciousness. This *adhyāsa* principle is pictured by Guru in his *Darśana Mālā* thus:

> That which is made manifest by the knowing function of Consciousness is superimposed.
> That which is not superimposed never becomes an object
> Of the knowing function of Consciousness.
> That which is superimposed is unreal.
> That which is not superimposed is the *sat* which alone is "That."
> — (v. 10)

What appears as the world is that which is superimposed on the Real Self. This is made clear in the words, "The world does not and cannot have existence on its own" (*na svataḥ eva bhāti*).

Analogies

Some basic concepts of Vedānta are well clarified with the help of certain analogies. Not only Vedānta but spiritual traditions all through the world resort to this method.

The Bible is one scripture that abounds in analogies. These are most advantageous when certain convictions can otherwise be arrived at only through cumbersome logical thinking or where no logical thinking avails at all. Analogies have the additional capability to reveal what is to be known as if visualized rather than as a logical conclusion. Analogy (*upamāna*) is accepted by Indian thinkers as a *pramāṇa* (valid means of knowledge) to be ranked between perceptual knowledge (*pratyakṣa-jñāna*) and knowledge through scriptural evidence or the words of authentic persons (*śabda-jñāna*). And more, while it depends on both perception and the words of authentic persons, both are dependent on it as well. This must be the reason that Vedāntins profusely make use of this *pramāṇa* whenever something is to be intuited indirectly (*aparokṣa-jñāna*) rather than as direct perception.

A few analogies that do not lose their novelty have constantly been used by Vedāntins ever since the inception of this philosophical vision in the Upaniṣads. Rope and snake, mother-of-pearl and silver, waves and ocean, clay and pots, mirage in a desert, gold and ornaments are some of these. Of these, the one of the mirage in a desert is advantageously made use of by the Guru here to reveal the unreality of the world-appearance. Though many are such analogies, each is used in a particular context of thinking or frame of reference. The analogy of a mirage is used where the point to be cleared is that the world is just an appearance and has no reality of its own. There are those who think of the world as real in itself, and, lured by it, think the worldly pleasures are what make their liveṣ meaningful. They are like those who see a mirage and, lured by it, go after it to quench their thirst. Just as thirsty deers, running after a mirage, happen to become exhausted, fall down and die, those who are in worldly pursuit happen to die without having known what real happiness is. This is suggested by the word *mṛgatṛṣṇābham*, rendered here as "like that of water in a mirage," literally meaning, "like the thirst of deers."

Is to be Properly and Intuitively Perceived (*darī dṛśyatām*)

The word *darī* in the original text means both "properly" and "cave." *Ātmā* is stated in the *Kaṭha Upanīṣad* as hiding as if in a cave (verse II.20). Consciousness in essence, *Ātmā* can never be said to be seated at any specific location. Therefore, only figuratively could it be conceived that it hides in a cave. Guru thus says, this secretly hiding *Ātmā* or Reality is to be properly known, or all the principles clarified in this verse are to be understood properly. When Vedāntins say, this is a secret wisdom, the secrecy in it is not something not to be disclosed to anyone, but is a secret that becomes revealed only to a fully competent seeker, who is also fully interested in it, and has full faith in it.

The second verse of the *Brahmavidyā Pañcakam* thus has clarified the Vedāntic problems, what *Ātmā* is (that it is *Brahman* itself), what it is not, that the visible world has no existence different from *Ātmā*. Both the questions asked in verse 1 have thus been answered fully in accordance with their dialectical inseparability. The remaining three verses will picture this *Ātmā* or *Brahman* as Existence (*sat*) in essence, as Consciousness (*cit*) in essence, and as Value experience (*ānanda*) in essence.

Verse 3

व्याप्तं येन चराचरं घटशरावादीव मृत्सत्तया
यस्यान्तः स्फुरितं यदात्मकमिदं जातं यतो वर्तते ।
यस्मिन् यत् प्रलयेऽपि सद्घनमजं सर्वं यदन्वेति तत्
सत्यं विद्ध्यमृताय निर्मलधियो यस्मै नमस्कुर्वते ॥

vyāptaṁ yena carācaraṁ ghaṭa-śarāvādīva
mṛt-sattayā
yasyāntaḥ sphuritaṁ yad ātmakam idaṁ jātaṁ
yato vartate ।
yasmin yat praḷaye 'pi sadghanam ajaṁ sarvaṁ
yad anveti tat
satyaṁ viddhy-amṛtāya nirmala-dhiyo yasmai
namas-kurvate ॥

That *sat* by which the being of everything,
Living or non-living, is pervaded,
Just as the being of pot, jug and the like
Is pervaded by the being of clay,
That within which the entire world pulsates,
That which the entire world is in essence,
That within which the born world has its being,
That unborn Substance into which everything
In the world gets transformed at dissolution,
That is to be understood by you as the Real (in you).
It is that Reality that those who are of blemishless minds,
Pay their obeisance to with their heads bowed
In order to attain immortality.

Brahman being *sat* in essence, is clarified by Guru in this verse as the Substance that pervades the being of the manifest forms of both the knower and the known world. What we call *jagat* (the world) is the flow of forms assumed by the one *Brahman* through Its creative self-manifestation. The word *jagat* literally means "that which is always going or changing." The history of thought ever since man began to think, is, in essence, the history of human efforts to discover the one changeless Reality that underlies and effects the beginningless and endless transformations taking place in this apparent world. This world was perceived by the ancient Greek philosopher Heraclitus as an eternal flux. The Western world is yet to find a final answer to the question of what is the Reality behind this flux. If at all the answer is found one day, they think, it will mark the end of the history of philosophical pursuits. But the seers of India found the final answer to the question thousands of years ago. One becoming fully convinced of it by realizing It as one's own *ānanda* experience, after accepting the words of the realized seers as true, is the goal of all spiritual pursuits in India. The history of Indian philosophy really consists of the story of the enlightened seers revealing their perception of the Reality and the later Masters interpreting them in order to verify and vivify the original seers' visions.

The world, because it is in a state of constant change, is not counted as real on its own, and, therefore, is thought of as unreal (*asat*). A flow is possible only when there is a liquid, for example water, to flow. Likewise, if the flow of the world is to take place, there has to be a causal Substance that flows. Heraclitus says, we cannot have two dips in the same river. When we bathe in a river, we think we are in the same river all through the process. But the water in the river constantly changes. We cannot have two successive dips in the same water. We have the feeling of dipping again and again in the same river only because we see the river as one, taking into account the water content of it and the geographical constancy of it.

The analogy preferred by Guru here is that of the one earth-content that fills the being of various utensils like pots, plates, jugs and so on. Just as one clay pervades the being of all such utensils, one Reality pervades the being of everything living and non-living in all the worlds. The form the Reality assumes is inclusive of the animating principle in living beings. That one Reality is the real content in me; that Reality is the real content in you. When we say, "everything living and non-living is pervaded," the pervasiveness is not like that of air in the atmosphere or water in a flooded area. The clay does not go to a pot and pervade it; on the other hand, clay itself assumes the shape of pots. It is in the existence of clay that pots, plates, jugs, etc. have their being. In other words, clay is the material cause, and pots, plates, jugs and the like are effects. Likewise, all the worlds and all the living and non-living beings in them, both mind and matter, are effects, and their material cause is the Reality we are in search of. It is within the being of that Reality, also called *Ātmā* and *Brahman*, that all the phenomenal worlds appear and disappear. Such is the Vedāntic perception. The words, "That within which the entire world pulsates" (*yasya antaḥ sphuritam*) does not mean therefore that it is like water in a pot or stars shining in the sky. As the possibility of a spatial misunderstanding exists, in order to avoid it, it is said immediately, "That which the entire world is in essence" (*yad ātmakam idam*).

The Vedāntic method is of searching for the material cause behind the apparent changeful world, the effect, and then perceiving the effect (the world) as not having its being as different from the causal Reality (*Brahman*), just as ornaments have no existence apart from gold. This stand of Advaita Vedānta is known as *sat-kāraṇa-vāda* (the theory that cause alone is real). Cause is seen here as the substance that constitutes and controls (*antar-yāmin*) the being of effects. Effects have no existence of their own; it is the existence of cause that appears as the effect.

The causal Substance undergoes no intrinsic change when the effects are seen in it. That is to say, the cause or *Brahman* becomes effects or the world, not through any evolution-process, and therefore the theory of evolution is not given any credence by Vedāntins. By the theory of evolution (*pariṇāma-vāda*) we mean, the causal Substance undergoes certain intrinsic changes and thus evolves into the form of effects. For example, milk, when cultured, gets curdled and becomes yogurt. This is evolution (*pariṇāma*). Cause here no longer remains the same. This theory of evolution has nothing to do with the modern theory of evolution known to biology. While the latter theory is related merely to biological species, the former is concerned with the entire world or all the worlds including living and non-living entities. That means, *Brahman* or *Ātmā* does not undergo any change in its essential content to appear as the world. Therefore, in the place of the theory of evolution, Vedāntins prefer "the theory of illusory appearance" (*vivarta-vāda*) to explain the origin of the world. *Vāda* means "theory" and *vivarta*, "an illusory form or unreal appearance caused by one's own ignorance (*avidyā*)." Understanding the cause-effect relationship as, cause undergoing no intrinsic change to appear as the effect, is called *vivarta-vāda*.

It could be wrongly construed, when we say the Vedāntins' way of thinking is *sat-kāraṇa-vāda*, that the external visible world is totally ignored as unreal as the causal *Ātmā* alone is real. But the differentiation of cause and effect itself is an imaginary creation of our analytical mind. Experiencing our own existence and experiencing the existence of the world involve no cause or effect. Immediately on having an experience what we usually do is to try to make that experience comprehensible to our thinking mind or intellect (*buddhi*), and in order to accomplish it, it (the thinking mind) creates this division. No one questions the correctness of this division and of the principle of causality itself. This division has for its basis our ignorance or *avidyā* only, which we have already examined. Transcending this ignorance and the cause and effect division created by it, and directly perceiving through intuition the non-dual Reality is the real task of the *sat-kāraṇa-vāda* of Advaita Vedāntins.

But what the thinking mind is familiar with is analysing any phenomenon it deals with in terms of cause and effect. The entire science of logic has for its basis the theory of causality. The final goal of Vedāntins, therefore, is incomprehensible to the logically thinking mind and transcends the realm of sense-perception. This cause-effect relationship could very well be mathematically conceived thus: the one Reality, when vertically viewed (*pāramārthika*) seems to be the cause, and the same Reality horizontally viewed (*vyāvahārika*) appears to be the effect. At the neutral point where the vertical and horizontal meet, meaning where the *pāramārthika* (the ultimate) and *vyāvahārika* (the transactional) meet, is the non-dual Reality. No differentiation of cause and effect, nor of *pāramārthika* reality and *vyāvahārika* reality, is relevant at that point. All this is suggested by the words, *idam-yad-ātmakam bhavati* (that which the entire world is in essence) (see figure below).

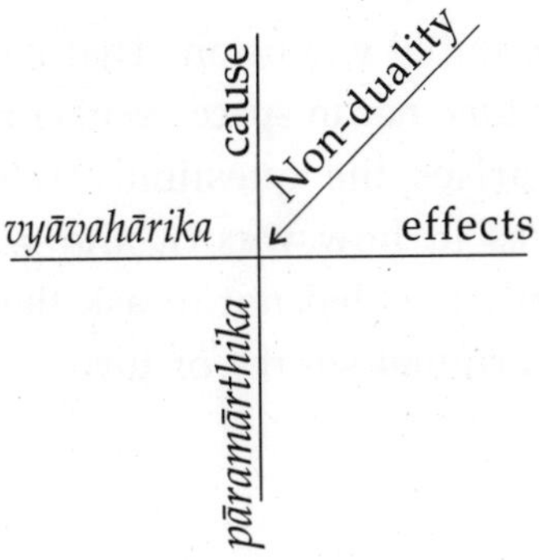

Creation, Sustenance, Dissolution

We constantly perceive every entity in the world as having a birth, a lifespan, and a death. For this reason, an impression has become stabilized in our mind that every worldly phenomenon, and the world as a whole as well, has a beginning, an existence for some time and a final dissolution. These three in Sanskrit are called *sṛṣṭi, sthiti* and *saṁhāra* or *laya*.

Modern scientists have their own view of the birth of the world. This world, in their opinion, was, in the beginning, a fragment that became detached from the sun during an explosion. This fragment in due course became cooled down, then living beings emerged upon it, which human beings mark the final stage in the long line of evolution. Such enquiries do not, in fact, lead us back to the original source of everything, and do not consider about where it ends. Instead, such happenings begin from somewhere in the middle of the process and end somewhere in the middle. A real enquiry into the origin of the universe should not be one that explains the origin of the earth or even of the solar system. The origin of galaxies also would not suffice. It should clearly state what was the original source of all these including the life principle in living beings. Theories like that of Big-Bang claim that the universe originated from a big explosion, and the expansion process begun thus is going on even now. The universe, according to such theories, will terminate as a result of a big implosion called the Big Crunch. Time, space and matter originated from the initial explosion. That means the explosion took place neither in time nor in space. Neither did exist any matter to explode. Then arises the question, "What was the thing exploded, when was it, how was it, and why was it?" Most scientists here simply decided not to ask these questions. This simply means, the original source of the universe still remains uncertain.

Vedāntins at the same time admit the existence of one causal Substance that is pure Consciousness in essence. Its mysterious power to unfold itself as matter and mind, as time and space, is also admitted. Admitting any mysteriousness is repugnant to true scientists, whose thinking is always linear, as a very long cause-and-effect-chain. Instead of resorting to this linear way of enquiry as in science, Vedānta perceives all these, from the galaxies to the human brain, as the manifestations of the one causal Substance, and as inseparable from that Substance or *Brahman*. It, in appearing as all the cosmic systems and everything in them, does not undergo any intrinsic change. It is like gold undergoing no intrinsic change when appearing as ornaments. Ultimately, creation, sustenance and dissolution are not real. They are mere appearances emerging in the one Substance *Ātman* or *Brahman* as a result of the beginningless and endless creative self-manifestation It undergoes. When one manifest form disappears and another appears, we merely think the former was a distinct entity and it died, and a new distinct entity is born. Really what exists always is *Ātmā* alone. Such an understanding concerning creation, sustenance and dissolution is known as *ajāta-vāda* (the no-creation theory). The *Bhagavad-Gītā* categorically says:

> That (Reality) is never born; nor does It ever die;
> Once having been, It does not cease to be either.
> Unborn, eternal, perpetual, ancient,
> It is not destroyed at the destruction of the body.
>
> — II. 20

Though our philosophical vision convinces us that the phenomena of creation, sustenance and dissolution are mere illusions caused by *avidyā,* still we see these events apparently taking place. This creation-dissolution concept involves a time-sense of something being born at a particular moment, existing for a while and dying at the end. We understand all events as taking place in time and space. As we closely examine and try to understand what is time and what is space, we realize that, instead of events taking place in time and space, time and space are two concepts we derive from the continuity and contiguity of events. We have time-sense only when events take place one after another. In an eventless state we have no time-sense. For example, during deep sleep we feel no time. And space-sense is derived from the contiguity of events. Many things existing simultaneously are events. Without simultaneous events we have no space-sense.

Locating a point on the surface of the earth is possible by making use of a map marked with latitudinal and longitudinal lines. Anyone can clearly locate a place by saying it is in such and such a latitude and such and such a longitude. Similarly the events we experience also have to be located in our memory. Such locating also needs a device; but we have already adopted it unconsciously. The vertical axis in that device is time, and the horizontal axis space. In other words, the vertical continuity of events is felt by us as time, and horizontal contiguity as space.

The idea that the creation of the world took place at a particular point of time or period, and that it will be destroyed likewise, is formulated in our mind as we start thinking of the subject. But we remain completely ignorant that it is the events of creation, sustenance and dissolution that cause the sense of time in us. With no events taking place, no time-sense is felt by us. In fact, time and space become a sort of veil that covers the Reality, rendering It invisible to us. Narayana Guru, in his *Jananī-Nava-Ratna-Mañjarī* (A Bouquet of Nine Gems on the Mother) makes this point clear as follows:

The delicate fabric woven
Out of time and the like
Envelops your Real form,
And for this reason
None do know the Real you,
O Mother, whose abode marks
The end of all the Vedas. — v. 5

We thus find it meaningless to think that the world was created at a particular time and will cease to exist at another. Such mistaken ideas have become deeply rooted in our mind because the symbolic creation stories narrated in our scriptures have come to be understood literally. Such stories should not be taken in the literal sense. The words in the text,

"That within which the born has being,
That unborn Substance into which everything
In the world gets transformed at dissolution,"

are to be understood with this background. If we begin our search for Reality by accepting creation, sustenance and dissolution as real at all, then the only stand we can take is that everything was born of the one causal Reality, everything has its being in that Reality, and everything merges back in that Reality at the time of dissolution. It is comparable to, pots, jugs, plates and the like being born of earth, they having their being in earth, and they becoming dissolved in the earth.

Does such creation take place gradually stage by stage, or does it take place instantaneously? The first stand is known as *krama-sr̥ṣṭi-vāda* (the theory of gradual creation), and the latter *yugapat-sr̥ṣṭi-vāda* (the theory of instantaneous creation). Advaita Vedānta subscribes to the latter and Narayana Guru is no exception. The instantaneous creation takes place in our consciousness always. The world disappears when we shut our eyes, and it appears again when the eyes are opened. Likewise, when the Consciousness becomes functionless, the world just disappears, and when the Consciounsness begins to function, the world also emerges. Narayana Guru in the *Darśana Mālā* says,

> The coming into being
> Of this world happened
> Not in gradual steps as from the sun.
> Instantaneously from the Self,
> Owing to its own wilful perception,
> Was the emergence, just as
> It happens when waking up from sleep. — I.9

Laya and *pralaya* are the Sanskrit words for dissolution. The latter word is also used to signify the Great Deluge. Hence the word in the present context may create the idea of the event of a great flood, and the entire world becoming submerged in it. This is a myth created in our mind by mythological legends which are really meant to be understood symbolically. The word *pralaya* literally means "proper fusion" and the prefix *pra* stands for "proper." The word thus in the philosophical context means only that the apparent individuated form merges back properly with the causal Substance, just as a pot, when broken, becomes part of the soil.

In Order to Attain Immortality

The Reality that pervades thus the being of everything living and not living, that is, the material cause of the appearance of creation, sustenance and dissolution, has to be birthless and deathless, and hence is immortal. Attaining that birthless and deathless state and making it one's own is the highest goal to which humans can aspire. The best way to attain it is to meditatively adore the one Reality, and to finally realize oneself in essence as already that Reality.

Those of Blemishless Mind Pay Obeisance to

Many of us go to temples or places of worship, and meditate on and worship God, standing before an idol, or symbol or even nothing visible. Some worship the sun at sunrise and sunset. We bow our head before those who deserve our respect. We greet our friends on meeting them. We unconsciously believe in all such contexts that we maintain a bipolarity with something other than ourselves. But only those having a transparent vision see the real principle behind this very common social custom. What relates me with others with such a bipolarity is nothing but the one immortal Reality or *Ātmā* that constitutes the being of both of us. Really it is not the other person we respect or greet, but the one Reality in both of us is what we honour.

To be Understood by You as the Real

That one Substance, the *guru* teaches his disciple, is to be understood as the ultimate Reality. We notice all through this verse that, of the *sat, cit* and *ānanda* that constitute the essential content of the Reality, it is the *sat* or Existence aspect which is considered here. If I say, I and the world I know do exist, then it is as *sat,* as manifest forms of *sat,* that both exist. This *sat* is beyond all dualities.

Verse 4

सृष्ट्वेदं प्रकृतेरनुप्रविशती येयं यया धार्यते
प्राणीति प्रविविक्तभुग्बहिरहम् प्राज्ञस्सुषुप्तौ यतः।
यस्यामात्मकला स्फुरत्यहमिति प्रत्यन्तरङ्गं जनै-
र्यस्यै स्वस्ति समर्थ्यते प्रतिपदा पूर्णा शृणु त्वं हि सा॥

sṛṣṭvedaṁ prakṛter anupraviśatī yeyaṁ
yayā dhāryate
prāṇīti pravivikta-bhug bahir aham prājñas
suṣuptau yataḥ ।
yasyām ātma-kalā sphuraty aham iti
praty antaraṅgaṁ janair
yasyai svasti samarthyate pratipadā pūrṇā
śṛṇu tvaṁ hi sā ॥

That Consciousness (*pratipat*) which,
After having created the world from Its own *prakṛti*
(Nature or urge for creative self-expression),
Itself enters the being of the very same world,
That which, as living organisms,

Assumes the role of the enjoyer of distinct objects,
That because of which
Oneself in deep sleep remains
Unconsciously conscious (*prājña*) of being happy,
That whose minute self-fragment glows
As I-sense in the interior being of everyone,
That for the sake of which
People wish well-being always,
That fullness of Consciousness is you in essence,
Understand clearly.

That last verse perceived everything as *sat* (Existence). The same *sat*, in essence, is seen as unconditioned Consciousness (*pratipat*) in the present verse. It may be easy to conceive a Substance that underlies the being of everything living and non-living. Still such questions as these remain unanswered: how does the Substance function consciously so as to manifest itself as a well-structured world? In human beings, one of such manifest forms, how do different functions take place at different states of waking, dreaming and deep sleep? An overall answer to all these questions together is that Reality or *sat*, in essence, is pure, unconditioned Consciousness. *Pratipat* is a Sanskrit word that signifies consciousness as does *cit*. Being a female gender word, in usage it could become *pratipadā*. This *pratipat* or *pratipadā* is seen all through this verse as the Substance that functions consciously everywhere. And the verse ends with the Master's instruction to the disciple, "You are that *pratipadā* or *cit* or Consciousness."

From Its Own *prakṛti*

It could be construed from the statement, "The world was created from its own *prakṛti*," that something called *prakṛti* exists apart from the non-dual Reality or *sat*. *Prakṛti* (nature) and *puruṣa* (person) are thought of as two distinct realities in the Sāṁkhya system. Vedāntins who insist on the existence of one Reality alone, on the other hand, consider *prakṛti* as the creativity of *Ātmā*. This creative urge finds expression as the phenomena of creation, sustenance and dissolution of the world as well as of individual beings. All such creative manifestations of *Ātmā* together are called *vibhūti*s in the *Bhagavad-Gītā* in chapter X. Such *vibhūti*s do not exist apart from the Self and have no being of their own, as ornament forms have no existence apart from gold. The *Gītā* shows how such *vibhūti*s materially form part of the Cosmic Body of *Brahman* or *Bhagavān*. As the *vibhūti*s have no existence of their own, they are illusory appearances. Because such appearances are caused to emerge in the Self, this creativity is often referred to as *māyā* inhering beginninglessly in the one *Brahman*. This *māyā* creates the impression of what really does not exist as existing. It causes various manifestations like *vidyā-avidyā, parā-aparā, tamas, pradhāna*, and of these one is *prakṛti*, as conceived by Narayana Guru in the *Māyā-darśanam* of *Darśana Mālā*. *Prakṛti* is defined by the Guru as follows:

> In the sense that it, by its very nature,
> Separates out the *guṇa*s in its own proper way,
> It is well-known as *prakṛti*,
> That, in essential content, is the three *guṇa*s.
>
> — IV.10

This *prakṛti*, while being inseparable from the one Self, causes the emergence of all the beings, living and non-living, within It; nor can it remain otherwise either, as is stated in the *Gītā* thus:

> Resorting to My own *prakṛti* and helplessly subject to it, I bring forth again and again the entire multitude of beings. — IX.8

Itself Enters the Being of the Very Same World

The Biblical story of God, after creating the world, breathing his own breath of life into the nostrils of the form of man, may come to our mind when we hear that Consciousness "enters the being of the very same world." Symbolically understood, the Biblical story signifies the very same principle the Guru mentions here. Vedāntins do not subscribe to the idea that God, after creating the world, stands apart as its controller and judge. Instead, the one Reality, in essence Consciousness, on assuming the form of the world, Itself functions as the conscious animating principle in all the beings including humans. What is portrayed here as *pratipadā* is nothing other than the Self-Reality that was seen as *sat* in the last verse. The act of entering is to be understood philosophically as pertaining to the realm of effects rather than to cause. Only then what is intended by the Guru here becomes evident to the intuitive eye of students. Consciousness, being the Reality that assumes the form of the world, already exists in every being created as their inner controller. Therefore Consciousness does not literally have to enter the beings.

In the Upaniṣads also we see the narration of creation stories, according to which *Ātmā*, *cit* in essence, after creating the world from Itself, is stated to be entering the very same world. For example, the *Taittirīya Upaniṣad* says,

> He desired: let me become many. Let me be born. He heated himself upon this desire. On being heated up, he created all this, whatever is here. Having created it, into it, indeed, he entered. Thus he became both actual and the beyond, the defined and the undefined, the founded and the unfounded, knowledge and non-knowledge, the true and the untrue. — II.6.3

Something done is felt to be well done when it gives full satisfaction. Whatever we do, if done with the perception that the satisfaction of doing it and the satisfaction the outcome gives are simply a sparking of the *ānanda* content of *Ātmā*, then it becomes well done. In this sense, the self-expression of *Ātmā* cannot be otherwise than well done, for self-expression always gives satisfaction. Therefore, the world that emerges as an expression of the creation urge in *Ātmā* is called *sukṛta* (well-made) in the same Upaniṣad:

> This world in the beginning verily was non-existent. Therefrom, indeed was the existent (world) born. It (*Brahman*) created Itself by Itself. Therefore it is called the well-made (*sukṛtam*). — II.vii.1

The word *prakṛti* used here could well be seen as related to the word *sukṛtam* of the Upaniṣad. In other words, this *prakṛti* is what is thought of as the *ātma-māyā* (My own *māyā*) of the *Bhagavad-Gītā* when it says:

> The unborn and undiminishing *Ātmā* though I am, the supreme controller of all that has come into being though I am, residing in My own *prakṛti,* I emerge as beings, owing to My own *māyā.*
> — IV.6

A passage in the *Svetāśvatara Upaniṣad* also could be remembered here:

> Understand *prakṛti* as *māyā* and the wielder of *māyā* as the Supreme Lord (*Parameśvaraḥ*). — IV.10

Śaṅkara admits that this passage of the Upaniṣad deals with the consciousness-content (*cit-svarūpa*) of *Ātmā*. He clarifies it as follows in his comments on the above-quoted passage of the *Taittirīya Upaniṣad*:

> It is because qualified by our perception that we know the external objects like pots. Likewise, the Self-content becomes experiential when qualified by certain kind of brightness of the intellect. Therefore it is often said, *Ātmā* remains in the cave of the intellect that is causal to any understanding. The same is signified here also. It is in order to make this point clear that it is said, "Having created it, into it, indeed he entered." One *Brahman*-Reality alone remains in the cave of the intellect in all the qualified manifest forms such as perceiver, hearer, one who reflects upon, the knower, and the like. The same is what the word *prāviśat* (he entered) signifies.

That *Brahman*, pure Consciousness in essence, enters everything created from Itself, suggests that the created world has no separate existence apart from the self-manifesting Consciousness or *Brahman*.

That Consciousness which . . . Unconsciously Conscious

Prāṇī is the Sanskrit word for living beings, literally meaning, "that which is endowed with *prāṇa* or vitality." Every living organism or *prāṇī* is but a conditioned manifest form of one unconditioned and undivided Consciousness or *pratipat*, as are non-living things. Of all such *prāṇī*s, humans are considered the most highly developed beings. The individuated consciousness of each functions in different states of waking (*jāgrat*), dreaming (*svapna*), and deep sleep (*suṣupti*).

Consciousness, as functioning in the waking state, knowing and enjoying external objects distinctly, is known as *vaiśvānara*. This enjoyment could either be agreeable (*iṣṭa*), disagreeable (*aniṣṭa*) or indifferent (*udāsīna*). The other extreme of the function of the individual consciousness is when it becomes fully absorbed into itself with no function at all. Though functionless, it enjoys unconsciously the happiness of sleeping soundly. That is why we say after a sound sleep, "I slept well, I did not know anything." The consciousness in this state that unconsciously experiences the happiness of sound sleep is known as *prājña*. In effect, the consciousness functions oscillating between these two extremes.

In the middle comes the dreaming state when the mind, urged by its own inner propensities (*vāsanā*s), aspirations and experiences gained in life, imaginatively creates objects from itself, itself enjoying them also. This is what we call dreams, and the functional consciousness in that state is known as *taijasa*.

The unconditioned Consciousness (*pratipat*) that creates all of us distinctly from Its own *prakṛti*, also functions in each of us as our distinct consciousnesses having different functional states. The Guru, in the verse, mentions only the *jāgrat* and *suṣupti* states, the middle one to be seen as included. Each such individual has a different way of experiencing the waking, dreaming and deep sleep states. Such differing potentials and possibilities by which each individual functions constitute their personal *dharma* (*svadharma*). Underlying all this is the one Reality or *pratipat* which is the material cause of all such emanations, and also functions as the I-sense in each individual in all the three states.

That for the Sake of which People Wish Well-being

Wishing each other well-being is a human behaviour. This habit reflects the natural human aspiration for happiness. *Svasti* (*su+asti*) is the Sanskrit word for well-being. To whom do we wish well-being? Is it toward individuals, or toward the one all-underlying Reality? Wishing well-being to the latter is meaningless. It already is *ānanda* (Happiness) in essence, as will be seen in the next verse. Equally meaningless is wishing well-being toward an individual, for as individuals, the one who wishes and the one who is wished for, are both unreal, as what is Real in both is but one Self alone. It is actually only because we are unaware of this oneness that we wish each other well in this way. Because of this ignorance, we perceive life as a process of alternation between happiness and suffering, while the desire of everyone is to avoid suffering and attain happiness. With this end in view we wish each other well-being. Philosophically, every such wish implies a prayer within us, "Let us perceive the one Self or *pratipat* that always exists as well-being, filling the being of both of us." The words, "That for the sake of which people wish well-being" is to be understood in this sense.

The *pratipat* or unconditioned Consciousness, which really cannot be understood, becomes understandable in its conditioned forms as cause and effects. With individuated form as the conditioning factor, the *pratipat* functions as all the altering states of mind and the I-sense in each of us. This one Consciousness has to be full in all respects, i.e., there is nothing outside Its bounds. If anything is there that does not come within the limits of this *pratipat*, it has naturally to be non-Consciousness; but, that it is considered non-Consciousness is also a conscious knowledge. That means, what we could think of as non-Consciousness is also within the bounds of Consciousness. Thus, Consciousness, in its nature and context, can never be other than boundless plenitude. Therefore the teaching is, "That Consciousness (*pratipat*) Itself is 'you'." Even the zest in you for knowing the Real is none other than a minute element of the manifest form of the very same Reality or *pratipat* you are in search of, functioning in the *prāṇī* that you are as the knowing conscious mind.

Thus is taught to the disciple the non-duality of the individuated self and *Brahman* or of the knowing consciousness and the known consciousness, or what is known as *Brahmātmaikya*. How the disciple should transform this teaching into his own experiential awareness as well as Happiness is what the next verse concentrates on.

Verse 5

प्रज्ञानं त्वहमस्मि तत्त्वमसि तद् ब्रह्मायमात्मेति सं-
गायन् विप्रचर प्रशान्तमनसा त्वं ब्रह्मबोधोदयात् ।
प्रारब्धं क्व नु सञ्चितं तव किमागामि क्व कर्माप्यसत्
त्वय्यध्यस्तमतोऽखिलं त्वमसि सच्चिन्मात्रमेकं विभुः ॥

prajñānaṁ tv aham asmi tat tvam asi tad-
brahmāyam ātmeti saṁ-
gāyan vipracara praśānta-manasā tvaṁ brahma-
bodhodayāt ।
prārabdhaṁ kva nu sañcitaṁ tava kim
āgāmi kva karmāpy asat
tvayy addhyastam ato 'khilaṁ tvam asi
saccinmātraṁ ekaṁ vibhuḥ ॥

With a properly calmed mind
Resulting from the dawning of *Brahman*-wisdom,
You may move around properly in all specific ways,
Joyfully singing, "Pure Consciousness indeed I am,"
"You (also) are that,"

"This *Ātmā* is indeed that *Brahman*."
How could there be for you then the bondage of *karmas*,
Whether already begun (*prārabdha*),
Accumulated from the past (*sañcita*),
Or those yet to be accumulated (*āgāmi*)?
Karma is itself unreal.
All such therefore are simply conditionings
Superimposed on the *Ātmā* that you really are.
You really are *vibhu*
(The one Lord in whom abide all becomings),
In essence *sat-cit*.

In verse 2, *Brahman* was pictured as the underlying Substance in one's own being. In verse 3 emphasis was given to the *sat* (Existence) aspect of *Brahman*, and in verse 4 the *cit* or *pratipat* (Consciousness) aspect was underscored. Now in the concluding verse, the same *Brahman* is potrayed by Narayana Guru as the realized Reality and Supreme Happiness of the disciple. Along with it the Guru lays bare the inner secrets of the *maha-vākya*s (great dicta) that enclose within them that core of Vedāntic wisdom.

All humans find themselves bound by their own *karma*s in some way. On realizing that all such *karma*s are not real in themselves, and are superimposed on the Self or oneself, one becomes released from the bondages caused by them as well. Realizing one's identity with the ultimate Reality that underlies the being of everything, and that causes the emanation of everything from Itself (*vibhuḥ*), (i.e., identifying with God) marks the ultimate limit in experiencing Happiness.

Mahā-vākyas (The Great Dicta)

The disciple, upon Self-realization, is asked by the *guru* to move around freely singing the *mahā-vākya*s (great dicta). The core-teaching of Vedānta is thought of as condensed in a few short sentences, known as *mahā-vākya*s, all appearing in the Upaniṣads.

Traditionally considered four in number, these dicta are, *tat tvam asi* (That thou art), *aham brahma asmi* (I am *Brahman*), *prajñānam brahma* (*Brahman* is Consciousness), and *ayam ātmā brahma* (this self is *Brahman*).

Of these, *tat tvam asi* appears in the *Chāndogya Upaniṣad* (6.10.12) appended to the *Sāmaveda; aham brahma asmi* finds place in the *Bṛhadāraṇyaka Upaniṣad* (1.4.10), attached to the *Yajurveda; prajñānam brahma* is in the *Aitareya Upaniṣad* (3.1.3) appended to the *Ṛgveda;* and *ayam ātmā brahma* in the *Māṇḍūkya Upaniṣad* (2) of the tradition of *Atharvaveda*. It thus becomes evident that one and the same wisdom is revealed in the Upaniṣads belonging to all the four Vedic traditions, and that the core of this wisdom is condensed in the four *mahā-vākya*s.

Of these dicta, *tat tvam asi* (That thou art) is in the form of an instruction given by a *guru* to his disciple, and hence is known as *upadeśa-vākya* (instructional dictum). The disciple, upon hearing the instruction, sits alone and contemplates and meditates *ayam ātmā brahma* (this self is *Brahman*). For this reason this dictum is considered *manana-vākya* (dictum for contemplation). This contemplation and meditation attains fulfilment in the realization *aham brahma asmi* (I am *Brahman*), and hence this dictum is termed *sākṣātkāra-vākya* (realization-dictum). The essential content of this realization is made clear in the dictum *prajñānam brahma* (*Brahman* is Consciousness), which is known as *svarūpa-vākya* (dictum revealing the essential content).

The nature of these *mahāvākya*s could well be differentiated in another way also. All the dicta are in the form of equations. One limb of these equations is always *Brahman*, and the other is a pronoun in the first three and *prajñānam* (Consciousness) in the final dictum. The three pronouns are of the second person, third person and first person (*tvam, ayam* and *aham* — you, this and I). *Prajñānam* transcends the realm of personal pronouns and is of the neutral order. This peculiarity, though originating from different *ṛṣis* (seers) who authored the Upaniṣads, suggests that what Vedānta ultimately teaches is the oneness in essential content of both the individuated self and the universal Self. That means, the universal Self and the individual self, whether conceived as first person, second person, third person, or as impersonal, have a common content, and in that content, which is unconditioned Consciousness, the two find oneness. This oneness is not merely an intellectual understanding, but is the direct experience of one's own oneness with the one Reality. This experience transforms one's life into that of *Brahman, sat-cit-ānanda* in essence, and no longer of the individual. One's own life is thus experienced as an everlasting flow of the *sat-cit-ānanda* song, as is evident from the *guru*'s words that ask the disciple to move around properly in all specific ways joyfully singing *prajñānam tu aham asmi* (pure Consciousness indeed I am), etc.

Though capable of being interpreted thus in a simple way, Śaṅkara, in his commentaries on the Upaniṣads and in his original works, prefers to resort to a semantic interpretation of the great dicta. Having an understanding of that interpretation also is a must for all Vedānta students.

Reflection on "*tat tvam asi*"

Śaṅkara takes the dictum *tat tvam asi* for example in order to interpret semantically all the dicta. The two limbs of these equations are meant to be dialectically perceived so as to intuitively experience the non-dual Reality that underlies both. Śaṅkara comes to this dialectical understanding after going along a circuitous route through semantics.

Śaṅkara, for this purpose, differentiates two kinds of meanings of sentences — literal meaning (*vācyārtha*) and indirect meaning (*lakṣaṇārtha*). Some sentences in any language are to be understood literally; some others are not so, being understandable only in their indirect suggested senses. The two limbs of the equation-like sentence *tat tvam asi* are *tat* (That) and *tvam* (you). The two words signify something entirely different and opposite to each other in nature, and hence what these denote can never be equated in their literal sense. In order to clarify the oppositeness of the two, both are subjected to a detailed study by Śaṅkara. These two studies, in the Vedāntic parlance, are known as *tat-padārtha-nirūpaṇa* (ascertaining the meaning of the term *tat*), and *tvam-padārtha-nirūpaṇa* (ascertaining the meaning of the term *tvam*).

TAT-PADĀRTHA-NIRŪPAṆA

The common experience of all of us is: I am different, you are different, that is different, and so on. But we have already seen in this *Brahmavidyā Pañcakam* that all such differentiated experiences occur in one Consciousness or Mind, that nothing has existence apart from that Consciousness, and that the separateness is the imaginary creation of *avidyā* (ignorance or nescience) which also could be called *māyā*.

This *māyā* or *avidyā* has two powers, namely, *āvaraṇa-śakti* (the power to put a veil over what is Real), and *vikṣepa-śakti* (the power to project something else on the Real). For example, when the mother-of-pearl is wrongly seen as silver, it is as if something veils the mother-of-pearl rendering it unseen by us. This is the *āvaraṇa-śakti*. Then the unreal silver is projected on the real mother-of-pearl so that silver is seen as the real. This is the *vikṣepa-śakti*. Likewise, our *avidyā* or *māyā* puts a veil on the Real *Brahman* or *Ātman*; thus *Brahman* always remains unseen by us. This is the *āvaraṇa-śakti* of *māyā*.

The same *avidyā* or *māyā* projects on *Brahman* the form of the world and thus we see the world as Real. This is the *vikṣepa-śakti*.

Because of these two *śakti*s (powers) we categorize Reality into cause and effect, mind and matter, genus and species, universal and particular, and innumerable objects and the ideas concerning them. Even when we see and understand the world thus, what is Real remains undivided and indivisible, imperceptible and even inconceivable. That undivided Reality is the object of our enquiry in Vedānta. That Reality, which is nothing other than *Brahman*, as something yet to be understood and attained, is referred to as *tat* (That).

As the effects of the above-mentioned *māyā*, we happen to see this Reality as the cause of creation, sustenance and dissolution of the world-appearance, as the indwelling controller of everything (*sarvāntaryāmin*), as omniscient, as omnipotent and as changeless. The word *Īśvara* (God) is used in Vedānta to denote *Brahman* so conditioned. While *Brahman* as such is ungraspable, *Īśvara* is the graspable version of the same. The Śaṅkara school of Vedānta, therefore, defines *Īśvara* as *Brahman* having become blemished by *māyā*. Such an *Īśvara* is what the word *tat* (That) signifies. Put otherwise, even when *tat* is conceived as pure, unconditioned Consciousness, the knower (*pramātṛ*) of the same remains as if different.

TVAM-PADĀRTHA-NIRŪPAṆAM

The word *tvam* (you) stands for the knower of the Reality, and is conceived as *jīva* (individual being or soul). A *jīva* is naturally bound by *saṁsāra* (the process of unceasing becoming), is subject to pains and pleasures, is of little power, knows only a little, is conditioned by the physical body, senses, inner faculties and the like, and is subject to change. Looked at thus, we see what is signified by *tat* and by *tvam* are entirely different and of opposite nature. Such a pair can never be equated in the literal sense. Śaṅkara, therefore, conceived the idea that the two are meant to be equated in an indirect sense (*lakṣaṇārtha*).

Indirect Meanings (*lakṣaṇārthas*)

Indirect senses are also of different kinds. One type is exemplified by the phrase *gaṅgāyām ghoṣaḥ* (the hamlet of cowherds in the Gaṅgā). We know that a hamlet cannot be located in a river. What is actually meant is that the hamlet of cowherds located on the bank of the river Gaṅgā. In modern times we say, he lives on such and such a street. Everyone knows that no one can live on a street. The literal sense of both the words *gangāyām* (in the Gaṅgā) and "on the street" is totally given up and a new suggested meaning grasped. Such indirect meanings are known as *jahal-lakṣaṇā, jahal* meaning "given up."

The dictum *tat tvam asi* is meant to convey the idea of the oneness of Reality. In the aforementioned *jahal-lakṣanā*, the literal sense and the indirect sense are related as the support and the supported. But no such support-supported relationship exists between *tat* and *tvam*. Therefore, the meaning of the dictum cannot be grasped by means of the *jahal-lakṣaṇā*. Still, just as the above-said example "in the Gaṅgā" is actually understood as, "on the bank of Gaṅgā," a certain alteration in the meaning of the words *tat* and *tvam* is needed to comprehend the real sense of the dictum.

Śaṅkara mentions another type of indirect sense also. The example cited is *śoṇo dhāvati* (red colour runs). The real meaning intended is "The red horse runs." The literal sense in this case is not given up, but a new sense is added to it. This type of indirect meaning is named *ajahal-lakṣanā, ajahal* meaning "not given up." The dictum *tat tvam asi* is not graspable in this kind of indirect sense either. The dictum is aimed at realizing the non-dual Reality, pure Consciousness in essence. Yet what the term *tat* signifies is beyond the range of perceptibility, while what *tvam* signifies is perceived directly. Eliminating this contradiction between the two is not possible just by adding a new sense to the literal one.

Now the only way left is by adopting a method that gives up the literal sense partly. When the contradictory part of the sense is given up, what remains emerges as the contradictionless oneness of these two. Such an indirect sense is known as *bhāga-tyāga-lakṣaṇā* (partly given up indirect sense) or *jahajahal-lakṣaṇā* (partly given up and partly not given up indirect sense). The best example of this in our day-to-day life that Śaṅkara cites is *so 'yam devadattaḥ* (This is that Devadatta). Semantically looked at, "this Devadatta" and "that Devadatta" are far apart spacewise and timewise. Therefore their oneness, though very simple, is arrived at by unconsciously negating the incongruence between the senses of "this" and "that." We can resort to the same method in the case of the dictum *tat tvam asi* also. The two terms *tat* and *tvam* differ in that the former signifies something beyond the range of perceptibility, while the latter denotes something directly perceived. To this contradictory nature is to be added the differences between *Īśvara* and *jīva* already clarified. Let us negate or ignore these contradictory aspects that are apparent. Then we intuitively perceive the common content of both, the absolute Reality that is beyond all contradictions. The realization of this Reality as one's own self-content is what the dictum *tat tvam asi* as well as the other dicta signify.

In Nataraja Guru's perception, the relation between the direct sense and the indirect sense in the case of *jahal-lakṣaṇā* is qualitative and in *ajahal-lakṣaṇā* it is quantitative. In other words, *jahal-lakṣaṇā* has a vertical dimension and *ajahal-lakṣaṇā* a horizontal one. The contradiction between the two dimensions is negated in the third kind of indirect sense.

Ontologically speaking, the underlying invisible Substance (*sat*) in both *tat* and *tvam* always remains one, while at the level of attributes (*bhāva*s) contradictions appear. By methodically negating all attributes we perceive the oneness of *tat* and *tvam* Substance-wise.

Śaṅkara, in order to find a comprehensible meaning to the *mahā-vākya*s, resorts to a very subtle semantic analysis. Narayana Guru, on the other hand, deals with the context in a very simple way without much intellectual exercise. He does it by giving stress to the Consciousness-content of what is ultimately Real. One and the same Consciousness, when conditioned by universal attributes is called *Īśvara* or God, and when conditioned by individual attributes, *jīva*. The homogeneous Substance in both is beyond all dualities, is eternal, is unconditioned, is free of all bondages, and is not something to be intellectually known, but is to be directly experienced as one's own being. The Guru says,

> That Consciousness which makes us know of all specific knowledge — we, in essence, are That. — *Aṛivu*, v. 11

In fact, finding a way of interpreting the *mahā-vākyas* does not emerge as a problem at all in the philosophy of Narayana Guru, as both "I" and *Īśvara* (God) are intuitively perceived as pure unconditioned Consciousness (*cit* or *pratipat*) having become conditioned. This basic Reality is stressed, when he says,

> What that one Consciousness is,
> Even That you are. — *Aṛivu*, v. 12

How the duality of the atomicity of *tvam* and the indivisible infiniteness of *tat* is transcended in an intuitive experience of the Self (*Ātmā*) is made clear by the Guru as follow:

> Atom and the indivisible infinite,
> Being and non-being —
> Such dual aspects become manifest
> (Because of the working of the creative urge).
> And afterwards (i.e., on realizing the secret of the cosmic urge
> and its sportive display),
> All dualities cease to be,
> And the experiences of being and non-being too,
> Losing all their bearings, become extinct.
>
> Atomicity disappears bodiless
> In the all-engulfing grandeur of the pure Consciousness or *Ātmā*,
> And therein one attains the plenitude of the indivisible infinite.
> Never known other than as the direct
> Intuitive experience of realization
> Of the stuff of pure Consciousness-effulgence,
> It is a silent ocean of nectar !
>
> — *Ātmopadeśa Śatakam*, vv. 96-97

What is this pure Consciousness-effulgence? Of what kind is it? How did it originate? Such questions do not arise at all. How it assumes the forms of both the knower and the objects known is portrayed by Guru in verses 11, 12 and 13 of his *Aṛivu*, a short Malayalam composition included in this volume. The functional nature of this Substance, and how one of such functions leads us to the final goal, are pictured in an analytico-synthetic manner in verses 36 to 42 of the *Ātmopadeśa Śatakam* (see also chapter 12 of *The Philosophy of Narayana Guru* by the present commentator). Śaṅkara, in this context, makes an attempt to soar high into the realm of the unthinkable from the realm of the thinkables, whereas Narayana Guru directly and intuitively experiences the unthinkable Reality within himself, and then perceives all the thinkables, both the universal and the particular, as the manifest forms of that unmanifest Reality. In other words, Śaṅkara's method here is that of ascending dialectics and Narayana Guru's a descending process in dialectical thinking.

Joyfully Singing (*saṁgāyan*)

The message conveyed by the *mahā-vākya*s is not just meant to be clearly understood. As was pointed out in the very first verse of the present work, it has to be made experiential as the Self-Reality that is unconditioned Happiness in essence, while living here and now. This intuitive experience does not perceive the incessant flow of life as a wild and rough path full of stones and thorns, but as a free-flowing dirge. The notes of a song have their highs and lows that follow a rhythm of their own, that can together render it a sweet one. Likewise, our life also should become transformed as a song of the Self, in which the pains and pleasures of life forming its highs and lows. The words "joyfully singing" (*saṁgāyan*) are to be seen as pertaining to this context.

Move Around Properly. . . (*vipracara*)

The ultimate limit of experientially realizing *Brahman* is what was pointed out so far in this fifth verse. Such an experiential perception of the ultimate Reality renders unreal everything that was till then thought of as the cause of all restlessnesses, worries and problems in life. Thus all the confoundedness of mind disappears. Even this experience of peacefulness is then felt to be nothing but a mode of expression of the one unconditioned Consciousness. The absolute Peace that results thus becomes well-founded in one's life. Nevertheless, one does not escape from the unavoidable necessities of the transactional world. On the contrary, all the vagaries of it are perceived simply as inseparably one with the Self-Reality, enabling one to correct whatever in one's life incongruent with the oneness of that Reality. This makes the flow of life in all its details fully in harmony with that realization, and makes of life itself a self-expression of the Reality thus realized. The activities natural to such a life do not make one bound, but enable one to perceive all such as various modes of expression of an absolutely liberated life. Therefore the *guru*'s instruction to the disciple virtually is, "Your life should become such." On this Narayana Guru says, "With a properly calmed mind resulting from the dawning of *Brahman*-wisdom, you may move around properly in all specific ways" (*vipracara praśāntā manasā tvam brahma-bodhodayāt*).

The word *vipracara* could well be interpreted in two ways here: one, "move around properly in all specific ways" — the prefix *vi* standing for *viśeṣeṇa* meaning "in all specific ways," and *pra* standing for *prakareṇa* meaning "properly," and *cara* meaning "You move around"; and two, "O brāhmaṇa (*vipra*), you may move around." The word *vipra* means "one who undergoes an austere life" (*tapo-vṛtti*). Though this latter sense is not unacceptable here, seen in the light of the words "while being in this world" (*atra bhuvi*) of the first verse, a fully liberated person moving around this world would become all the more relevant.

Karmas

That a person's *karmas* (actions) affect his or her fate in the next incarnation, and that a person's innate propensities called *vāsanā*s depend on his or her *karma*s of many previous incarnations, supposedly form one of the basic tenets of Hinduism. Buddhism also subscribes to this idea. Hindus think, such *karma*s are of three categories: *sañcita-karma*s, *āgāmi-karma*s and *prārabdha-karma*s. The admissibility or otherwise of this belief from the scientific point of view has not been established. Modern genetics acknowledges that, through the sex chromosomes of the male and female, the innate characteristics accumulated through many previous generations are handed down to the new child begotten by the two. In other words, the *karma-vāsanā*s in a newly born child are a blend of certain of the *karma-vāsanā*s of numerous generations in the family trees of both the parents. You cannot fully free yourself from these *vāsanā*s, but it is possible to modify or purify them. Such innate propensities in an individual, whether understood religiously or genetically, constitute the *sañcita-karma*s or accumulated actions of the past.

We are bound to prepare ourselves to perform whatever *karma*s are unavoidable in practical life in the future, in accordance with our inborn innate propensities as well as the characteristics that have been acquired by us as a result of education and past experiences in life. Such expected *karma*s of the future are called *āgāmi-karma*s. To put the same in terms familiar to Indian mythology, all the *karma*s performed in your present life create in you new *vāsanā*s and these decide the nature of your next incarnation and the *karma-vāsanā*s in it. Such a possibility in future incarnations is known as *āgāmi-karma*s.

We also perform certain actions to ensure our existence in this world, and such *karma*s we initiate are given shape by our innate propensities as well as our new ideas and imagination. All such *karma*s already begun are known as *prārabdha-karma*s. The fruits of such are bound to be enjoyed or suffered by ourselves. Such *karma*s are often compared to an arrow already released from the bow that is yet to reach its target. Having been released, it necessarily must hit its target. Similarly, the *prārabdha-karma*s having been begun, no one can escape from their results. On one becoming a *jñānin* (enlightened person) and thus a *mukta* (liberated person) one's seeds of all the *sañcita* and *āgāmi-karma*s that cause future incarnations get completely roasted, but the *prārabdha-karma*s remain to be enjoyed or suffered in the present life. This is how scholars explain the phenomenon that liberated *jñānin*s also happen to have pleasures and pains in life, and also sometimes have to suffer severe bodily pains especially towards the end of their lifetime. Such is the view maintained by almost all the scholars of all the schools of Vedānta.

Narayana Guru, on the other hand, perceives this issue also purely from the point of view of Wisdom, i.e., of the non-duality and immutability of the Self-Reality. Viewed thus, *Ātmā* has no *karma*s. A realized person, being *Ātmā* itself, also has no *karma*s. All the *karma*s, whether *sañcita, āgāmi* or *prārabdha,* are simply superimposed (*adhyasta*) on the non-dual Self in our state of ignorance (*ajñāna*). Vedānta, as everyone agrees, is not meant to teach *ajñāna*. A *jñānin,* i.e., a knower of *Brahman,* being *Brahman* Itself, and *Brahman* having no *karma* of Its own, the knower of *Brahman* also has no *karma* of one's own. A *Brahman*-knower, therefore having to enjoy or suffer the fruits of any kind of *karma*s, be it *sañcita, āgāmi* or *prārabdha,* is meaningless. Conceiving otherwise is really a sort of promiscuous mixing up of *jñāna* with *ajñāna*.

For a *karma* to exist, its doer (*kartā*) must also exist. No *karma* can exist without a doer of it. The idea that one has to suffer or enjoy the fruits of one's actions implies that one is the doer of those actions. This is a notion caused by *ajñāna. Brahman* is no doer of actions, and the *Brahman*-knower has no sense of being the doer of actions. Then either of the two to have any *karma* of its own or his/her own is meaningless. The imaginary *guru,* therefore, asks the disciple who supposedly has already attained Wisdom, "How could there be for you then the bondage of *karmas* whether *prārabdha, sañcita* or *āgāmi*? *Karma* is itself unreal." When *karma* is itself unreal, how can it have subdivisions?

Adhyāsa (Superimposition)

Karmas, as we have just seen, are all unreal in themselves. Likewise, the entire world, in which alone *karmas* are relevant, is also unreal as was seen in verse 2 above. How should we then treat what we perceptually experience and conceive as ideas within ourselves? Vedāntins consider all these as simply superimposed (*adhyasta*) on the one Self. What is this *adhyāsa*? Śaṅkara utilizes the whole of the "Introduction" to his commentary on the *Brahma-Sūtras* to clarify what is *adhyāsa*. For this reason, this "Introduction" is often referred to as *adhyāsa-bhāṣya*. His stand could be summarized as follows:

The two notions "I" and "you," as subject and object, are of opposite nature as are brightness and darkness, and therefore, the two coming together and attaining unity is impossible. Much less possible is the unity of their characteristics. Therefore, attributing the subject and its characteristics on the object, as well as attributing the object and its characteristics on the subject is wrong. Yet it is common practice to attribute subject and its characteristics on the object and vice versa, without discriminating subject, object and their respective attributes, and thus we happen to say, "I am such and such a person," "That is mine," and so on. Seeing, thus, what is unreal as real is called *adhyāsa*. It signifies that the remembered form of a prior experience becomes seen elsewhere in another experience mistakenly (*smṛti-rūpaḥ paratra pūrva-dṛṣṭāvabhāsaḥ*).

The analogy used by almost all the schools of Indian thought to clarify the nature of *adhyāsa*, that means, how the unreal happens to be seen as real, is that of the mother-of-pearl and silver. What our eyes get into contact with is the mother-of-pearl. Silver exists only in our memory, as it was seen somewhere else previously. This silver in the memory is projected on the mother-of-pearl which causes mistaking it for silver. The silver seen thus is superimposed (*adhyasta*). This superimposition (*adhyāsa*) happens only when three circumstances coincide.

1. Though there is sense contact with the real object — in the example, the mother-of-pearl — owing to lack of specific knowledge about it, the knowledge of it remains merely generic, as of something that could be referred to as "this"
2. The knowledge of similarity.
3. The memory of what is superimposed.

The Vedāntin's stand on how *adhyāsa* happens could be summarized as follows: we become unable to perceive the specific nature of the real thing (mother-of-pearl) our eyes get into contact with, because of certain defects of our eyes. Then arises in our mind the memory of something else similar (silver) that we have seen somewhere else previously. In this condition, because of ignorance, the real object (mother-of-pearl), in an undefinable way creates the silver-impression. This is followed by the idea of silver getting formulated in consciousness. Though no silver is created there, the experience "I see silver here" thus takes place. Likewise, though what we really see is *Brahman* or *Ātman* (the Self), because of our ignorance of ourselves, the Self remains hidden from our view, and in an undefinable way It creates the impression of the non-existent world superimposed on Itself. As is the entire world superimposed on the Self, so are *karma*s also superimposed on the Self, because *karma*s take place only in the world.

Sat-cit in Essence

The non-dual *ānanda* experienced as one freely moves around in life, is what this concluding verse expounds, and this experienced *ānanda* can never be something non-existent or empty of content. It, on the other hand, marks the plenitude of Existence. This *ānanda* experience exists in Consciousness or *cit*, and Existence is called *sat*. Therefore, the theme of this stanza, the *ānanda*-experience, is depicted as *sat* and *cit* in essence.

Ātmā is Itself *sat, Ātmā* is *cit,* and *Ātmā* is *ānanda,* as Vedānta defines It. This does not mean that *Ātmā* is an entity constituted of these three factors. On the other hand, the Existence (*sat*) of *Ātmā* is experienced as *cit* and *ānanda; Ātmā* being Consciousness (*cit* or *pratipat*) in essence is experienced as one's own existence (*sat*) and *ānanda* at the same time. *Ātmā* being *ānanda* in essence is an experience in *cit* that alone ultimately exists (*sat*). *Ātmā* being *sat* and *cit* in essence was clarified separately in verses 3 and 4 above.

You Really are *Vibhuḥ*

Vibhuḥ means "that in which all the beings (*bhūtis*) have their being" (*sarva-bhūti-saṁyukte vibhuḥ*). God in this sense is sometimes referred to as *vibhuḥ*. The disciple is taught here, "You are that *vibhuḥ*." That means, the disciple is expected to realize, "I am the Self (*Ātmā*) or *Brahman* that is the one abode of all beings."

Tvam (you) and *vibhuḥ,* as we have already seen, are dialectical counterparts, one being individual and the other universal. Equating these two by their mutual cancellation or by negating the individual and universal conditioning factors from each, unfolds unto our intuitive dialectical vision the non-dual *sat-cit-ānanda* essence of the Self or of oneself. To put the same in common parlance, the duality between *bhakta* (supplicant) and *Bhagavān* (Lord) is transcended as is indicated by the following prayer of Narayana Guru in his hymn named *Sadāśiva Darśanam* (The Vision of Sadāśiva or the Eternally Auspicious God).

> O God, please keep in mind
> That this humble one has no other desire
> Than attaining to the state of You
> And I being one, at this very moment.

Part II

Advaita Dīpikā
(Lamp of Non-duality)

Introduction

NARAYANA Guru's original works, whether philosophical poems or hymns, are all imbued with the essence of non-dualistic (Advaita) perception. In the *Ātmopadeśa Śatakam* (One Hundred Verses of Self-Instruction) in the Malayalam language, he presents his philosophy of non-dualism comprehensively with all relevant philisophical problems dealt with in his own original and systematic way. In the Sanskrit work *Darśana Mālā* (Garland of Visions) he follows, on the other hand, more or less the traditional way, though the garland-shaped structural scheme is something hitherto not conceived by any predecessor of the Vedāntic tradition. Summarizing the core of Vedānta philosophy in five verses is what he does in *Brahmavidyā Pañcakam* (The Science of the Absolute in Five Verses). His other purely philosophical works are *Aṛivu* (Consciousness), *Śloka-trayī* (Triad of Verses) and *Advaita Dīpikā* (Lamp of Non-duality), each answering a specific major problem that arises from the Advaita philosophy.

The first eight verses of *Advaita Dīpikā*, the work we examine here, give stress to one basic stance crucial to Vedānta: that one causal Reality alone has real existence, and that Reality in essence is pure and unconditioned Consciousness. The world, according to this view, is unreal. Then arises a problem: even after becoming fully convinced that the world is unreal, it continues to be perceived by the senses; why is it so? The next seven verses answer this question succinctly, and the last two verses give us directions as to what kind of spiritual discipline enables us to solve this problem for ourselves.

The finality (Self-realization) of Vedāntic teaching is not derived from logic. So too, the solution to the problem raised is not based purely on logical reasoning. It is rather the intuitive penetrative eye of dialectical wisdom that resolves the problem.

The fixed idea that the world exists as it appears to be is the root cause of all problems in life. Vedānta teaches: what really exists is not the world, but is Consciousness or *Ātmā* alone. What appears as the world, including the problems in life that form a part of it, are simply imageries that appear and disappear in the Consciousness-Reality because of its own *māyā*. Treating them seriously is the mistake we make. Contemplation on these lines makes life peaceful, contented and stable. Giving a helping hand to seekers who tread this contemplative path is the sole purpose of this short commentary.

Text, Translation and Commentary

Verse 1

per āyiram pratibhayāyiram iṅṅavaṭril
ārāl eẓum viṣyam āyiram ām prapañcam
orāykil ner itu kināv uṇarum varaikkum
nerām uṇarnn aḷav uṇarnnavan ām aśeṣam ׀

Names in their thousands, mental images in their thousands,
And the corresponding inalienably emerging objects in their thousands —
These together constitute the world.
As long as not reflected on properly, it seems real,
Just as dreams persist to seem real so long as the dreamer does not awaken;
But when he awakens, the entire dream becomes merged into himself.

Advaita Dīpikā (Lamp of Non-Duality) is the name of this philosophical poem. *Dvaita* (duality) is the state in which one perceives or admits two realities or more-than-one reality. *Advaita* is the opposite of *dvaita,* and means the state in which not two is perceived. A perception constituted of countlessly multiple entities is the world we are familiar with. Considering all such apparent entities as real on their own is what *dvaita* signifies in Indian Philosophy. Advaita, on the other hand, is the perception of one underlying Reality in all that appears as many. Then the question arises, "What is that one all-underlying causal Reality?" This question is where the real search begins.

Dīpa means "lamp," and *dīpikā* is a little lamp. A little lamp, when lit, makes a bit of the surrounding area clearly perceptible. Here too is lit a little lamp — the lamp of non-dual perception, shedding light within a clearly conceivable area of thought. As a result, a basic doubt gets resolved. This is a doubt that arises from the very core of what Vedānta ultimately teaches: why does the world continue to be perceived by the senses even after one becomes convinced that it is unreal?

Seekers have always emerged throughout the world. Two are the questions they try to answer: "Who am I?" "From where did this world come into being?" Though seemingly different, the two questions are mutually complementary. Finding an answer to the former takes one to the conviction that the Reality that underlies one's own being is what constitutes the essential content of the whole world as well. Conversely, the search for the causal source of the world answers the question "Who am I?" also, for every individual being is an inalienable part of the world. The one Reality that underlies the being of oneself and the being of the world thus becomes revealed. To live as an embodiment of that Reality is known as *sākṣātkāra,* the nearest English word being "Realization."

Narayana Guru adopts a different approach in each work to unveil his philosophical vision. The *Ātmopadeśa Śatakam* (One Hundred Verses of Self-Instruction), the most important and most comprehensive of his Malayalam compositions, is an attempt to answer the question, "Who am I?" In the *Advaita Dīpikā,* on the other hand, the reflections begin as a search for the causal Reality that underlies the world-appearance. A specific question issuing from the conclusion thus arrived at, is then asked in verses 9 and 10, and answering it is what the rest of the work does.

That this world is an aggregate of countless names (*nāma*) and forms (*rūpa*) is a classical concept as old as the Upaniṣads, the most ancient source books of Vedānta. Going still deeper than this traditional concept, the Guru here thinks of the world as constituted of innumerable names, innumerable mental images and the correspondingly innumerable objects of perception.

What modern science thinks of as the world is the sum total of all physical entities physically perceived by our sense organs. And that physical world is boundlessly expansive. Do the objects thus perceived really exist as they are perceived? We are not sure. Even if granted that they do exist so, they do not become part of the experienced world unless an experiencing mind or consciousness functionally exists. And in that mind numerous ideas should get formulated, each corresponding to an object. This domain of ideas or mental images has to be as extensive as the objective world. World-experience thus is a two-faceted functional situation in which the endlessly expanding perceptible objects form one facet, and the corresponding endlessly expanding world of mental images forms the other. One facet is meaningless without the other.

Every object in the perceptible world has a corresponding image in the perceiver's mind. The Guru calls it *pratibhā*, literally, "a corresponding bright image." Every image thus formulated is usually given a name. Whenever the name is articulated, it helps recall the image of the object. So too, encountering the same or the same type of objects again recalls back the former mental image and the name, enabling us to recognize the encountered object. As far as man, the living being who communicates through languages using words, is concerned, the inseparable oneness of these three — names, mental images, external objects — constitute the experienced world.

Ideas get formulated in our minds; names doubtlessly are devised by minds; and the external perceptible objects, as we will see soon, are nothing but mind or consciousness-substance manifesting itself. The three, in short, are nothing but one unconditioned Consciousness becoming variously conditioned. Therefore, what really exists is none of these three, but one unconditioned Consciousness alone. This truth becomes revealed only to an enlightened seeker. Until thus enlightened, the world as it appears would seem real; the mental images would seem real; the names would seem real.

One of the peculiarities of human mind is that it dreams. Scenes common as well as uncommon in ordinary life are often seen in dreams. They may be believable or unbelievable, pleasant or unpleasant. They are all mere dreams, not real. Yet their being unreal becomes revealed only upon waking. Until then all those scenes would be counted as real. Where do those seemingly real scenes disappear upon waking up? Nowhere else than in the one who was dreaming. Those scenes thus do not just cease to exist but only disappear in the dreamer who continues to exist.

Human mind and human life pass alternately through three states: waking, dreaming and sleeping. All of these and their experiences are nothing but various dream-scenes seen by one unconditioned Consciousness. A dream has no existence apart from the dreamer's mind, itself assuming the form of dreams. This world is an eternal dream dreamt by the one pure and unconditioned Consciousness, also called *cit*.

No dreamer is aware of the fact that what he sees is a mere dream. So too, one who is engrossed in the world-experiences that pass through the alternating three states, does not realize that what one continuously perceives is a prolonged dream, that those scenes are not real on their own. This ignorance, in Vedānta, is known as *ajñāna*. Waking up from this ignorance is comparable to the waking up of a dreamer. Only on this waking up one realizes that what one was till then perceiving as the world is merely one pure Consciousness (*cit*) manifesting itself variously, and that its existence is merely dream-like. Who we imagine ourselves to be, is simply part of that dream.

Whose dream is this, called the world? Of the one pure and unconditioned Consciousness or *cit*. Whose Consciousness is it? No one's; it is simply the non-dual Consciousness that unfolds itself as all experiences. Though ultimately inconceivable, when conceptualized, it can be seen as cosmic as well as individuated. In the former aspect it is known as *Brahman* (the Absolute) and in the latter as *Ātman* (the Self). The cosmic aspect at times is also called *Īśvara* (God) or *Parameśvara* (the Supreme God) as the context demands. Thus it could also be said, this world is a dream dreamt by *Parameśvara*, as the Guru himself conceives in the beginning verse of the *Darśana Mālā*, his most important philosophical poem in the Sanskrit language. He says:

> In the beginning, non-existent indeed was this world. Thereafter the dream-like upsurge of everything was caused by *Parameśvara* by His sheer will. —v.I. 1

Woken up from this dream, what remains would be *Parameśvara* alone, *Brahman* alone, *Ātman* alone, I alone. In the absence of this "I," in the absence of the perceiving "I," the very existence or non-existence of this perceptible world is of no relevance. Such is the line of reflection in the next verse.

Verse 2

ner alla dṛśyam itu dṛkkine nīkki nokkil
veṛalla viśvam aṛivām maruvil pravāham
kāryattil nilppat iha kāraṇa-sattayennye
veṛalla vīciyil irippatu vāriyatre ।

Unreal becomes the visible world seen devoid of the perceiving subject.
None other than a mirage seen in the desert land of Consciousness is this world.
None other than the causal substance is real in the being of effects,
Just as what is real in waves is water alone.

Of what sort is the reality or validity of the visible world was examined in verse 1; the conclusion being that it is similar to that of a dream. The formulation of dreams takes place in the mind of a person who sleeps. In the absence of such a mind no dream happens. This point is made use of here to enter into one of the central ideas of Vedānta.

First, how the subject and the object or the perceiver and the perceived are related is considered. The perceiving Consciousness is then thought of as the causal Substance, and finally how cause and effect are related is cogitated upon.

The perceiver, the perceived and perception are the three factors always involved in every event of knowing. In the Sanskrit language these are known as *dṛk, dṛśya* and *darśana.* Together they are known by the term *tripuṭi* (tripartite factors). The perceiver (*dṛk*) here is none other than the dreaming mind of the last verse, and the perceived, the world constituted of names, mental images and external objects. The claim the Guru makes here is that the latter is unreal in the absence of the former. Take, for example, the case of something being directly perceived. It gains the status of being the perceived only when sensed by the eyes. Unless thus perceived, the thing is not the perceived (*dṛśya*) at all. That the thing will exist even when not perceived is our common notion. Yet someone else seeing it is its basis. Asserting the existence of something not yet perceived by anyone anywhere, not yet even imagined by anyone, makes no sense. In short, the existence of "the perceived" is meaningful only when perceived by a perceiving eye or a knowing mind. "Devoid of the perceiving subject," therefore the Guru says, "the perceived world is unreal." The perceiving mind, in other words, is what makes the world real.

What then is undeniably real? The knowing Mind alone — Consciousness alone. It is in this Consciousness that the dream-sights mentioned in the last verse get formulated. The world, in other words, has only a dream-like reality. What really exists is the dreaming Consciousness or Mind alone. The dreams we are familiar with are not ceaseless. The dream called the world, on the other hand, is not of that sort; it continues to loom as real even after knowing that is not real. The unrealness of the world is therefore clarified further with the help of yet another analogy — that of a mirage. Water would be seen flowing in a desert land seen from a distance in broad daylight. Our knowing that it is just a mirage does not make its appearance vanish. Likewise is the world — even after realizing it to be unreal, it continues to appear real.

What is the grand desert land in which appears this grand mirage, the world? It is the pure, unconditioned Consciousness (*cit*). "I am the perceiver," and "The world is the perceived" simply form the opposing facets of one and the same grand mirage. In other words, "I am the perceiver" and "The world is the perceived" are ideas that get formulated in one Consciousness alone. The very same Consciousness, functioning properly, becomes aware of the unreality of the subject-object duality and realizes their appearance as dream-like or mirage-like. It thus becomes evident that the knowing Consciousness (*dr̥k*) alone is real. The known object, of which the subject-object duality is but a part, is unreal. Ontologically speaking, *dr̥k* or the knowing Consciousness alone is the causal Substance that has its own existence. The experiences, "I am the perceiver" and "The world is the perceived" are all effects. In this specific sense, *dr̥k* or the knowing Consciousness is the cause and *dr̥śya* or "the perceived" is the effect.

The coming into being of anything should be from some source called "cause," and what emerges out of the cause is called "effect." In the case of making a pot, for example, clay is the cause and the pot the effect. Clay cannot assume the form of a pot on its own; a potter has to work on it. The potter too thus is a cause. Clay then is called the material cause (*upādāna-kāraṇa*) of pot and the potter is its incidental cause (*nimitta-kāraṇa*). Our concern here is not the making of pots, but the creation of the world. If the world is an effect, in the place of the pot, what is the clay-like substance out of which it emerged? And who was the creator? There being no causal reality other than the one Consciousness existing, both the causes have to merge in one, which also is known as *Brahman* or *Ātmā* or even the Supreme God. *Brahman* (the Absolute) or *Parameśvara* (the Supreme God) or *Ātmā* (the Self), therefore is considered the material-cum-incidental cause (*abhinna-nimitta-upādāna-kāraṇa*) of the world, in Vedāntic terminology.

The effect pot has no existence apart from that of the cause clay. So too the world's existence is inalienable from that of the causal Substance — Consciousness. As clay assumes the apparent forms of many pots, so too one Consciousness manifests itself as the entire world. Thus the world has no existence apart from Consciousness. Another example very dear to Guru to clarify the inseparable oneness of cause and effect is that of waves and ocean. The water of the ocean is the cause, and the waves are mere apparent, momentary forms that emerge in it. What is real in waves is water alone. No wave exists apart from water. Likewise, the world is the total of the ripple-like forms that emerge in the ocean of Consciousness. No world exists apart from It.

Substantiating this point from the perspective of modern science is what the next verse does.

Verse 3

vāsassu tantuv itu paññiyit ādi-mūla-
bhūta-praghātam itum orkkukil ipṛakāram
bodhattil ninnu vilasunnu maru-sthalattu
pāthassu pole paramāvadhi bodham atṛe ।

Cloths are nothing but yarn; yarn is nothing but fibres;
Fibres are nothing but primeval elements clinging together;
Thus envisioned on and on, it becomes revealed
That everything becomes apparent out of one Consciousness,
As water is seen flowing in a desert land.
Ultimately what exists thus is Consciousness alone.

Being a *ṛṣi* of the ancient wisdom tradition of India notwithstanding, Narayana Guru was a product of the Age of Science, and his thinking was imbued with its spirit. Analytical searching is the method most familiar to science. Even such an enquiry leads us to the conclusion that the one causal substance that underlies the appearance of everything is nothing but consciousness, and that is what Guru underscores in this verse with all the preciseness of a scientific mind. Consciousness alone is the causal reality even in what we consider as inert matter. For example, take a piece of cloth. Taken apart, it turns out to be yarn, and the existence of cloth disappears in the existence of yarn. Yarn, in turn, when analysed is found to be cotton fibres in content. It is these fibres that assumed the form of yarn and cloth. The fibre can be analysed further, taking our search to subtler levels of existence. The ancient Indian scientific mind conceives that all physical entities are constituted of five basic elements — earth, water, fire, air and space — none of which does exist physically anywhere in their pure state (*tanmātras*), for they are too subtle to be physical. All actual physical existences are their various compound forms. The pure states of the elements that underlie physical reality, in other words, exists only as ideas in our consciousness. Individual consciousness is nothing but a functional mode of one universal Consciousness. It is in the existence of this Consciousness that the existence of physical elements are imagined, and they, in their turn, make the physical entities and the world appear as real. What ultimately exists, thus, is Consciousness alone, itself assuming the form of basic elements, fibres, yarn, cloth and so on, and finally the world as well.

Let us now look at what constitutes the fibre from the point of view of modern science. Carbon atoms form the basic content of a cotton fibre. And atoms as such have never been seen by anyone, neither with naked eyes nor microscopically. Their undeniablity is demonstrated by mathemetical calculations of scientists. Such calculations are considered real simply because they work. Every atom has been found to be constituted of a nucleus and a few electrons revolving around it. Electrons are negative energy in essence and the nucleus positive energy. Some minuter particles also have been traced out by scientists as forming part of the nucleus. The existence of all these particles is merely conceivable and theoretical, never perceptible. Yet they are so real that their fusion as well as fission results in the release of energy so immense that it can devastate huge cities at one stroke. That these theoretically existing energies must have a unified field in which they find unity is a dream of scientists, which has not yet been actualized even theoretically. The existence of energy particles, their multiplicity, their unification, all are theories and thus have their being only as functions of the thinking mind or consciousness. Thus the fact that consciousness alone is the one all-underlying reality is admitted, though through the back door, even by modern science.

The ancient Indian way of thinking as well as the modern scientific search for reality thus takes us to one and the same conclusion: what is ultimately real is Consciousness (*cit*) alone. How can this subtle Consciousness/Reality assume the appearance of the gross world? The answer is that the appearance of the world is mirage-like, caused by *avidyā* (ignorance). The world, we that form a part of it, our thinking and theorizations, and even atom bombs, are just mirage-like visions seen in the infinite desert-land of Consciousness.

Verse 4

vṛittistham ām aṟivil viśvavum ill atinṟe
vittām avidyay atum illa viḷakku vannāl
addikkil eṅṅum iruḷ ill uṭan aṅṅu vartti-
viṭṭal viḷakku poliyunn iruḷum varunnu ।

In the Consciousness that underlies all functions
Does exist no world, nor ignorance, its causal seed;
When the lamp shines, no darkness remains thereabout;

The burning wick blown out, the lamp gets extinguished and darkness appears too.

That even a very common physical object like a piece of cloth, when closely examined, is found to be pure and unconditioned Consciousness in essence, is what was laid bare in the last verse. To always function is but natural with Consciousness. Functions constantly change, and as a result the experiences that get formulated in Consciousness also incessantly alter, giving the impression that the objects experienced also are fleeting. Ornaments, whatever their forms assumed, never cease to be gold in essence. So too, our ever-altering experiences, whatever their forms, never cease to be Consciousness in essence.

In the case of the piece of cloth we examined in the last verse, cloth's existence ceases to be or it disappears in the existence of yarn; its non-existence alone remains. Likewise, the yarn's existence is not found in the cotton fibre; only its non-existence remains. So too, the being of none of these would be found in the existence of Consciousness, the ultimate Reality. Though not existing, there is an inherent possibility in Consciousness for all these to appear. Such a non-existence of an effect in a cause, prior to the former's emergence is known as *prāg-abhāva* (anterior non-existence). For example, the *prāg-abhāva* of pot exists in clay. Likewise is the *prāg-abhāva* of the world in the existence of pure Consciousness.

That the *prāg-abhāva* of the world exists means, the world does not really exist, and hence the words, "In the Consciousness that underlies all functions, does no world exist."

How does the world that is simply non-existent, appear to exist? Because of *avidyā* (ignorance). What is *avidyā?* That possibility of error because of which one does not perceive what is really, real and perceives the unreal as real, is called *avidyā.* Under its influence it is but natural that one does not see Consciousness as real and does see the apparent world as real. As a result we happen to think that each of us, while being only transitory functional modes of expression of one Consciousness, has our own separate existences. Consequently we feel, the meaningfulness of life depends upon others and other objects. The contact with them, if favourable, is thought of as making life meaningful, and, if unfavourable, as making life miserable. Life then is felt to be fearsome, and the most fearsome of all phenomena is death. Death, at whatever cost, should be avoided — such is the way we treat it. One ultimate means alone avails to avoid death as well as to be saved from all fears: getting rid of *avidyā,* the cause of all of them.

How to get rid of *avidyā*? First we should find out where it exists. If it does exist anywhere at all, it should be in the one Consciousness for the simple reason that Consciousness alone has real existence. To think that *avidyā* (ignorance or the absence of true knowledge) can exist in Consciousness is simply absurd. And nothing other than Consciousness has existence either. Ultimately thus, *avidyā* can have no existence of its own, and hence the words, "Nor does ignorance, the causal seed of the world, exist."

What then is it that we call *avidyā*? It is simply like calling the absence of light, darkness. Darkness has no being. Brightness can be present or absent. Darkness is merely the name given to the absence of light. *Avidyā,* likewise, is the absence of *vidyā* (knowledge).

If Consciousness alone exists, then how can there be absence of knowledge? Consciousness or knowledge, in fact, does not cease to exist nor does it disappear. Simply we remain oblivious of the reality that Consciousness alone exists. Our seeing or not seeing Consciousness as what really exists does in no way affect the existence of Consciousness as such, but doing so affects us. Not seeing what really exists, causes us to think of what is not real as real and to live accordingly.

Why do we then not see the real as the real? Suppose you go to a jewellery shop to buy ornaments. There you examine the type of ornaments you need, looking for the particular design you like. All ornaments are different in your perception. But the jeweller sees all of them as just gold in different forms, and he fixes their price simply by weighing the gold content in them. Likewise is our case. Our perception of us and of the world is so conditioned that we see each of us and everything perceptible as different realities, never seeing the one all-underlying Substance. This conditioning is called *avidyā*. We have to decondition ourselves to see all this differently looking apparent forms as one Reality manifesting itself variously. And that Reality is what we just now saw as Consciousness in essence, and is popularly known in Vedānta as *Ātmā* (the Self) and *Brahman* (the Absolute). Deconditioned thus, we find all the endlessly multiple entities as merging and disappearing in the being of the one *Ātmā* or *Brahman.* The most intriguing factor is that without assuming such modes of appearance, the one Reality/Consciousness (*Ātmā* or *Brahman*) cannot exist pure and simple. And as with gold, the very manifest forms end up becoming a veil that hides the one Reality from being perceived. The potential for such self-hiding self-manifestion is mysteriously inherent in the one Reality, and this mystery is what is known as *māyā*.

One way alone is open before us to remove the darkness of *avidyā,* as is the one way of bringing forth a lit lamp to remove ordinary darkness. Bringing forth the lamp of non-dual wisdom (*Advaita Dīpikā*) dispels the darkness of *avidyā*. Then alone it is revealed that the world that appears has no existence of its own, nor does *avidyā,* its causal seed, and that everything is a magic-like *māyā*.

A lit lamp sheds its light all around; so too if the lamp of wisdom is lit in life, then no *avidyā* can overrule it. The world will then be found to have no real existence. No suffering, no fear, not even the fear of death will then have any place in life. Nonetheless, our predicament is such that even though the lamp is already within us, it is as though it has been extinguished. The lamp in us needs relighting. Otherwise, life will remain totally submerged in the darkness of *avidyā*.

Verse 5

ārāikil īyulakam ill itavidya tattvam-
orātavarkk it ulakāy vilasum bhramattāl
ārāl viḷakk erikil illa piśācit andha-
kāram bhayannavan iruṭṭu piśācu polām ׀

Closely examined, this world is found non-existent,
it being mere *avidyā.*
To those who are ignorant of Being as such,
It looms as the world simply because of delusion.
When a lamp is lit nearby, no ghost appears to be,
But for those afraid of darkness
The very same darkness looms as a ghost.

Why are humans roused to think of the meaning of life? Everyone intends to live happily, but the happiness they dream of is never enjoyed to its fullest. Though dreaming of a happy state, at times one plunges into the depth of unimagined miseries. By no means and at no cost it is possible to keep out suffering in life absolutely. For this reason human beings live in fear of suffering. Given the unavoidable difficulties and distresses of life, how can we live free from fear? This is a fundamental problem in life for which everyone knowingly or unknowingly is in search of an answer. Some are fully aware of the seriousness of the problem; some are not. Either way they need a solution, and the only possible solution is what the present verse suggests.

What is ultimately Real (*sat*) was brought to light in the first four verses, and that Reality (*sat*) is Consciousness (*cit*) alone. Fear and suffering are caused by events that happen in the world. We too were born as part of the world, as part of the beginningless and endless flow of events that take place in what really exists. Every event or the outcome of every event reacts with other events or the outcome of other events. That is the way the unfoldment of events takes place in the Reality.

Consciousness (*cit*) in essence, this Reality can never remain inert and inactive. Always alive and active, it manifests itself as newer and newer apparent forms, one after another, and one continuing into another. The Reality, being Consciousness in essence, must also know what takes place in Itself.

This Reality, while being *sat* and *cit*, is also *ānanda* (Value experience) in content, and hence evaluating every event as desirable, undesirable or indifferent is but natural within Its self-unfolding and self-knowing function. Desirable events cause happiness, undesirable events unhappiness or suffering. How to avoid the latter is the problem before us.

Reality (*sat*) being Consciousness (*cit*) in essence, is always functional, and hence gross and subtle phenomena appearing and disappearing in Reality (*sat*) is but natural. We form a part of it. The aggregate of this constant flow of events is what we call the world. The Sanskrit word for world is *loka*, meaning "that which can be looked at." What is ultimately Real in all such perceptibles, as we have already seen, is *cit* alone. The real cause of all suffering and fear in life, in short, is our habit of treating the perceptible world as real in itself. Realizing Consciousness alone as really existing transforms the world, all the events in it, we individual beings who experience them, the actual feeling of happiness and suffering, all into mere ripples that appear and disappear on the surface of the boundless ocean of Consciousness. Knowing what is ultimately Real — which is *sat, cit, ānanda* — is the one and only way that saves us finally from all the miseries and fears of life.

Every wave is inseparably one with the occan, i.e., it has no existence apart from the ocean. So too, we individuals, the world, events in the world, the happiness and suffering they cause, which are all mere waves that emerge and remerge in the ocean of Consciousness, do not exist apart from that Reality. Whatever the transformations that take place in It, they are all really that one

Substance in essence. Yet, we remain completely oblivious of being that Substance, even as we remain as It.

Why is it so? Because *avidyā* veils from us the reality that we are all essentially one Consciousness even now. The result is that we perceive the apparent phenomenal manifestation of Consciousness or *Ātmā* — what we call the world that has no existence of its own — as real, and remain ignorant of what we really are in essence. Mysteriously self-concealing is the functional dynamism of *Ātmā.* Knowing is one of its many functions. This function may result in right knowledge or wrong knowledge. The possibility of the latter type of knowing, particularly concerning what is real, is what is to be understood as *avidyā.*

To get rid of suffering and fear in life, first we have to become aware that we are being misguided by *avidyā*. How is it possible while we are already under the spell of *avidyā*? There are masters who have already transcended the bewitching spell of *avidyā;* they will guide us. Narayana Guru was one such. Hence his assuring words: "Closely examined, this world is found non-existent, it being mere *avidyā.*"

Once this message of the world-being-not-real is heard of from a *guru*, what we need is to search for what is really Real. When an ardent seeker meets a real *guru*, the *guru* leads the seeker to the Real as well. What thus we attain finally is termed *tattvam* here. *Tat* means "That," standing for the Reality we are searching for. *Tvam* is a suffix meaning "the state of something being itself." *Tattvam* thus means the state in which "That" or Reality is itself pure and unconditioned, rendered here as "Being as such." Knowing *tattvam* thus means becoming aware that one Consciousness alone exists underlying all appearances. Unless and until thus knowing *tattvam*, one continues to count the world as real. The *tattvam* realized, one becomes enlightened that everything is nothing but one Reality or Consciousness unfolding itself incessantly, just as all ornaments are different forms that one gold-substance assumes.

Wrongly understanding the apparent forms as real is what is known as *bhrama* (delusion). It happens only when reality and unreality are not discriminated. In such an indiscriminate state of knowing, one may be taken for the other and it is called *bhrama*. This error simply vanishes upon knowing what the Real is. The certainty we come to thus is known as *pramā*. Getting rid of *bhrama* and attaining *pramā* is what we need. As bringing in light is the way to dispel darkness, so too getting rid of *bhrama* is to be attained by dispelling the darkness of *avidyā* by bringing in the light of wisdom (*jñāna*).

What is wisdom? I, the individual, realizing that what is real in me is the ultimate Reality alone. That Reality is Consciousness; thus I am Consciousness. It then becomes revealed that the one Consciousness that I am unfolds itself as everything everywhere as well, and that is what we call the world. The grossest aspect of that manifestation is what we call matter, and the subtlest aspect, mind. Realizing thuswise constitues the essential content of wisdom.

Fearing ghosts in the dark is something common among humans. No one then thinks patiently whether such a being called ghost exists or not. Yes, it does exist: really, it is none other than the ghost of ignorance in each of us. What is perceived as a ghost in ordinary darkness is nothing other than the darkness itself. Hence the way of freeing someone from the fear of ghosts is not arguing with him in order to convince him that ghosts do not exist, but is to simply bring forth the light. Likewise, freeing human beings from fiendish fears and sufferings is to be accomplished by bringing forth the lit lamp of wisdom, or else the lamp getting lit on its own.

Verse 6

uṇṭillay ennu muṛa māṛiy asattu sattu
raṇṭum pṛatītam it anādi-tamas svabhāvam
raṇṭum tiraññiṭukil illay assattu rajju-
khaṇḍattil ill uragam uḷḷatu rajju mātṛam ।

The real and the unreal — each appears in turn as though existing and not existing;
Both are phenomenal appearances that are but the beginningless darkness manifesting itself:
Closely looked at, both appearences have no being and thus are unreal;
There is no snake in a piece of rope; what exists is rope alone.

We live in this world, where we perceive and experience everything around us. That we do exist, that everything we encounter exists as such, which is the idea we usually have, is experienced by consciousness. The being of all experiences is in consciousness alone, as functional modes of consciousness alone.

Going deeper to the level of subtleties, we see that what is directly perceived with our senses is not the real, but what underlies it is the real. It was in that sense it was stated in the last verse, "Closely examined, the world is found to be non-existent." That too is a knowledge. In other words, that the world exists is an experience and that the world does not exist also is an experience, and as experiences both have their being in consciousness. This consciousness, underlying both, in essence is the ultimate Reality and is beginninglessly and endlessly functional. As a result emerges the experience, "This world exists." Moreover, Consciousness unfolds itself as the world it experiences as well. As the other side of this comes the experience, "This world is unreal." The all-underlying Consciousness has in it the inherent potential to unfold as ourselves and create in us the impressions "The world is real," and "The world is not real."

As these impressions alternate, we get confused as to what is real and what is unreal. In order to avoid this the Guru warns us, "Both are phenomenal appearances." The original word for "phenomenal appearance" is *pratīti*. It means "that which has no existence of its own, but makes the impression of existing." "The world is real" and "The world is unreal," in other words, are both phenomenal appearances. Then ultimately what is real? The one Consciousness in which the two phenomena appear together alone is Real.

How do such appearances, that are opposite in nature, emerge in the one Reality? Although Consciousness is Effulgence in essence, there is inherent in it an element of darkness that conceals from itself its own true nature and content. What happens when darkness prevails was seen in the last verse: Ultimately what is real will not be perceived; non-existent ghosts will be seen, and we get scared. Likewise the one beginningless and endless Reality — Consciousness — is not perceived and instead what is perceived are the alternating phenomenal appearances. The darkness that causes this concealment is called *avidyā*. The all-underlying Reality is beginningless and endless. The *avidyā* inherent in It is also beginningless, but it is not endless, for it ends with knowing its nature and how it functions, with intuitively perceiving the one Consciousness that alone exists, oneself becoming merged in It.

All appearances are the darkness of *avidyā* manifesting itself. The original word for "manifesting itself" is *svabhāva*. *Bhāva* means "manifest form," and *svabhāva*, self-manifestation. The word also means "characteristic of" which implies, manifesting itself as the world of dualities is characteristic of *avidyā* (darkness). All appearances in this sense are just darkness manifesting itself. Nothing, we know, is visible when light radiates in pure space. Whatever is distinctly seen is some form that obstructs the free radiation of light rays. Such forms, in principle at least, are the opposite of light (darkness) in essence. All visible forms are thus darkness materialized. In the place of ordinary light, what is Real is Consciousness. The darkness inherent in It, materialized, assumes the form of the appearance of the real-unreal opposites.

Surprisingly enough, nothing is said in this verse about the one Reality, for all that is to be said was stated as early as at the end of verse 3. It needs no further clarification. Therefore, instead of repeating it, an analogy is given here that helps one intuitively perceive the Reality: the well-known rope-snake analogy. No matter how many times, how many people, mistake a piece of rope for a snake and become frightened, it never really becomes a snake. It continues to be the rope. Likewise, whatever the various theories and hypotheses scientists and philosophers formulate concerning what is Real, these ideas never affect what really exists. Such theories are nothing but ideas that took shape in the ever-existing Consciousness. The very same Consciousness appears as the world theorized about as well as the theorizing mind. This certainty attained, one feels, one merges back gently into the Reality, also represented by the syllable *AUṀ*, wherein no preference for the ideas of the real and the unreal has any role to play.

Verse 7

asty astiy ennu sakalopari nilpatonne
satyam samastavum anityam asastyam ākum
mṛttin vikāram at asatyam itinkal okke
varttippat orkkil oru mṛttitu satyam atre ।

"This exists," "This exists," thus what has existence above everything
Alone is Real; everything else is fleeting and thus unreal.
The changeful apparent forms that clay assumes are all unreal;
The clay that underlies these forms alone is found to be real when well thought of.

Ultimately what is Real? Answering this one question is the task all philosophers and scientists have before them. An infallible method acceptable to all has to exist in order to discriminate the real from the unreal. The present verse clears the path of this method in a scientific way by delineating the characteristic features of the real and the unreal.

We began the present enquiry admitting the existence of the apparent world and examining its essential components. It is changeful, and this is the reason for distrusting its realness. What then is to be counted as real? That which ultimately exists, that which eternally exists, is real. The apparent world does not seem to be real ultimately, for an element of insubstantiality is evident in what appears to be. A piece of cloth, for example, disappears in the being of yarn. Yarn, in turn, disappears in the existence of cotton fibre, and fibre finally in the constituent elements. These elements too ultimately disappear in the being of Consciousness. The being of Consciousness, on the other hand, has nothing causal behind it in which It disappears, for It is conscious of its own beingness. Thus we are provided with an infallible path leading us to what is ultimately real, through which we arrive at the certainty we are in search of. Almost same is what the modern science resorts to in its search for reality, except that scientists do not admit that names, mental images and objects together make up the world. The aggregate of perceptible objects alone, in their perception, constitutes the world. And what ultimately underlies the material appearance — energy — is thought of by them as real.

Modern science too, thus in principle, admits, what really exists is that which we finally come to when advancing our search like, "This is real," "This is real." Yet, what essentially that reality — energy — is, remains a conundrum. Vedānta, by defining the unreal as that which is changeful and fleeting, helps us in this matter. How does this criterion help us evaluate the conclusion science has arrived at? Is the reality thus arrived at, particle or wave, changeless or changeful, eternal or fleeting, one or many? Though the scientists wish it to be one, the energy they actually came across is not one, but of many forms, each different in its intensity and nature. The lifespan of some of them is less than even a hundred-thousandth fraction of a second. Such dissimilarities as weak force, strong force and neutral force have also been discovered among them. In short, the ultimate reality scientists know of is not one, not eternal, and not changeless. Provable both as particle and wave, and for that matter, as substance and no-substance, it remains a mystery for them. What does then underlie these mysterious, fleeting, changeful, multiple forms of energy? The conclusion Guru comes to in the present study is that the underlying factor is the Consciousness that knows all these forms of energy.

In order to help us methodically decide what eternal Reality ultimately underlies all the apparent existences, Guru here conveniently makes use of the pot-clay analogy, which is very famous in classical Vedānta. Pot, pan, plate, cup, or whatever be the apparent form one clay-substance assumes, they never cease to be clay in substance, and clay never ceases to be clay either. Likewise is the Consciousness-Substance (*cit*) that assumes the forms of countless names, countless mental images, and countless perceptible objects. Even when appearing as all these, It never ceases to be Consciousness in essence, nor does Its existence ever cease to be.

The one everlasting Consciousness (*cit*), what ultimately exists (*sat*), radiantly manifests itself everlastingly. This radiant self-manifestation of Consciousness is known in Vedānta as *bhāna*. It causes the unfoldment of Its own *ānanda* content as pleasurable, painful or indifferent experiences as well. This is true whether one realizes it being so or remains completely ignorant of it, as is clarified in the next verse.

Verse 8

ajñāna-veḷayilum asti vibhāti ranṭum
ajñātam alla sukhavum vilasunnu mūnnum
rajju-svarūpam ahiyoṭum idantay ārnnu
nilkkunnatinn iha nidarśanam ām it orttāl ।

Even when in ignorance
One's *asti* is never unknown;

So too is *bhāti* (*vibhāti*);
And so too is one's *priya* (*sukha);*
Thus all these three always find expression.

When the rope's content is associated
With the idea of snake, it
Assumes a new this-ness.

Well considered, this analogy
Illustrates the aforesaid.

Asti, bhāti, priya are three conjoined technical terms of Vedānta. *Brahman* or *Ātmā* is defined as *sat, cit, ānanda*. These three, as an individual experiences, are signified by the terms *asti, bhāti,* and *priya. Sat* means "Existence," and is experienced by an individual as "I exist." This experience of self-existence is referred to as *asti,* meaning "something exists." The essential content of self-existence is pure Consciousness (*cit*) — the consciousness of beingness, effulgence in essence. Never remaining inactive, it incessantly finds expression as stream-like experiences. This function of *cit* is named *bhāti* meaning, "the shining forth of something." Every such experience is more than an event of knowing. It involves an evaluation also, relating the object known to one's own value notions or likes and dislikes, and thus treating it as pleasurable, painful or indifferent. This phase of the evaluating function of consciousness denotes "the state of being dear" termed *priya. Asti, bhāti, priya,* in other words, are three facets of every individual's conscious beingness.

Take the case of an ignorant person. He is not at all aware of the one Reality that exists above all that is perceivable and conceivable. Such a person takes the perceived world as real. (That all such visibles are unreal we have already seen.) Those who perceive thus are called *ajñānins* (the ignorant). *Ajñāna* (ignorance) is the wrong knowledge of treating the unreal as real. The mental function that causes *ajñāna* is what is known as *avidyā* (nescience).

Ajñānins also have the sense of existence — the sense of self-existence and the sense of the world's existence. They too thus experience beingness (*asti*). Likewise, the act of knowing goes on constantly within them also. They are aware of the changing world as well as of themselves who perceive the changing world. The individual consciousness or mind finds expression as all these experiences without interruption. This is called *bhāti*. Each such act of knowing or experiencing, even in the case of the ignorant, is an event of evaluating what is experienced in terms of pleasure, pain or indifference as well, the manifest form of the *ānanda* content of *Ātmā*. *Priya*, thus, is not absent in the knowing function even for the ignorant.

A *jñānin* perceives his/her own existence, his/her experiences, his/her pleasures and pains, merely as the *asti-bhāti-priya* facets of his/her own being. Such a one sees the cosmic counterpart of his/her own being as what we call the world, the constantly changing unpredictable facets of its appearance, and the pleasures and pains it entails. An *ajñānin*, on the other hand, is incapable of thinking or of being concerned with the ultimate Reality. Yet in an *ajñānin*'s case too, the *asti- bhāti-priya* trio is not irrelevant. The difference is that such a one remains quite ignorant of its place in his/her life.

The Guru, in order to illustrate this point, resorts to the well known rope-snake analogy. The context in the analogy is that of mistaking a piece of rope in twilight for a snake and then becoming frightened. In the perception of one who sees correctly what really is there, the rope alone has existence, rope alone is cognized as existing, and it is not at all frightening. He therefore remains fearless. The one who mistakes it for a snake also has his own *asti*-experience (that the snake exists), *bhāti*-experience (that he sees a snake) and *priya*-experience (that it is a frightful being). Only that the trio in the latter case is much different from what is true for the *jñānin*.

In other words, both when a *jñānin* perceives Consciousness alone as real and when an *ajñānin* sees the world as real, the trio of *asti-bhāti-priya* is equally relevant — that consciousness exists, that consciousness functions, and that from consciousness well up pleasures and pains, are equally true. It's only that the former is aware of it being so and the latter is not. We should remember that these three (*asti-bhāti-priya*) are none other than the individuated facets of *sat-cit-ānanda.*

Verse 9

viśvam viveka-daśayinkal aẓiññu sarvam
asvastham ākilum at-indriya-dṛśyam ākum
dikkin bhramam viṭukilum ciram iṅṅivanṟe
dṛkkinnu dikku punar aṅṅane tanne kāṇām ।

The entire world, in the state of discriminative awareness,
Becomes separated out as having no existence of its own.
Still it continues to be perceptible to the senses.
Even after becoming free from the confusion of directions,
To the viewer's eye, the confused directions
Continue to be the same.

Verse 10

satyattil illay ulakam sakalam viveka-
viddhvastam-āya piṟakum vilasunnu munpol
nistarkkam-āy maruvil ill iha nīram ennu
siddhikkilum vilasiṭunn itu mun-pṟakāram ।

Really the world has no existence;
yet it looms as real as before
Even after being completely annihilated as a result of
discriminative awareness.
Even after becoming fully convinced that,
Doubtlessly, no water is present in mirage,
It looms to be so as before.

That of mistaking a piece of rope for a snake was the analogy relied on in verse 8. Bringing forth a light makes the apparent snake disappear and reveals the real rope. The snake will be seen no longer, and thereafter only the rope is seen. But such is not the case with the world. Even after discriminating the real and the unreal, and becoming certain that the world has no existence, it contiunes to appear. It continues to be perceived by senses. Laying bare this problem with the help of two analogies is what verses 9 and 10 do. Its solution forms the rest of the work. A real *jñānin* intuitively perceives the world that never ceases to appear and the one all-underlying Reality (*sat*), non-dually. The Guru does not deny the apparent existence of the world. The apparent world, on the other hand, is the form in which the one Reality exists. Such is the perception of a *jñānin*. Being a part of the world, one cannot realize one's oneness with Reality by denying one's own existence. On the contrary, realization is to be done through intuitively perceiving oneself as well as everything else as one Reality become manifest. Suggestive of all this are these two verses that occupy the very centre of this composition.

We have already established that what ultimately exists alone is Real. Whatever is other than That has therefore to be unreal. This was underscored by the statement, "everything else is fleeting and thus unreal" of verse 7. Even after attaining this conviction, the world continues to appear as it did when one was still an *ajñānin*. How is it so? We'll see this question answered in the remaining verses. Here, in the present two verses, the nature of the problem before us is simply shown.

Many, on arriving at unfamiliar places, get confused as to which is the east and which is the west. The south is sometimes taken for the east. Seeing the sun rising the following morning clears all such doubts. Despite this, one may continue to feel, "Here it seems the sun rises in the south." This is because the confounded sense of directions had become fixed in one's mind. Such ideas become fixed in us concerning knowledge of the world also. Vedānta calls it "conditioning" (*upādhi-paricchinnatā*) of knowledge. Though pure and unconditioned in essence, Consciousness never remains functionless. Functioning appears in conditioned forms which in no way affect the essential purity of Consciousness. Such conditionings are simply superimposed on the Real and are known as *adhyāsa*. That which appears in conditioned forms is then called *adhyasta*, and the unconditioned Reality *anadhyasta*.

Someone becoming confounded about directions in no way affects the real directions of the compass. Likewise, even when the superimposed appearances are seen in what is Real, the unconditioned Reality remains unconditioned, unaffected. This point is further clarified in verse 10 with the help of the mirage-analogy. Water appears as rippling in desert lands in the midday light. Knowing well that no water exists there does not make the appearance of the mirage vanish. Nor does our seeing the water there or our knowing well that no water is there, affect in any way the real nature of the desert either. Our understanding alone is what undergoes change.

"Really the world has no existence" is the enlightened awareness a *jñānin* attains, and is suggestive of the basic stand of the Advaita school of Vedānta. It is almost equivalent to Śaṅkara's famous words *brahma satyam jagan-mithyā* (*Brahman* alone is real; the world is unreal). Yet this philosophical or rather logical conviction does not put an end to perceiving with our senses the world as existing.

"How to explain this?" is the problem the Guru poses here. The need of addressing this problem, hitherto unasked in any major Vedāntic text, might have been the inspiring force behind writing the present work.

Verse 11

jñānikku satt-ulaku cittu sukha-svarūpam
ānandam allanṛtam ajñan-it-apṛakāśam

kāṇunnavannu sukham astitay-ārnna bhānu-
mān-arkkan andhan-iruḷārnnoru śūnya-vastu ।

In the perception of the enlightened,
What appears as the world is but *sat* alone.
It is *cit* as well, so is it *ānanda* in essential content.
It never is insubstantial.
Yet it being so is not evident to the unenlightened.
The existence of the sun, easily perceptible to the sighted,
Is simply a darkish vacuity for the sightless.

Discriminating the real and the unreal was the main presentation in the first half of the present work. The conclusion thus arrived at was this: pure and unconditioned Consciousness (*cit*), as the one all-underlying Substance (*sat*), alone exists on its own. The apparent world has no existence of its own and hence is unreal.

Why is it then that, even after knowing thus clearly and definitely, the world continues to appear as real to the senses? This is the major problem posed in verses 9 and 10 that form the very middle of the work. How the world thus appears to be real to sense preception is adjudged by a *jñānin* (an enlightened one), the central point of the answer to the question, is what we see in the present verse. The remaining verses are a sort of elaboration appended to what this verse conveys to us.

The Guru clarifies the point with the help of an analogy. As the sun shines in the sky on a bright day, it radiates its light everywhere, and everything in the world becomes perceptible because of its light. Still such a sight is perceptible only to a sighted person. No blind person can see it. For the blind even such a sight appears to be a void of darkness. Likewise is the case of the Sun of Consciousness, the Sun of *Ātmā*. It incessantly manifests Itself as all the world. The enlightened one, with the inner eye of wisdom open, perceives the one Consciousness or *Ātmā* alone as assuming the form of, manifesting Itself as, everything, all together forming what we call the world. In other words, a *jñānin* is fully aware that what is seen as the world is nothing but *Ātmā* or Consciousness.

Reality, as the abstract substance that underlies all appearances, having no form or name of its own, is termed *avyākṛta* (the unmanifest), literally that which has not yet been made into specific forms. In the state in which it has assumed specific, perceptible, understandable forms, it is called *vyākṛta* (the manifest). For instance, gold as a substance is *avyākṛta*, and it becomes *vyākṛta* as it appears in the form of various ornaments. So too, *Ātmā* is *avyākṛta*; the world is simply its *vyākṛta* form. A *jñānin*, therefore, sees only Consciousness or *Ātmā*, *sat-cit-ānanda* in essence, alone as manifesting Itself as the perceived world.

What is ultimately Real is called *sat* in Sanskrit. The one and only ultimate Reality, *Ātmā*, thus is definable as *sat*. *Ātmā*, as *sat* has inherent in it the immense potential and urge to unfold Itself as the world. For this reason, It never remains unmanifest. *Ātmā*, thus become manifest, is what we call the world which on its own is unreal (*asat*). A *jñānin* sees in the unreal, apparent, world the one Real, unmanifest, *Ātmā* alone manifesting.

What in essential content is this one ultimate Reality (*sat*)? It is Consciousness in essence. *Cit* is the Sanskrit word for consciousness. *Ātmā* thus is definable as *cit* as well. This *cit*, as abstract reality, is *avyākṛta*, and having become *vyākṛta* assumes the form of all kinds of knowledge — knowing the world as existing, termed *avidyā*, as well as knowing the world as not existing, termed *vidyā*. In other words, both *vidyā* (knowledge) and *avidyā* (ignorance) are different, mutually exclusive, manifestations of one *cit*. Sense experience — in the present case, of experiencing the world as existing — is also none other than a particular manifest form of *cit*.

Sense perception always involves more than an event of knowing something. Along with knowing, evaluating what is perceived in terms of the perceiver's value notions, and relating it with one's likes and dislikes in life, pleasure and pain, also takes place. One likes the object if it is pleasurable, dislikes it if painful, and feels indifference if it is neither pleasant nor unpleasant. Whatever the resultant feeling, relating the known object to one's happiness and suffering always takes place, and it takes place nowhere else than in Consciousness, the essential content of *Ātmā*. This evaluating aspect that serves as a measuring rod for discriminating pain and pleasure, is what is called *ānanda* in Vedānta. Put conversely, it is the *ānanda* content of *Ātmā* that manifests itself as our pleasures and pains. A *jñānin*, therefore, sees only the *ānanda* aspect of his own beingness — Ātmā — becoming *vyākṛta* in all pleasant and painful experiences in the perceived world. In short, in the perception of a *jñānin*, the world that continues to be perceived even after realizing its being unreal, is nothing but the manifestation of the *sat-cit-ānanda* content of *Ātmā* (the Self). The apparent world, in other words, is nothing other than *Ātmā* manifesting Itself.

This apparent world thus is not insubstantial, nor is it chaotic and orderless either. This is the reason why it is called the cosmos. The one all-underlying Reality, when manifesting Itself as the lawful and harmonious cosmic order, is called *ṛta* in Sanskrit. Hence the Guru's words, "It never is *anṛta*," rendered here as "It never is insubstantial."

In short, the self-manifestation of the one Consciousness, the all-underlying Reality, *sat-cit-ānanda* in essence, is what an enlightened person continues to perceive as the world. The perceiver and the act of perceiving are also none other in essence. What really happens in sense perception is not the event of one perceiving another; it simply is the one Consciousness-Reality unfolding itself as the perceiver, the perceived object and the act of perceiving, and all these three once again realizing their essential oneness.

This truth is not apparent to all. For a *jñānin*, on the other hand, it is something as clear as broad daylight. It would not be a *jñānin* who asks, "Why does the world continue to be perceived even after one realizes it to be unreal?" Some basic stands of Vedānta are founded on experiential, dialectical awareness (*yoga-buddhi*). Those who ask for such explanations, in the usual course, rely on logical thinking alone, with no idea about the dialectical awareness of *jñānins*. Such doubts are never answerable logically. On the contrary, the doubts vanish altogether on one's becoming enlightened. The Guru therefore warns, "Yet it being so is not apparent to the unenlightened."

Verse 12

vitt-onnu-tān vividham-āy vilasunn-itinkal
arthāntaram ceṛutum illa viśeṣam-āyi
rajju-svarūpam aṛiyāt-iruḷāl vivarta-
sarpam ninaykkil itu rajjuvil ninnu veṛo ।

One seed alone is it that manifoldly manifests itself;
In the manifest, no other meaning content at all exists.
When one, ignorant of the rope-reality, thinks of it as a snake,
Does it become existent apart from the rope?

The Guru restates the philosophy of non-dualism (*advaita*) in the present work, as the answer to the question, why the world continues to be perceptible to the senses even after realizing its unreality. That the apparent world is unreal does not mean that nothing has existence. One Reality does exist, and as we saw in the last verse, in essence it is *sat-cit-ānanda*. It is what unfolds itself as the world perceptible to the senses, as the perceiver and his senses, and as the act of perceiving. A *jñānin*, therefore, intuitively sees only one *avyākṛta* Reality — *Ātmā* or Consciousness — as become *vyākṛta* and having assumed the form of all these three.

A very tiny seed of a banyan tree grows into a huge, endlessly branching tree that can live many centuries. Countless are the leaves and fruits that bud in it and grow old, and fall down year after year; yet the tree continues to exist. The extremely subtle seed has inherent in it all these potentials. Comparable to this is the phenomenon of life. Countless individual beings, organic and inorganic, form the leaves, flowers and fruits of the tree of life. They bud, they exist for a while, and they disappear, whereas the tree of life continues to exist endlessly. Life, in other words, is an eternal phenomenon that continues through the birth and death of individual beings. The aggregate of those beings, in their gross form, is what we call the world.

Reality is not what is visibly apparent; the invisible one Substance that underlies all the changing forms is the Reality. The apparent pot-form is not the real; the clay that assumes the pot-form is the real. The one Reality that assumes the form of the world and life is what we saw in the beginning as Consciousness in essence, and in the last verse as *sat-cit-ānanda.*

Whichever the ornament-form gold assumes, it never ceases to be gold; nor are ornaments real on their own except as forms assumed by gold. Similar is the unreality of the world and the reality of *sat-cit-ānanda.* The world's apparent existence is as the ever-changing manifest form of that one absolute Reality, also called *Brahman* in Vedānta. The world, whatever its visible and knowable forms, whatever names given to them, never ceases to be the one *Brahman* in essence. Hence the famous Upaniṣadic dictum *sarvam khalvidam brahma* (everything here indeed is *Brahman*). Such is the vision that the Guru's words enshrine.

The Vedāntin's stand that the visible world is unreal only means that the form of the world perceived by the senses has no existence on its own. All such forms are superimposed on *Brahman,* which alone really exists. Even when assuming the form of and appearing as the world, the causal Reality continues to be the same. This phenomenon of effects perceivably appearing while the causal reality undergoes no intrinsic change, is known as *vivarta* in Vedānta, exemplified best by the rope-snake analogy.

Someone seeing a piece of rope as a snake does not in any way make any intrinsic change in the real rope; it continues to be the same. The perceived snake has no existence apart from the rope either. The snake is simply a form superimposed by the perceiver on the rope, and hence is *vivarta*. Likewise, the *sat-cit-ānanda,* become *vivarta,* appears as the world to the one who does not see the former. In short, when one, owing to ignorance, does not see *Brahman* as *Brahman,* It appears to him as the world.

To become convinced of this one needs simply to analyse what is perceived. Putting emphasis on this point is what the Guru does in the next verse.

Verse 13

oronnatāy avayavam muẓuvan piriccu
veṛākkiyāl ulakam illa vicitṛam atṛe
veṛākum īy-avayavaṅṅalum evam aṅṅott-
ārāykil ill-akhilavum nija-bodha-mātṛam ।

Entirely separated out one after another and one step after another,
The world, lo and behold, ceases to be!
Those separated-out-parts too, further enquired into, cease to be real.
Everything thus is but the self-aware Consciousness, the Real, alone.

The knotty problem we are trying to resolve here is this: the world appears to be real to the senses even after one becomes convinced of it being unreal; why is it so? Answering it, verse 11 pointed out that what appears to the senses as the world is nothing but one Consciousness or *sat-cit-ānanda*. That this one causal Reality alone is what exists underlying all that appears to be, that the visible world does not exist apart from or other than as a manifest form of that one causal Reality, was underscored in the last verse. The Guru, in the present verse, pinpoints how one can become enlightened and resolve the otherwise perplexing problem by the method of analysis well familiar to modern science. Such analysis has to be an open one, unconditioned by preconceived notions and prejudices.

Looked at from afar, a forested range of hills will look like a single entity having a bluish hue, shaped according to the nature of its hilltops and valleys. Come very close, and what we see will be neither the forest nor the hills nor the one overall shape, but we will see wildly growing trees and undergrowths, green in colour. When the forest is seen, the trees go unnoticed. When the trees are seen, the forest disappears. Similar is the case with perceiving the one Reality and its innumerable manifest forms. The Reality seen, the manifest forms become unreal. The manifest forms noticed, the Reality disappears. The forest, in the example, stands for the universal and trees for the particular. Not stopping the analysis at the particular, let us go on with our analysis further, as was seen in verse 3 above. Then we see that the piece of cloth loses its existence in the being of yarn; yarn loses its existence in the being of cotton fibres; cotton fibres lose their existence in the being of basic elements; the basic elements lose their existence in the being of Consciousness, which is not analysable further. That which has analysable constituent parts thus is unreal. The undeniably existing Reality, the one indivisible the Reality, is Consciousness alone, which the Guru calls here *nija-bodham*. *Nija*, in the Sanskrit and Malayalam languages, means "one's own" as well as "the real." The word thus means "one's own consciousness — the Reality that is Consciousness," rendered here as "the self-aware Consciousness, the Real."

The "I" sense of each individual entity, the consciousness that is conscious of its own beingness, in essence is none other than this one Consciousness, the ultimate Reality. Perceiving It as Real requires an intuitive, penetrative eye.

That the mutual eclipsing of appearance and reality, the part and the whole, of is owing to *avidyā* (ignorance), and that the one

Consciousness-Reality continues to exist after this *avidyā* and its effects vanish, is given emphasis in the next verse.

Verse 14

nūl-āṭa-tannil udakam nura-tannil evam
hā lokam āke maṛayunn oravidyayāle
ālocanā-viṣayam-āyitu tanre kārya-
jālattoṭum maṛakil uṇṭ-aṛiv-onnu mātṛam ।

Yarn is what is real in cloth;
Water is what is real in foam;
Lo and behold ! Similar is the way the world ceases to be real,
For it (the seeming duality) is caused merely by *avidyā*.
Meditatively examined, it (*avidyā*), along with its effects, becomes extinct;
Still a lone Reality continues to be: the one Consciousness.

The Guru, carrying on the answer to the question, how the world continues to be perceived by the senses even after becoming convinced of its unreality, gives further clarification with the help of two analogies. The first is again that of yarn and cloth. What is real in cloth is yarn alone. Thus yarn is reality and cloth appearance. Seeing the cloth eclipses the reality of yarn, and seeing yarn eclipses the appearance of cloth. The fact, nevertheless, is that the two are inseparable; even after understanding yarn to be real, the cloth continues to appear as cloth, no one having taken the trouble to take the yarn apart.

The other analogy is that of water and bubbles. It is the eternal water-substance that assumes the fleeting form of bubbles. Actual separating out of bubbles from water is impossible; their separateness has meaning only as an idea.

The same is true with the apparent world and the Consciousness-Reality also. Separating them out is not possible, their separateness being mere human ideation. Without the

Consciousness-Substance the world never appears to be; without appearing as the world, the Reality never remains purely abstract either. The Reality, in Vedānta, is known as *sat,* and appearance *bhāva*. Thinkers, biased by either, create theories of correlating the two. Only between two separately existing entities is any correlating necessary and possible. Imaginarily separating the inseparable and then trying to put them together reasonably is the mistake these thinkers make. This imaginary separation happens unawares only because of the *avidyā* (nescience) they are still subject to. This *avidyā* is defined by the Guru himself elsewhere as "that mental function by which the Self (*Ātmā*), the Real, is taken to be unreal and the non-self (*anātmā*), the unreal, is taken to be real." Water and foam are inseparable; *sat* and *bhāva* are inseparable; reality and appearance are inseparable; and cause and effect are inseparable. The lamp of non-duality (*Advaita Dīpikā*) becoming lit within alone makes transparent the inseparable oneness (*advaita*) of the apparent world and the Reality. The meditative search for that illumination is what is referred to in the original text as *ālocanā* and freely rendered here as "meditatively examined."

The extinction of *avidyā* thus attained results in the vanishing of the dualities of appearance and reality, cause and effect, *sat* and *bhāva,* subject and object, and the like. What remains then is only the Effulgence of the non-dual being of Consciousness. The manifest form of this Consciousness or *Ātmā* alone is what perceived as the world, as the phenomenon of life in it and its pleasures, pains and problems. Its being so remains concealed to us only because of *avidyā*.

Verse 15

ānandam astiy atu bhātiy-at-onnu tanne-
tān anyam orkkil atu nāsti na bhāti sarvam
kānal-jalam gagana-nīlam asatyam abhṛa-
sūnam ninaykkil gaganam paramārtham ākum ।

Ānanda alone manifestly exists (*asti*);
It alone manifestly shines (*bhāti*);
That one alone is oneself;
Considered as other than oneself, what manifestly exists would seem not to exist;
The whole world then would seem not manifestly shining.
The mirage-water, the skyblue,
The bloom of the sky — all these are simply non-existent.
The ultimate reality in them, when well thought of, is sky alone.

The answer to the vital problem this work tries to solve, is this: one Reality — Consciousness — alone has its own existence. It is Its existence that manifestly shines as the existence of the world, a phenomenon inherent within It. One understanding Consciousness alone as real does not stop its self-manifesting. This is the reason for the continued perceptibility of the world even after becoming convinced of its unrealness.

The one all-underlying and self-unfolding Reality, as we saw in verse 11 above, is definable as *sat-cit-ānanda*. These three become manifest as individuated beings and are directly experienced by the very same individuated beings as *asti-bhāti-priya* as was seen in verse 8 above. The *sat* (Existence) aspect of the Absolute or the Self is experienced as one's own existence (*asti*), *cit* (Consciousness) aspect as one's own altering states of mind (*bhāti*), and the *ānanda* aspect as pleasures and pains.

Ānanda, as the essential content of the absolute Self, is itself here conceived as manifesting as all the three — *asti, bhāti* and *priya,* for *ānanda,* as existing, is *sat* as well, and as conscious experience is *cit* also. Anyone of these three (*sat, cit, ānanda*) could also thus well be considered as manifesting individually in beings as *asti, bhāti* and *priya.* Treating the Self as of *ānanda* content is all the more significant here in view of the joy of the self-unfoldment of the Self — the creation of the world. This is going to be depicted in the next verse.

It is the self-aware *ānanda*-beingness of the absolute Self that, become manifest, appears as the existence of every individual entity, as every mental state, and as every value sense. The individual who perceives the unreal world as continuing to be perceived, is no other Substance in essence, the world he perceives too is no other in essence. The perceiver's existence and the perceived's existence are thus really one Existence. In other words, what is perceived as the world is nothing more than the perceiver's existence extended. Seen as apart from oneself, the world, theoretically, becomes unreal; but seen as not apart from the Self, from oneself, the world is as real as oneself. Realizing one *Ātmā* alone as real does in no way make oneself unreal; such is the case with the world one perceives.

The puzzle we deal with here becomes relevant only upon seeing the world as existing separately from oneself, only when the Reality is treated as an object to be known. Then the world being unreal may sound like meaning, that the Reality manifesting Itself as the world should not have happened. Such denial of the world virtually implies denying the existence of oneself, an impossibility. A realized person, a *jñānin*, perceives the world and himself continuing to appear to be as one *Ātmā*'s various manifestations. In short, the puzzling question, as is with almost all questions in Vedānta, arises from the ignorance of the questioner. Rescued from this ignorance, one feels the meaninglessness of the question and becomes enlightened oneself to the non-duality of the world and Reality or *sat-cit-ānanda*. Sky or space is given as an example of it. Remaining imperceptible and one, it appears as the unreal water seen in the mirage, as the blue hue of the sky, and even as imaginary flowers blooming in the sky. All these are mere illusory phenomena (*pratibhāṣa*), yet they are not alike in being unreal. The water seen in a mirage is almost tangible. Not so is the blue of the sky; it is far away and its seeming existence is due to the distance it involves. When approached, it recedes into the depth of space. It is this unreal skyblue, reflected, that appears as the flowing water in mirage as well. The flower that blooms in the sky, on the other hand, is merely a human fantasy. Yet all of these have one causal ground: the space or sky. The unreality of the world could also be thought of as of any order, yet it has one Reality which remains unchanged. That is Consciousness, *Ātmā, Brahman* or *sat-cit-ānanda*. As long as the Reality exists, the phenomenal appearance of the world, of life with all its pleasures and pains, the perceiver included, continues. The *Advaita Dīpikā* (Lamp of Non-duality), as the title of the work suggests, is none other than the dawning of the inseparable oneness of *sat-cit-ānanda* and the world of actualities, as in the case of the oneness of water and waves.

How the one Reality — *Ātmā* — unfolds itself and appears as the world unceasingly is answered in the next verse.

Verse 16

ātmāvil illay-orahamkr̥ti yogi-pole
tān māyayāl vividhamāy vihariccitunnu
yogasthanāy nilayil-ninn-iḷakāte kāya-
vyūham dhariccu vihariccitum iṅṅu yogī ।

Ātmā is devoid of I-sense.
It, as with a *yogī*, owing to Its own *māyā*,
Sportively unfolds Itself in varied forms.
A *yogī*, unmoved from his state of
Being well-founded in *yoga*,
Assumes myriad forms, sportively moving around.

That innumerable names, innumerable ideas and innumerable corresponding objects comprise the world, that it has one underlying Reality that alone has everlasting existence, and that that Reality is Consciousness in essence, were all detailed in the first half of this work. That one Reality is here named *Ātmā*, the most crucial word in the philosophy of the Guru, and which the Guru uses in the present work only once. The word

"Consciousness" — *arivu* or *bodham* in the original — conveys the idea of something inconceivably abstract while being brightness in essence, whereas what *Ātmā* signifies is the directly experienced actual beingness of oneself. The word *ātmā* is derived from the verb-root *āt,* meaning "to pervade." The substance that pervades the being of something — for example, clay in a pot — is its *ātmā.* The substance that pervades one's own being, as with all else, is nothing other than Consciousness.

The way the one Consciousness — *Ātmā* — unfolds Itself as the subjective as well as objective world is always thought of as a mystery often described in Vedānta with the help of the concept of *māyā.* In the present case, it is compared by the Guru to the phenomenon of *siddhis* (psychic powers) seen at times in the lives of *yogīs*, himself an excellent example. A *yogī* is a person in a state of *yoga,* the state of being fully absorbed, the state of realizing oneself fully as pure Consciousness in essence. A *yogī* is one who is already inseparably absorbed in the pure Consciousness that is the essential Substance in the entire cosmos, thus fully identified with the whole. In such *yogīs* are seen at times unworldly attainments known as *siddhis*, for example, being seen at two places simultaneously. This phenomenon is conveniently made use of by the Guru to show how mysterious is the way of the unfoldment of the world.

How *Ātmā* unfolds Itself and appears as the world becomes clear if one understands how a *yogī,* remaining oneself, appears to be in different places at the same time. A *yogī*'s self-understanding, by necessity, is entirely different from that of a commoner. The former lives by perceiving oneself as fully one with the whole, as a wave with ocean, and the latter by perceiving oneself as a separately existing entity among other such entities. It is such perception of the latter that makes the *yogī* seem to exist separate from them and to be miraculous. What is normal and natural with a *yogī* is something uncommon and supernatural in the perception of a non-*yogī.* "I am everything" is the common and natural experience, a *yogī* is always imersed in. One, then, sees oneself in everything and everything in oneself. The state of this natural full identity with everything, to a commoner, looks like the *yogī* appearing here and there at the same time. He counts it as a *siddhi. Yogī*s, in other words, do not *show* any miracle; what is natural with them is merely *seen* by non-*yogī*s as miracles. Yet such phenomena seen in them are no mere mental fantasies of the spectator either.

In his well-known book *Jonathan Livingston Seagull*, Richard Back portrays how the natural beingness of a *yogī* is seen by others as a miracle. Jonathan the seagull practises flying at the highest speed possible. The maximum speed attainable in this world having been attained, he reaches another world where the highest speed he knows is only something very common. A master who can teach the maximum speed attainable in that world lives there. He, finding a real seeker in Jonathan, teaches him the secret of attaining the highest speed. To increase flying speed means to decrease flight time, and by bringing down flight time to zero one reaches the maximum speed attainable. Making flight time zero means reaching somewhere in no time, in other words, being at two places at the same time. The master who taught this secret to Jonathan dies very soon, but the latter practises it on his own and finally actualizes it. And then the other seagulls in the community began to see Jonathan as sitting here and there at one and the same time. So is the case with *yogī*s too. They feel themselves as existing everywhere; the non-*yogī*s perceive them as existing simultaneously at more than one place they are interested in and nowhere else. Leaving aside the individualness (*ahamkṛti*) of a *yogī*, then what is seen as the miraculous phenomenon is nothing but the one *Ātmā* assuming the form of and appearing as many. In this sense the Guru says, "*Ātmā* is devoid of I-sense. It, as with a *yogī*, owing to Its own *māyā*, sportively unfolds Itself in varied forms." A *yogī*, counted as an individual being, experiences himself as unfolding and appearing as the world; and counted as the one Reality, *Ātmā* becomes manifest as the world, Itself undergoing no intrinsic change. This self-unfoldment of *Ātmā* is nothing more than a sport for It — an occasion for experiencing the joy of bringing out and seeing for Itself all the potentials hidden within.

Sat-cit-ānanda in essence, *Ātmā* never remains inactive, never remains without unfolding Itself as the world. And for this very reason, It remains hidden from our perception. This mysterious self-hiding self-manifestation of *Ātmā* — we the perceivers forming part of it — is known in Vedānta as *māyā*. Though non-existent in itself, it causes *Ātmā* to appear as the world and as we see the world.

What we always perceive, what we continue to perceive even after becoming convinced of the unreality of the world, in short, is *Ātmā* alone. We, the perceivers are also nothing but *Ātmā*. *Ātmā* seeing *Ātmā* Itself is what happens, for nothing other than *Ātmā* exists. *Ātmā*, by the unfolding Itself and assuming the form of the world, we the perceivers and the act of perceiving included, provides for Itself an occasion for perceiving Itself. Confounded by *māyā* as we are, we think we are perceiving the world. Logical reason is not what controls this mysteriousness of *Ātmā*, for reasoning is simply part of its manifest forms, and hence *Ātmā* never becomes revealed to reasoning. Those who transgress logical reasoning, through intuitive perception, realize themselves being *Ātmā* in essence, no more doubt remaining. This point is given special emphasis to in the next verse.

Verse 17

ajñāna-saṁśaya-viparyayam ātma-tattva-
jijñāsuvinnu dṛḍhabodhan-itilla tellum
sarpa-pratīti phaṇiyo kayaṛoy itenna
tarkam bhṛamam kayaṛu kāṇkil itilla tellum |

Ignorance-originated doubt resulting in confoundedness
Arises in those who are still seekers of Self-Reality or the

Reality that oneself is.
It never occurs even in the least with those who are well stabilized in enlightenment.
The doubt as to whether the apparent snake is snake or rope
Is because of confoundedness;
On seeing the rope, it has no chance to arise at all.

Humans, in the wisdom context, could well be classified as three groups: the ignorant (*ajñānins*), the seekers (*jijñāsus*) and the enlightened (*jñānins*). The totally ignorant one has no desire at all to know what is real in oneself, what is real in the world, and therefore the doubt as to whether this or that is real does not arise in such a one at all. Doubt arises only in the minds of those who have already entered the path of search for Reality. Such seekers are called *jijñāsus*. The enlightened ones (*jñānins*), of course, have no doubt at all.

The non-dual perception of Reality (*advaita darśana*) is unravelled in the present work as the solution to a specific issue: why do we continue to perceive the world with our senses even after becoming fully convinced that the world is unreal? The world, as we saw in the last verse, is nothing other than *Ātmā* become manifest, induced by no I-sense. Then what is it that we perceive with our senses — the world or *Ātmā* become manifest? That it is the latter is the truth. Yet we are completely unaware of it being so. This state is what is known as *ajñāna* (ignorance). The Self-Reality (*Ātma-tattva*) remains Self-Reality even as It assumes the form of the world, we the perceivers included. And, therefore, the enlightened (*dṛḍha-bodha*) perceives *Ātmā*'s existence alone in all that appears as the world, as its perceiver and as the act of perceiving. Only in the one who is yet to realize the Self does arise the above said perplexing question. Nevertheless, such a one is a seeker, for he/she yearns to clarify his/her doubts.

Ajñāna (ignorance) is the state of not knowing the Real as the Real, of not knowing *Ātmā* as the Real. Seeing *Ātmā* and misjudging it as the world happens because of the *ajñāna* in the seeker. A *jñānin,* on the other hand, sees *Ātmā* as *Ātmā* though appearing as the world, and hence the question raised here is of no relevance for such a person. The ultimate solution to the problem, thus, is not looking for a reasoned-out answer, but is attaining *jñāna* or Self-Realization. The Guru again tellingly makes use of the rope-snake analogy to bring this point into relief. Only those who are not certain that what lies before them is simply a piece of rope, have the doubt whether it is a rope or a snake. No logical reasoning helps them in coming to a decision. Seeing the rope and getting rid of the confusion is the only solution. The same is true in the present case also. What I see always everywhere is *Ātmā* alone; this world is the form in which *Ātmā* manifests itself — this certainty realized, one becomes free of the doubt, "Why do I continue to see the world?"

The Guru suggests a sort of contemplative practice in the next verse in order to help the seeker get rid of the confounded state he is in.

Verse 18

munne kaṭannu viṣayam-pṛati vṛtti munnil
ninnīṭum āvaraṇam-ām tira nīkkiṭunnu
pinnīṭu kāṇum aṛivum pṛabha-tanre pin-poy
kaṇṇenna-pol aṛivu kāṇukayilla tāne ।

The contemplative function of mind,
Advancing before every object of perception,
Removes the veiling curtain in front;
And then is seen the one Consciousness.
The eyes do not go behind and see
The illuminating principle that enables the eyes to see;
So too Consciousness does not see Itself.

As we saw in the last verse, our final goal is to become enlightened. This means, becoming fully convinced that one causal Substance alone unfolds Itself as everything in all the worlds, and perceiving that Substance alone in all that is apparent. That one causal Substance is none other than pure, unconditioned Consciousness, or *cit*. Even the one who understands all this theoretically may continue to perceive the unreal world as existing, not the real Consciounsess-Substance. This seems to be a conundrum in the mind of the seeker who still is ignorant, but not in the mind of an enlightened one. Becoming enlightened saves one from this conundrum as well. The contemplative practice that helps the seeker already aware of the unreality of the world to attain this goal is what the present verse concentrates on.

We, on seeing a pile of gold ornaments, naturally may like to classify them as, "This is a chain," "This is a bangle," "This is a ring," "This is a stud" and so on, forgetful of the fact that all of these are but gold and thus one in essence. Seeing a chain as a chain, not as gold, happens because the chain-form becomes a sort of veil put on the gold-substance. And the potential to assume this self-veiling form is inherent in gold. Likewise is the world-form that puts a veil on *Ātmā*, keeping the latter unnoticed and creating the impression that the former does exist. In order to see the gold substance, one has to mentally eliminate the visible chain-form. Similarly, the world-form that obstructs a direct vision of *Ātmā* has to be eliminated mentally in order to intuitively perceive It. Only upon removing the front curtain does what happens within a drama stage gets revealed. Likewise, the removal of the world-curtain enables the seeker to perceive what is really within: *Ātmā* playing the world drama.

The potential to assume the form of ornaments is inherent in gold; so too has *Ātmā* inherent in It the boundless potential to unfold Itself beginninglessly and endlessly as the world. This mysterious potential is known as *māyā*, and devoid of it *Ātmā* never exists either. Owing to this *māyā; Ātmā* assumes the function of knowledge, necessitating the presence of objects to be known (*viṣayas*). *Ātmā* assumes the form of *viṣaya*s as well, again owing to *māyā*. The appearance of the knower along with his act of knowing, and also of the object, are like the front curtains of a drama stage. Remove them; then what becomes revealed is pure and unconditioned Consciousness or *Ātmā*. It is neither the knower's knowing nor the object known; It is the one Substance that fills the being of both. That Substance alone has real existence. I am That. Everything is That. One who realizes thus is the enlightened.

Does the enlightened one know clearly and distinctly what Consciousness or *Ātmā* is? No, for It never is an object of knowledge. As the knowing function goes on in consciousness, the Consciousness causal to it remains unknown to that function, and it is in this sense Vedānta holds that the ultimate Reality is unknowable. A familiar example that can shed light on this point is the case of our own eyes. Eyes, because of their illuminating power, see other objects, but the very same illuminating power ever remains invisible to them. Nevertheless, Consciousness or *Ātmā* remaining unknown objectively is not a hindrance to one experiencing oneself as That in essence and existing as That.

No logical reasoning, no critical acumen, helps one to remove the above-mentioned veil. Opening one's own inner eye, the intuitive eye of wisdom, alone helps, as is underscored in the next verse.

Verse 19

kāṇunnu kaṇṇ iha tuṛakkil aṭaykkil andhan-
tān ullil mevum aṛiviññu varāykayāle
jñānam puṛattu taniye varikilla kaṇṇu
veṇam varunnatinu kaṇṇinu kāntipole ।

One sees when the eyes are open;
When closed one remains simply blind;
For the consciousness within does not find an outlet.
Wisdom, likewise, does not become revealed on its own,
For it needs an eye,
And that eye should be luminous as well.

The philosophical problem this work mainly deals with, and its final answer, have all been made sufficiently clear. What we perceive constantly is not the world, but is merely the aggregate of the countless forms, both subtle and gross, in which one Consciousness or *Ātmā* manifests Itself. Such truth is revealed only to a *jñānin*. Only those who are endowed with the penetrative eye to go beneath the veil and see what is within become *jñānins*. The veiling curtain is nothing other than the appearance of the phenomenal world. Just as in the case of removing the veil of the ornament-form and seeing the gold-reality, this veil has to be removed. Then alone it becomes clear that what appears as the world is nothing but *Ātmā*. This perception requires an intuitive eye. This eye has to be bright and has to be kept open as well. Unless so opened, no final solution to the problem dawns, or else all ends up as an experience like that of one who tries to see something with his eyes closed.

Many may exist who attempt to find a cogent solution to the problem by relying on logical reasoning. Such attempts will continue endlessly and the problem will remain unresolved. But at the opening of the intuitive, penetrative eye of wisdom, the veiling curtain becomes removed and then the question also vanishes needing no answer. What then remains is this experience alone: Consciousness remains conscious of Its own existence.

Part III

Aṛivu

(Consciousness Examined)

Introduction

To know, to think and let know are the features that differentiate humans from other beings. Devoid of this faculty, humans are just like any other animal. Every knowledge is a functional mode of consciousness, and without it there will be no awareness of one's own existence nor that of the world. This consciousness could be seen as of two dimensions — one, the individuated and the other, the universal. From the efforts we make to ensure sufficient food to eat, clothes to wear, a comfortable abode in which to live, and other activities of self-preservation at one extreme, to the never-ending efforts we make to know the secret of the world at the other — all such are functions of the consciousness of individuated beings. Let us now think of the consciousness that universally underlies the entire cosmic system. Many energy particles combine together in an unalterable and preconceived systematic way to form an atom of every physical element. Whether energy is a particle or wave, that is to say, whether matter or non-matter, is decided not by the energy we examine, but by the examining mind. This is a well admitted fact by modern Theoretical Physics. At the other pole of it we notice countless galaxies and nebulae together forming a boundless universe. Though inconceivable to the human mind, this universe apparently has a structural coherence of its own despite all the explosions and implosions that take place in it, and the unpredictable changes happening even at its minutest level. This indicates that a consciousness fills the being of the entire universe. Thus, individually as well as universally conceived, the world and the life system in it is supported by an inherent consciousness.

What is this all-controlling and all filling consciousness? How are consciousness and the objects it becomes conscious of related? Is consciousness one or many? Will there be a world existing without a knowing consciousness? How far is the extensiveness of consciousness? How can we know the real nature of this consciousness? Will this consciousness decompose and cease to be as all physical objects do? What existed before something being known? We know that we know. Is not-knowing a knowledge or non-knowledge? Did the objective world emerge first, and consciousness arise out of it, so that it could make the very world its object? Or, do the two always remain together? Or else, did consciousness originate first, and then the objective world emerged out of it? Is it not consciousness that gives room to exist for the very space that gives room for everything to exist? If so, is it not in consciousness that the entire universe has its being? Will the world exist, if no one exists to know it? Is there anything that is not comprehensible to knowledge? Where did consciousness originate from? Where does each specific knowledge originate from?

Who am I who knows, "I am a being who knows?" Under which category could consciousness be included when subjecting it to analysis? How does the experience of knowing emerge — by the knowing mind entering the object known, or by the known object entering the knowing mind? How are consciousness and I related? Am I consciousness itself? Or, is consciousness simply a quality of the entity called "I"?

How are the objects of knowledge to be understood analytically? How are the sense organs, because of which we are aware of external objects, and consciousness related? Each object of knowledge and the objective world as a whole, apparently have respective structural perfections. Does the consciousness that knows them also have the same structure? Is consciousness something analysable? Do such questions have definite answers? Or, is it altogether an answerless mystery?

Numerous are such questions that consciousness creates about itself. Narayana Guru, in this pithy and short composition, answers all such questions as part of depicting a comprehensive vision of the functionally existing Consciousness-Reality.

The questions are answered in a dialectically conceived way rather than resorting to logical reasoning. That means, the basic stand that *Ātmā* or *Brahman,* unconditioned Consciousness in essence, is the one all-underlying Reality, is made a firm basis for the solution to all problems. If this forms one pole of the dialectical situation, at the other pole is placed each of the problems, and a solution to them is arrived at by relating each to the one firm basis.

That *Ātmā* is Consciousness in essence, is accepted by almost all the Upaniṣads; and the evidence of it is our own direct experience. Narayana Guru gives special emphasis to this aspect in all his philosophical works. He proves logically also how it is one Consciousness alone that unfolds Itself as everything, particularly in his *Advaita Dīpīkā* (The Lamp of Non-duality). In fact, this one stand makes it easier to solve many philosophical problems as well as the problems of actual life.

This work is an original contribution of Narayana Guru to world philosophy in general and Indian Philosophy in particular, for no such in-depth philosophical examination of consciousness seems to have been undertaken till now either in the East or in the West, other than a few psychological studies of the human mind that have guided different schools of Western Psychology. A work having a personal mark of the Guru's own, its each word is filled with the clarity of a comprehensive vision of the one ultimate Reality he realized. The original word for consciousness in the Malayalam language in which it is written, is *aṛivu.* Every line of this work of fifteen verses and sixty lines, begins with the word *aṛivu.* We apologize for not being able to be as strict in this translation as Guru was in the original. It is to the strictness of sense rather than to the format that we give importance in the translation. The original is written in a musically recitable metre called *Gīti*.

We have tried our best to make the commentary as simple as possible; yet the subtlety of ideas in it does not yield to the simplicity of language. The reader, in order to comprehend the real intention of Guru, would have to read repeatedly each verse and its commentary, and meditate on it, before proceeding to the next. A familiarity with the Guru's *Ātmopadesa Śatakam* (One Hundred Verses of Self-Instruction) along with *The Philosophy of Narayana Guru*, a study based on the above work, and also *Advaita Dīpikā* that forms part of this book, is recommended before making use of this work for one's spiritual pursuit.

Such cryptical works of great seers charged with the intensity of high philosophical vision, are not amenable to logically convincing commentaries. It is a myth that logic is the only way of scientific thinking which helps you attain certainty. For these reasons any attempt to convincingly comment on such works will become futile even if they go on endlessly. No commentary will be the last word either. The present commentary is also to be considered in this light. This explains why the present commentary is written while another by Guru Nitya Chaitanya Yati, my *guru* and predecessor, is already available. The present one could well be treated as an appendix to that. It is our earnest wish that more enlightening commentaries on this work will appear in the future also.

It is one Consciousness that governs the entire world. When we say "Consciousness" (with capital 'C'), we do not mean any state of mind in which we are conscious of something. On the other hand, it is the one pure and unconditioned Consciousness-Substance that assumes the form of all such mental states. As the present work itself reveals, that one Consciousness is the Substance that appears as what we call the visible material world as well. It is the very same unconditioned Consciousness that becomes conditioned and appears as the mental states of such unique, enlightened seers like Narayana Guru, and sow the seeds of revolution in human understanding, both at the personal and social levels. In fact, it is the revolution that happens within the depths of human understanding that are then reflected as the revolutions in society. Such apparent social revolutions are easily taken notice of by observers. But the revolution causal to them happens within those who are enlightened, and it always remains unobservable. Discovering the nature of that unobservable inner revolution alone helps you understand, who and what a great *guru* like Narayana Guru is.

In the particular case of Narayana Guru, the social revolution that took place in the State of Kerala as inspired by him is easily noticed and appreciated by historians, but the awareness-revolution that took place within him, as revealed in the present short composition, remains yet to be properly appreciated by historians of philosophy. His philosophy is neither a repetition of the already existing schools like that of Śaṅkara, Rāmānuja and Madhva, nor a compendium of all such philosophies. He precisely and concisely re-presents the Upaniṣadic vision in terms easily understandable to the mindset of a modern man. The present work shows clearly how original his way of thinking is.

Text, Translation and Commentary

Verse 1

aṛiyappeṭum itu veṛall-
aṛivāyiṭum tiraññiṭum neram
aṛiv itil onnāy atukoṇṭ-
aṛivallāt eññum illa veṛonnum ǀ

The known "this" is no other,
It, when closely examined, also
Reveals itself to be Consciousness in essence.
Thus the Consciousness-Substance in both these
(The known and the knower) being one alone,
Nothing other than the one Consciousness
Ever has real existence anywhere.

Expansion:

Whatever becomes an object of knowledge that could be referred to as "this" has no real existence apart from the knowing consciousness. Closely examined, all such objects are found to be different manifest forms of Consciousness. The Consciousness that assumes the form of the knowledge of the existence of objects, and the Consciousness that functions as the knower, are not two. Therefore, no reality other than one Consciousness exists anywhere at any time.

We human beings think and know, and let others think and know. Doing both these alone makes us real human beings, for humans are defined as thinking animals. Making human life satisfactory also requires our knowing and letting others know.

Why do we think? We have a feeling that something exists, our own existence not excluded, and that feeling is what makes us think. The experience of nothingness would not make us think. Even in the case of the experience of nothingness, the existence of that experience is undeniable. Thus the feeling that "something is" makes us ask, "What is it that exists?" Is it what we perceive with our senses that really exists? Or, is it merely an illusory vision? Aren't we sure that the canopy we see over the sky is really unreal? Still we continue to see it with our eyes. Then, is it not possible that everything that we perceive with our eyes is a similar illusory vision?

As all such doubts arise, an intense desire to know what really exists takes root in us. The emerging of all sciences, all philosophies, all mystical visions, is a result of this human urge. In spite of all these efforts, we are yet to arrive at a final and convincing answer to the fundamental question of what really exists.

Something apparently exists that becomes an object of knowledge; anything that does not exist never becomes so. It could be asked, isn't it possible to think of your having money in your pocket even when your pocket is empty? Yes. But the money you think of then, though not in your pocket, is not non-existent. It is the existing money that you are thinking of even then. Something called money exists. The characteristics and utilities of it could make you imagine it being in your pocket, even when you have no money with you. Suppose what we call money has not become part of human life, or that no such thing exists, then you will have no chance to think of it being in your pocket. Therefore, it is the existing money, not the non-existent one, that you think of.

The Known "This"

Now we have to know what is it that really exists. This enquiry became necessary because of our feeling that something exists. That about which we have the feeling of existence is called an object; the Sanskrit word for it is *viṣaya*, here designated by the words "the known 'this.'" What Guru tries to teach us in this verse is that this object, in the ultimate sense, has no existence apart from Consciousness.

This world's existence, as far as I am concerned, is "as I am aware of it"; for you it is "as you are aware of it." To assert that a world no one is aware of exists, is meaningless. A world I personally am not aware of may exist; then someone else should have being to be aware of it. If no one else exists to know of it, at least God would be aware of it. Whether mine, yours, of someone else, or of God, all awarenesses are events occurring in Consciousness. Every knowledge is a distinct, specific mode of functional appearance of the indistinct Consciousness, as are all feelings and emotions. That means, knowledges, feelings, emotions, do not exist apart from Consciousness. The existence of the world, the object we know, is in the form of our experiences or awarenesses. To be more specific: objects in the world are perceived with our senses; all senses enable us to have different experiences — all concerning a single world; the aggregate of such experiences gives shape to the world each one of us perceives. All experiences, admittedly, take place in Conscisousness. In other words, the physical world we perceive, even its materiality, is nothing but a specific mode of expression of one Consciousness.

This much is about the experience of the world in general. Now let us examine the case of every specific experience like, "This is a pot," "This is a plate," etc. that forms part of the world.

Suppose something you have never seen or known before is shown to you and you are asked, "What is this?" You will never be able to say what it is. Why is it so? Simply because you recognize something as such and such only when the object shown was already known to you. In your act of recognizing something, you are really *re-cognizing* something that has previously been *cognized*. On your having sense-contact with something, you pick up a previous experience of the same sort from your memory, and project it on and identify it with the object you now get into contact with. Such is the way you recognize something. For example, when you see a chair and recognize it as a chair, you first get into contact with the chair. Then the chair-experience you had before is picked up unconsciously from your memory and is projected on the object before you and then you recognize it as a chair. Is it not, then, something in your memory, in your mind, that you see as if it exists outside? If so, is it not our mind, our consciousness, that becomes experienced as external objects?

Now let us take the case of the whole of the external world you constantly see directly with your eyes. What is actually within the bounds of your visual area is a small semi-circular region, and everything beyond it remains unperceived. Though we consider the latter also as part of the *visible* world, its real existence is in your imagination as an extension of what you directly perceive. That means, of the infinitely extensive *visible* world, what is actually visible is merely a minute part of it, the rest of it is in your mind. You consider the latter also as part of the *visible* world merely because of the possibility of directly seeing it if you reach where it is. Something existing in the imagination of the mind means its existence is in consciousness.

Let us now examine what is within the visual area. It is filled with objects, and each of them, as we have already seen, is distinguished as such and such by bringing out the idea you have already in your mind and projecting it on the entity you come into contact with. All the ideas are different functional modes of one single Consciousness, and they are projected outside and perceived as objects. It is Consciousness alone that is perceived by Consciousness. This is what happens when you see objects within the visual area.

Take the case now of seeing a single object within the visual area. For example, a rose is before me, and I recognize it as a rose. What are the factors I notice enabling me to distinguish it as a rose? Its colour, its shape, its fragrance and the like are those factors. All these are not really the rose; these are only different qualities of the rose, the qualified. Whatever I perceive directly, whatever I know of it, is not the qualified rose but the qualities of the rose. That means, the qualified rose is not perceived, but my experience is of having seen it.

This is the case with the entire world as well. We perceive the world to have countless qualities. While what we know are only the qualities of the world, the qualified world remains not directly known. Yet the existence of the qualified world is undeniable, and our experience is to see it.

Where does this world that we experience then exist? The object, the world, is merely an idea we formulate in our mind, as the rose is an idea I formulate in my mind, with the qualities perceived being instrumental. That means, the qualified object's existence, the existence of the world, is in consciousness. The Guru himself summarizes this stand in verse 32 of his *Ātmopadeśa Śatakam* as follows:

> Whatever is known is not the all-supporting Substance,
> But is only its attributes,
> For the said Substance remains always imperceptible.
> The earth and the like (all perceptible and hence attributes)
> Therefore do not have real being of their own.
> What really is, is the one all-supporting *Ātmā*
> Or Consciousness pure and unconditioned,
> In essence simply effulgence alone.
> This is to be recalled constantly.

Now where do the qualities we directly perceive exist? We think at least the qualities must exist outside. But how is it possible? The qualities can exist only where the qualified is. To say that a rose is here and its colour is somewhere else is meaningless. If the qualified exists in our consciousness, then the qualities also have to exist in consciousness itself. If both the qualified and the qualities exist in consciousness, then what do we perceive as existing outside?

That is what is counted as *māyā* in Vedānta. A mysterious creative urge inherent in Consciousness makes it appear both as the qualified and the qualities. Really what we call "outside" where the objects are thought of as existing, as well as "inside" is also nowhere else than in Consciousness. Seen holistically, Nature, the total of the self-unfoldment of the one Reality, has no inside or outside. Both these are concepts we have created with the knowing individual as the norm.

Thus, closely looked at, we realize that what appears as the objective world is no more than the variegated and never-ending creative self-expression of the one Consciousness. The Guru, therefore, says, "The known 'this' is no other."

Nothing Other than the One Consciousness Ever has Real Existence Anywhere

Along with my knowledge of the object, I have also the experience that I am the one who knows, that I am the subject. Who is this "I," who knows? My first impression is that I am the one who is sitting at the desk and writing; but apparently it is my body that occupies the chair near the desk. This body is merely mine; it is not myself. Whatever I could predicate as "mine" never becomes "I" because these are all possessed by "me." Really I am the one who owns all that is mine. Thus, my sense organs, my mind, my intellect, and even my soul are not "I" as these are all "mine." Even the self that is thought of as "mine" is not the real Self.

Who or what then is this "I" who owns all these? It is merely a Consciousness that cannot even be counted as mine.

An object really becomes an object, it is to be remembered, only when a subject knows it, otherwise it is no object at all. That means, it is the subject, consciousness in essence, that makes an object. Similarly, a subject becomes a subject only when an object is perceived. The act of perceiving is the interlink between the two. Perceiving is a function of consciousness. Put otherwise, Consciousness is the one substratum both in the subject and the object, or Consciousness is the Reality that unfolds itself as both. Everything thus is Consciousness in essence.

The task undertaken in this composition is a close study of this Consciousness. We have just seen how what we consider as the object is really Consciousness in essence. Who knows such an object? The very same Consciousness. The final certitude we arrive at and the ultimate benefit of knowing are also experienced in Consciousness. That means, nothing outside the amplitude of Consciousness happens either in human life or in the world. The present study is no exception. Consciousness is called *cit* in Vedānta.

Every knowledge is about something that exists; likewise the consciousness that knows also exists. The existence of something is an experience we have. Even when we experience that there is no jar on a table, it is the knowledge of jar's existence that allows us to make this judgement. All experiences are different forms in which consciousness functions. Seeing, touching, tasting, smelling, hearing, imaginations, emotions are all experiences, and even the materiality of the physical world is so. Every experience admittedly is a manifest form of consciousness. Thus nothing exists apart from Consciousness. What ultimately exists is called *sat* in Vedānta.

We face difficult situations in life; these worry us. Such situations arise when the coming together of subject and object do not agree with our likes and dislikes. These likes and dislikes, in their turn, have their being in consciousness and they depend upon one's value concepts. This value-sense is known as *ānanda* and it, like *sat* and *cit*, also constitutes the essential content of consciousness.

As we have already seen, creative self-unfoldment — owing to its own *māyā* — is inherent in Consciousness, and it happens at all the three levels of *sat*, *cit* and *ānanda*. As *sat*, it manifests as all the objects, both existent (*sat*) and non-existent (*asat*). As *cit*, it becomes unfolded as all knowledges and experiences of the subject;

such knowledge could either be true knowledge (*vidyā*) or untrue knowledge (*avidyā*). As *ānanda,* it appears as both happiness (*sukha*) and suffering (*duḥkha*). Having this holistic vision enables us to perceive all the trials and tribulations of life as well as the happiness we feel, merely as part of the sporting of one Consciousness. This awareness alone ensures enduring peace in life. Guru himself, in his *Ātmapodeśa Śatakam* asserts:

> A divine sport going on beginningless
> In the one pure and unconditioned Consciousness (*Ātmā*)
> Indeed is all this! —v. 34

Verse 2

aṛivill ennāl illīy-
aṛiyappeṭum-ennat uṇṭit-ennālum
aṛiv-onn-illennāl-īy-
aṛivet aṛivinn atill aṛiññīṭām ׀

In the absence of a knowing consciousness,
The known can have no being.
Even if granted that the "known" has being
Also when not being known,
Which is the consciousness to which occurred
The knowledge of such an existence?
No such knowing (without a knowing consciousness)
Can ever there be as is convincingly understood.

Expansion:

> Unless the knowing consciousness exists, no known object would exist. Suppose the known object exists with no consciousness to know of it. That the object exists thuswise is also a knowledge. Which is the consciousness in which this knowledge occurs? No such knowledge is possible with no consciousness to know of its existence.

The first verse showed clearly that one Consciousness alone has real existence, and that the existence of everything else is nothing other than the one Consciousness become variously self-unfolded. On the other hand, modern science teaches us that it was matter that emerged first, and consciousness appeared later as a by-product of it. That means, matter can exist with no consciousness existing to know of it. The present verse examines the validity of such a notion.

Though all of us conveniently say "the world," no one exists who knows the entire world. What is within the bounds of our knowledge of the world is merely a minute part of what really exists. The rest of it remains outside the bounds of our knowledge. That we do not know it does not make that unknown part of the world non-existent. Whether we know of it or not, it remains there always. Such is the notion we have of the world or of what exists.

All that we directly perceive, we usually take as real. The assumed proof of it is that we have the experience of it. That means, our experience is what makes the existence of something certain or uncertain. In the absence of a consciousness experiencing it, the existence of something does not become certain. All experiences have their being in consciousness. Thus it is as the various manifest forms of consciousness that everything we know exists.

Then, what about that which is outside the bounds of knowledge? Does it also exist in consciousness? We already know that what we do not know is more than we do. We know that nothing outside the known area is clearly known to us. This is also a knowledge, and we know this only because the knowing function takes place in us. We discriminate that this much is known to us and the rest is not known to us. This discrimination also is performed by consciousness. Suppose no consciousness that performs the action of knowing exists at all. Then the differentiation of the known and the unknown also does not occur. The notion that something becomes the object of knowledge, and some other things do not become so, also becomes meaningless unless the action of knowing occurs.

Something gains the status of being an object only when it is known. If matter alone is what exists, its existence is known to a consciousness, and it also becomes an object or part of the objective world only when known by a consciousness. With no knowing of it, matter existing and not existing are equal. When consciousness performs its knowing function, if a particular thing does not come within its ambit, then it remains an unknown object. That means, the known and the unknown have being only when consciousness exists with its knowing function.

Modern science that bases itself on materialism teaches that, whether I or you or anyone knows about it or not, the world that becomes an object of knowledge exists independent of the knowing mind. Let us admit it to be so. Still, that such a world exists also is a knowledge. Which is the consciousness to which this knowledge occurs? With that consciousness not existing, the independent existence of the world becomes meaningless.

So much about knowing the world. Now let us look at knowledge knowing itself, or rather consciousness becoming aware of itself. Then the object known is consciousness itself. Who is then the subject? It is myself. Am I not consciousness itself in essence? Yes. As we become aware of consciousness, we very often forget that the object of knowledge is none other than the subject who knows or the knowing consciousness itself. Thus even while remaining one indivisible consciousness, it is thought of both as subject and object, allowing the thinking process go on. Such a division of the knowing consciousness and the known consciousness, while Consciousness remains indivisibly one, happens because something veils the real Consciousness so that it is not perceived. This veil that causes the apparent division is called *avidyā* (nescience) in Vedānta. Only to those in whom this *avidyā*-veil is removed does the secret of non-duality of Consciousness become revealed. The duality of the thinking consciousness and the consciousness that is thought of simply vanishes upon this revelation. Until the removal of the *avidyā*-

veil, such arguments continue like the subject is real or the object is real. In fact, it is where this *avidyā* reigns that such arguments, particularly about Consciousness or Reality, can play their role. If the consciousness that is the object of knowledge exists apart from the knowing me, then there would be none to know that consciousness. But it is not the actual case, for consciousness is constantly being known. That means, consciousness and I are simply one. This subtle point is clarified by Guru himself in his *Ātmopadeśa Śatakam* as follows:

> Pure Consciousness (*aṛivu*) and "I" (*Ātmā*) —
> These two are one alone
> In the perception of the one who has become free of the veil (of *avidyā*);
> Others go on arguing for or against.
> If "I" (*Ātmā*) could be taken as something
> Other than pure Consciousness,
> Then there would be no one to be conscious
> Of that Consciousness. — v. 99

This hidden principle implied in making consciousness our object of knowledge is equally true with making the external world so. The objective world, as we have already seen, is also Consciousness in essence. Knowing the world, then, means knowing the Consciousness. The existence as well as the non-existence of the world becomes meaningful only to a knowing consciousness. That consciousness cannot be non-existent, for no non-existent consciousness can know. Both the existence and non-existence of the world are thus not beyond the bounds of Consciousness.

In short, without knowledge or consciousness existing, no object of knowledge can exist. Logically speaking, I become the knower and an object becomes the known only when the knowing function of consciousness takes place. In its absence, neither do I gain the status of the knower, nor does the thing known gain the status of the known. That means, when no knowing happens, neither the subject exists nor the object also exists; but both exist when knowing occurs.

Verse 3

aṛivinn aḷav-illāt-et-
aṛiyām aṛivāy-atum viḷaṅṅunnū
aṛivil eẓunna kināviṅṅ-
aṛivāyīṭuna vaṇṇam aṅṅellām ।

That which is known with no means of knowledge,
Shines always as the effulgence of pure Consciousness.
All the dreams that well up within one consciousness
Have being only as (functional modes) of the very same consciousness.
So is the case with everything.

Expansion:

There exists a knowledge that we gain without help from any of the valid means of knowledge (*pramāṇa*s) such as sense perception, inference, etc.; it is the knower knowing himself or herself. We may also experience that it shines as pure effulgence. That means, as the objects known are really Consciousness in essence, so is the knowing subject also Consciousness in essence. The objects we see and enjoy or suffer in dreams, become formulated in our consciousness, and they do not exist apart from that consciousness. The same is the nature of the existence of objects known and of the knowing subject — both emerge from Consciousness and both do not exist apart from Consciousness.

We noticed in the first two verses that what appears as the objects of knowledge is nothing other than the one Consciousness which in turn is but the *Ātmā* of Vedānta. All objects become known to us when they are subjected to a sort of measuring up, with our act of knowing as a measuring rod, where our sense organs, mind, reasoning faculties, memories, value sense and the like serve as aids. But the knowledge each of us has about ourselves is not so. It does not depend upon any such measuring rod or any aid. It is the event of the knower simply remaining aware of his or her conscious existence, a knowledge which we cannot define as the knowledge of so and so about such and such a thing with such and such a means of knowledge. In other words, it is simply the event of consciousness remaining self-luminous. But instead of directly experiencing the self-luminousness of oneself or of Consciousness or of *Ātmā,* what we wrongly do in our ignorance is to make it also an idea, that is, of "I" knowing "myself." To be short, what shines both as the object of knowledge and the subject of knowledge is nothing other than the self-luminuous Consciousness or *Ātmā* alone.

To see dreams is a human phenomenon. (We are not quite sure about it in the case of other animals.) What do we see in our dreams? Certain things or events or visions given shape to unconsciously by our own consciousness. All such visions are of living nature as well, and while they reflect our value notions in life, they also fulfil certain bodily and mental conditions or needs of the moment. No one would dare to claim that such dream-visions have existence apart from the dreaming mind or consciousness.

Who enjoys a sweet dream or gets frightened by nightmares? It is ourselves. To be more precise, it is our own consciousness. That means, what appears as the objects perceived and the perceiving subjects, in the case of all dreams, is our own mind or consciousness. No dream-vision, thus, is outside the range of consciousness; neither is the perceiver of dreams so, nor the act of dreaming.

The same is the case with our waking state also, the state in which we supposedly experience our life. It is in that state that we are aware of the existence of the visible world as well as of the mind that knows about it. Both are experiences, and thus are merely different conditioned functional modes assumed by one unconditioned Consciousness. Both forms of awareness have no existence apart from the one causal Consciousness. Seen thus, our life-experiences as a whole are nothing more than a prolonged dream.

Only upon waking up do we realize that what we were seeing till then was merely a dream. Until waking up, we wrongly think that what we are experiencing has real existence. When dreaming, we do not take those visions as dreams. Likewise, even as we are fully engrossed in our worldly affairs, we remain completely oblivious of the reality that all such are mere dreamlike appearances emerging in Consciousness. Instead, we think all those visions are real happenings, the idea which creates all problems. Our waking up from this prolonged dream is what we call attaining wisdom or Self-Realization. Only upon such awakening do we realize that the world we were counting as real until then was merely a dream. Then the problems which were tormenting us also will become part of that unreal dream. Such a new awakening should be our goal.

Do we, in the usual course, create an idea of the world in our mind by consciously measuring it with the measuring rod of consciousness? No. We remain ignorant even that any understanding we gain is a sort of measuring and evaluating. (The only exception to this rule, as we have already seen, is the case of knowledge knowing itself.)

A heap of grains is measured by making use of a bushel. The size of the bushel decides how many bushels of grains we have measured out. The same is true with our knowing the world and ascertaining its meaning as well. The world, and the phenomenon of life that forms part of it, are measured usually by us and evaluated by us by making use of our faculties of seeing, hearing, smelling, tasting and feeling, and also of imagining, fancying and logical reasoning. That means, all such faculties together form the bushel for measuring the world in our case. The nature and value we perceive in the world depend upon the ideas and imaginations with which we conceive of it, using all these faculties for the measuring rod.

With some, very insignificant matters are sufficient cause for them to commit suicide, either by consuming some poison, by hanging themselves or resorting to some other means. Some others face all difficult situations with a calm mind; nothing of the vagaries of the external world torments their inner peace. Though both these types of people get into contact with the same world, and live in the same world, their visions of the world are much different. That means, the standards with which both measure the world are different.

There are certain standard measures or valid means of knowledge, that our functional consciousness has itself devised in order to ascertain the certainty or otherwise of what we know of the world as well as of life. Such standards, in India, are known as *pramāṇas*. No such means of knowledge helps us arrive at a certainty about the very consciousness that functionally devised such means in order to ascertain its own knowing faculty. Narayana Guru therefore says,

> Ineffable and unthinkable is this
> Infinite and unresolvable (non-duality),
> How can any *pramāṇa*
> Be of any avail with regard to It ! — *Ātmopadeśa Śatakam*, 94

One could live with the enlightened awareness that all the experiences and knowledges we have of life and in our life have no reality other than as the incessant modes of expression or self-manifestation of the one ineffable and unthinkable Reality or Consciousness. On the contrary, one could also live one's life guided by the notion that everything we encounter, experience and know, are real in their own right.

Two sets of people here perceive and evaluate one and the same world, and develop two different attitudes towards it, and arrive at two different conclusions about it. Which of these two perceptions is the right one? A difficult question indeed to answer. Besides the fact that the nature and meaning of the existence of the world depend on the understanding and value perception of the perceiver, no absolute nature or meaning is definitely discernible to the human mind. The former is a relative concept of the world. What exists absolutely, and is meaningful absolutely, is one Reality alone — the one unconditioned Consciousness not measurable with any *pramāṇa*. That means, everything measurable and perceptible is nothing but the relative aspects of the one absolute Reality or Consciousness, that manifests Itself by becoming conditioned in the form of various sense perceptions, ideas, imaginations, emotions and the like, that is to say, by Itself assuming various names and forms. It is this conditioned aspect of Consciousness that makes the world appear to be an entity having a name and a form, or rather as an aggregate of all names and forms. These do not have being apart from the one Consciousness. Put otherwise, all that we experience as the world and the worldly, are merely dreams emerging in the one unconditioned and absolute Consciousness.

As we are well aware, the visions seen by a dreamer in his or her dreams, are, in a way, an outcome of the creativity of his or her consciousness functioning with the actualization of happiness as the primary goal. The same is true with the unconditioned Consciousness-Reality as well. It too is inherently creative. At no time does It remain inactive and thus never ceases emanating something new from Itself. This creativity is called *prakṛti* in Indian Philosophy — *kṛti* meaning "activity," with the prefix *pra* standing for "proper" (*prakarṣeṇa*). Thus the word *prakṛti*, though translated as "nature," really means, "proper activity." Any activity will be absolutely "proper" only when it happens impelled by nothing else. This creative urge, having become self-actualized, is what we call the visible world. This creativity is also aimed at happiness — it is the happiness of perceiving Its own infinite potentials. This means, Consciousness knows Itself with no standard measure or *pramāṇa* as an aid. And as a result of this self-expression of Its own creative urge, the entire world appears to be to Itself. Guru, in his *Ātmopadeśa Śatakam*, portrays this picture as follows, answering the question, why does *Ātmā* or Consciousness create the world from Itself?:

Pure Consciousness (*Ātmā*),
In order to actualize
The potentials hidden within,
Transforms Itself assuming the forms
Of various specific manifestations such as the earth,
And moves spiralling up and down and back and forth,
Making many an apparent form emerge,
Like the glowing figures of a spiralling fire stick. — v. 33

Even when appearing as the world It does not cease to be Consciousness in essential content, and what appears to be is the self-manifestation of the one Consciousness. The entire world experience is thus the ever-changing various apparent facets of the one Consciousness, as is pictorially depicted also in the *Viśvarūpa-darśana-yoga* (The Yoga of the Vision of Cosmic Form) of the *Bhagavad-Gītā* in its chapter XI. Nothing other than Consciousness thus exists as Real.

This one Consciousness is termed *cit* in Sanskrit, and Itself is the essential content of *Brahman* or *Ātman* of Vedānta, often defined as *sat-cit-ānanda* (Existence-Consciousness-Value-experience). As *sat* (Existence or Reality) It appears as the existence of the visible world, subjective as well as objective; as *cit* (Consciousness) It manifests both as *vidyā* (true knowledge) and *avidyā* (untrue knowledge); as *ānanda* (Value-experience), It becomes conditioned as happiness and suffering.

Our attempt here is to know the Consciousness (*cit*) that serves always as the measuring rod for all knowledge. Why can't this Consciousness also be measured out? For no other reason than that That itself is the measuring rod. A bushel cannot be used to measure the bushel itself, but it does not mean that the bushel is non-existent. Likewise, though Consciousness cannot be measured out by making use of Itself, Its self-luminousness is always the most direct of all our experiences. All other experiences we have, have this one *cit* for their essential content.

Verse 4

aṛivinu niṛav uṇṭennāḷ
aṛiv-allātuḷḷat eṅṅ-irunnīṭum?
aṛiv-etenniṅṅ-atu poy-
aṛiyunn-aṅṅenn it eṅṅ-irunnīṭum?

The being of Consciousness is all-inclusive plenitude.
Then, where else can exist anything that is not Consciousness?
Where could that Consciousness be found if searched for by asking,
"What is (that one) Consciousness (that alone exists)?"
As though it were something existing externally?

Expansion:

Ātmā, unconditioned Consciousness in essential content, that shiningly manifests as the one who knows as well as the object known, alone has all-pervading existence. How can what we think of as the non-self (*anātmā*), then, ever exist other than in *Ātmā*? The non-self, therefore, has no existence of its own. What is it that we all *Ātmā* or Consciousness thus? Where does it exist? Such enquiries do not take us anywhere near a definite answer, for it is the very same *Ātmā* that makes the enquiry assuming the form of the enquirer. *Ātmā*, thus, is not something that we can search for and find out.

That what abides in the being of everything known is none other than Consciousness, was shown in verse 1. Verse 2 made it clear that the known object does not exist if no consciousness exists. It was thus established by the method of agreement and difference that what appears as the known is nothing other than Consciousness.

It is with the aid of certain valid means, known as *pramāṇas*, that we arrive at certainty with regard to anything. But Consciousness remaining conscious of Itself, is not some knowledge gained by any such means. It simply is the self-awareness of

Consciousness. It requires nothing external as an aid. The self-awareness of Consciousness is also thus Consciousness in essence. That means, the underlying Substance in both the object of knowledge and the subject of knowledge is one unconditioned Consciousness alone. That Consciousness is the one Reality that has all-pervading existence, and It can never be searched for and found out as if it is something "other." This is the one argument made in this verse.

Consciousness is the one Substance that pervades everywhere, abiding as the being of everything apparent. That means, Consciousness alone has all-inclusive plenitude. Then, where else can what we think of as non-self or non-consciousness exist? In other words, if you think that something other than Consciousness exists, then where does it exist? Is it not one Consciousness alone wherein all such can exist? What exists in the being of Consciousness, necessarily has to be Consciousness in essential content. That means, if at all something that could be thought of as other than the Self or Consciousness does supposedly exist, that existence has necessarily to be in Conscioussness, as a functional mode of Consciousness. In short, what we usually count as not-consciousness does not exist outside the being of Consciousness.

We have the sense that our knowledge is very limited. We sense this by taking into account only the amplitude of information collected so far in our memory. The plenitude of Consciousness discussed here may also be perceived from this limited perspective. Really, the amplitude of our consciousness, even in its individuated aspect, is unthinkable. How then can the amplitude of the unconditioned Conusciousness is thinkable?

Suppose my knowledge has a limit of its own. It could well be compared to a circle. Then what I think of my consciousness is that its range is within the bounds of that circle; then whatever is outside those bounds cannot be knowledge. But it remains a fact that, I knowing that what is beyond the bounds of that circle is not knowledge, is also a knowledge. That means, what is not knowledge, what is considered beyond the bounds of knowledge, also is within the functional amplitude of consciousness. Thus, even our individuated consciousness, in its functional range, is of such a boundless extensiveness as to include within it what is known as well as what is not known.

Then what about the universal Consciousness? Let alone then the case of the non-dual or absolute Consciousness?

Our final goal is knowing the all-underlying Reality; and that Reality, as we have already seen, is unconditioned Consciousness in essence. The questions we ask ourselves, when searching for something would be as follows: what is the object we are in search of? Of what kind is it? How is it to be known? Where can we find it? Answering such questions really constitutes the core of our search. Here the Reality we are in search of is the Consciousness that fills everywhere. Being so, how would it be possible to know it as though it were located somewhere? It, in other words, should not be searched for as an object that could be found at any particular location. Being the Substance that fills everywhere, it should be the one that fills the being of the knower also. That means, the object we are in search of itself functions as the knower or as the knowing mind. The knower or the knowing mind, in order to know the ultimate Reality, therefore, does not have to search for It anywhere outside, but has only to turn to himself or herself, or the mind turn to itself, and directly perceive It as the Substance in the being of himself, herself or itself.

We usually gain a definite knowledge of anything with the help of certain *pramāṇa*s or valid means of knowledge, and for this reason, due consideration to *pramāṇa*s forms an important section in all the Indian schools of philosophy. The nearest equivalent to it in Western Philosophy is epistemology. *Pratyakṣa* (perception), *anumāna* (inference), *upamāna* (comparison), *arthāpatti* (presumption), *anupalabdhi* (non-perception), and *śabda* or *śruti* or *āgama* (scriptural evidence) are the *pramāṇa*s acceptable to

Vedāntins. Some schools do not admit all these, whereas some others add *aitihya* (customary legends) and *smṛti* (memory) also to the list. Yet all these *pramāṇa*s apply only in the context of someone knowing something else. In the context of the knower knowing oneself, on the other hand, the help of all such *pramāṇa*s is of no avail, and one's attention becomes interiorized towards oneself. This culminates in one experiencing oneself, and so becoming lost in the lustrous oneness of the knower and the known. As the Guru puts it himself in his *Ātmopadeśa Śatakam* (verse 14), this experience is comparable to a lamp that shines incinerating the threefold factors of knowledge (the knower, the known and the event of knowing). The same brightness would then be convincingly felt to be the Reality we are in search of. No amount of meandering in this world in search of it would help us arrive at this conviction.

Verse 5

aṛivil-irunnu keṭunnīl-
aṛivām ennāl it eṅṅ-iṛaṅṅīṭum?
aṛiviney aṛiyunnīliṅṅ-
aṛiyun-nerattu raṇṭum onnāyī ।

Pure Consciousness never becomes reduced to something else.
If pure Consciousness alone is,
Then what else could this (world) be reduced to?
The pure Consciousness that the world is,
In the usual course does not become known.
When known, the two (the Consciousness and the world)
Attain inseparable oneness.

Expansion:

Consciousness (*cit*), as we have seen, is the one Reality that exists everywhere and appears as everything. Whatever be the form in which It appears, It never steps down from being Consciousness and becomes something else, just as gold does

> not cease to be gold when it appears as ornaments. The first impression we have of the world is not that it is nothing but Consciousness itself, but that it is something known to consciousness. If Consciousness alone is the one Reality, then where can the world emerge to be other than in Consciousness? If something comes out from somewhere it has to be Consciousness that comes out of Consciousness to remain Consciousness Itself. In the way of thinking we are familiar with, we do not think of the world and ourselves as being but one Consciousness. But, what happens when we realize what that Consciousness is and its real nature? Then we realize also that, that Consciousness and this world are not two, that the former is the Reality and the latter the form in which It appears. An apparent form does not exist apart from the substance that assumes that form.

Something we individually have become aware of, as we know, cannot be reduced to non-knowledge; it always remains in our memory. The same could be understood in its universal sense as well. Then we could say, knowledge or consciousness does not become reduced to non-consciousness in any way.

The first four verses made it clear to us that Consciousness alone has real existence. It is Consciousness alone that assumes the form of everything subjective as well as objective, universal as well as individual. What ultimately exists never gives up that status nor becomes reduced to non-existence. That which always changes is the external apparent forms, and not what ultimately exists.

This point could be clarified with the help of an analogy given in the *Chāndogya Upaniṣad*. A goldsmith takes a piece of gold and gives it the form of a beautiful chain. Later, on finding that this chain has become out of fashion, it is molten and reshaped into a new chain or some other ornament in accordance with demand. The real substance in such ornaments is gold, and it continues to exist without giving up the status of being gold, even as the ornament forms change. We and the world of which we are an inseparable part, together are to be seen in the place of changing ornament forms. A gold-like Substance exists underlying all these apparent forms. That this Reality is nothing other than unconditioned Consciousness, is the lesson we learnt so far from this short work of Narayana Guru. The *Chāndogya Upaniṣad* compares the ever-changing process of the one Consciousness-Reality passing through many changeful apparent forms, to the phenomenon of a caterpillar moving forward leaving behind its hold on one tip of grass and seizing the hold of another without itself undergoing any fundamental change.

Consciousness, thus, is the all-pervading and all-underlying Substance in all that appears to exist. This Reality assumes the form of everything, as the subject as well as the object, as the subtle as well as the gross, as mind as well as matter, as names as well as forms, as the entire universe as well as the phenomenon of life in it. Whatever the form in which Reality appears to be, none of these forms exists eternally. One Substance or Consciousness alone is what eternally exists and it never ceases to be Consciousness, regardless of the variety of forms in which It manifests.

Though such is the truth, it is the externally perceived forms that we take to be real. We thus remain oblivious of the truth that an invisible Substance underlies the being or pervades the being of all that is perceptible. To go back to our gold-ornament analogy, we are well aware of the truth that gold is the substance in the being of ornaments. Do we see with our eyes the real substance called gold? No, though we have the impression that we directly see gold. What really is the gold's own form? It has no form of its own, but assumes whichever form we give to it. Irrespective of such altering forms, gold remains the unalterable substance. What then is the unalterable form of the unalterable gold? It has no such unalterable form. That means, the unalterable gold is really formless. Has anyone perceived with one's own eyes something formless? No, for only something that has a form is perceptible.

The substance in the perceptible ornament forms is, therefore, imperceptible. Likewise, the substance underlying the being of the visible world also is invisible, and we have already seen that It is pure Consciousness in essential content. Yet in the normal course of events we do not experience Reality in this way.

What appears as ornaments is nothing but gold. Everyone knows that gold and ornament forms are inseparably one. That is to say, knowing gold holistically means knowing ornament forms also, for the potential and possibility to assume all ornament forms is inherent in gold. It is one gold-substance, that assumes all the countless forms of ornaments. After knowing thus we'll never be able to see or think of gold and ornament forms as separable entities or truths. Their separateness is merely the creation of the reasoning mind of humans. The same is what happens when we become enlightened on the nature and content of the all-filling Consciousness or *Ātmā*. Attaining this enlightenment means, seeing the entire world in the one Consciousness, as the aggregate of the multitudinous forms assumed by the one Consciousness-Substance (*cid-vastu*). It is Consciousness Itself that is perceived as the world. Put otherwise, the one Substance in all that is perceptible as forming the world, is Consciousness alone. The world thus has no existence separable from Consciousness. The Guru asserts this point in his *Ātmopadeśa Śatakam* (verse 20) as follows: "The world has no existence separable (from the primeval Reality or Consciousness)." The world is simply Consciousness self-manifesting. The two, thus, really are not two. The separateness of the two is also a man-made concept, but never perceived anywhere. To put the same in terms of causality, the causal Substance is Consciousness, and from It nothing other than Consciousness emanates as effects. That the world and the Consciousness-Substance (*cid-vastu*) are not two, forms the core of the philosophy of non-dualism (*Advaita*) according to Narayana Guru.

All that we considered as related to the universal Consciousness, will be found to be true with our individual consciousness as well. Something we have come to know never becomes non-knowledge. It is one individual consciousness that is aware of everything that one knows, and that consciousness never ceases to be consciousness either.

Of what sort will be the state in which consciousness makes an attempt to know itself? The object to be known, then, is our consciousness, and the subject who makes the attempt to know is also our consciousness itself. We are well aware also that there are not two consciousnesses in us. Then, when do we know ourselves perfectly? The certainty of having known our own consciousness is experienced when we realize that the very consciousness that makes the attempt is itself the consciousness that is being known. That is to say, the knowing consciousness and the known consciousness becoming merged in the non-dual Consciousness is where self-knowledge attains perfection.

The implication is that Consciousness never becomes non-existent, and never remains unmanifest either. The Sanskrit word *abhāva* denotes both "non-existence" and "the unmanifest state." The *abhāva* implied in the present verse is what in the Nyāya System (Indian Logic) is known as *pradhvaṁsa-abhāva,* one of the four kinds of *abhāva*s (non-existences) postulated by that system. *Pradhvaṁsa-abhāva,* literally means "posterior non-existence." It could be clarified with the help of an analogy. A pot, when broken, becomes transformed into shards, or it continues to exist in the form of shards. Therefore, as the Nyāya System holds, the pot-shards, have in them the posterior non-existence (*pradhvaṁsa-abhāva)* of the pot. But, clay, the real substance in the pot, does not have non-existence at any time. The words in the text of the verse, "Pure Consciousness never becomes reduced to something else," in philosophical terms, implies that Consciousness has no posterior non-existence. On the destruction of the pot what ceases to exist is the pot-form alone, not the clay. Likewise, at the dissolution of the apparent forms, only visible aspects cease to exist, the one invisible all-underlying Consciousness continues to exist without being reduced to anything else. Consciousness, thus, is not subject to *pradhvaṁsa-abhāva*.

Whatever be the form clay assumes, it never becomes reduced to a state of not being clay. Whatever be the ornament form in which gold appears, it is never reduced to not being gold. Similarly, even when the visible world undergoes transformation, the underlying Substance or Consciousness, neither ever ceases to exist nor is transformed into something else. In short, Consciousness, the ultimate Reality, is not subject to any kind of *abhāva*.

Though the word *abhāva* does not form part of the text, the idea clearly is implied in the verse. As was mentioned above, *abhāva* could also be understood as the state in which there is no *bhāva* or manifest form. The invisible, eternal gold's existence is always in some visible, fleeting form. Without assuming such forms gold never exists as an actual entity, and without the eternal gold existing, no transient ornament form can appear to be either. Similarly, without manifesting as the transient world, the eternal Consciousness or *Ātmā* cannot exist, and without Consciousness or *Ātmā* existing the world cannot appear to be. The ever-existing Consciousness (*cit*) in this context is treated as *sat* (Existence), and the fleeting world phenomena as *bhāva*. The state in which no *bhāva* is assumed could also be termed *a-bhāva*. Realizing the oneness of the eternal Consciousness-Reality (*sat*) and the transient world form (*bhāva*) is the core teaching of the philosophy of non-dualism (*Advaita*). In mathematical terms, this non-duality could be symbolically portrayed as the "0" point where the vertical axis representing the eternal Reality, and the horizontal axis standing for the world appearance, meet. The *Bhagavad-Gītā*, underscoring this vital point, clearly says:

nāsato vidyate bhāvo nābhāvo vidyate sataḥ ।
ubhayor api dṛṣṭo 'ntas-tv anayos tattva-darśibhiḥ ॥
— II.16

The unreal cannot manifest itself; the Real never exists without manifesting itself; the inherent truth of these two has thus been perceived by the seers of ultimate Reality.

Verse 6

aṛiyum munp etennāl
aṛiv-illātonnum iṅṅirippīlā
aṛivaṛraṭin et-atiruṇṭ-
aṛivennāl onnum iṅṅu kāṅmīlā ।

If asked, "What was existing before knowing?"
The answer is, "Without Consciousness existing nothing can have being (before and after knowing)."
How can the unknowable (pure Consciousness) have bounds?
If Consciousness alone is all that is,
The reality of everything else just vanishes.

Expansion:

It could be asked, "What existed before Consciousness found expression as specific experiences and the experience of the world?" The only possible answer would be that with no Consciousness existing to manifest Itself and to know, no state of being prior to knowing can be thought of. Being what existed before knowing and after knowing, Consciousness-Really is unknowable. What is unknowable thus is boundless as well. When it becomes self-evident that the unknowable and boundless Consciousness alone has ultimate existence before and after knowing, what seemingly exists here, and now forming the visible world, becomes non-existent.

We understood from the last verse that Consciousness alone exists after the event of knowing. Now the present verse brings to light that Consciousness alone existed even before knowing.

What Was Existing before Knowing?

Suppose I see an object I have never seen before. I make efforts to know what it is and finally come to a clear understanding of it and what it is good for. What existed before my arriving at this clear understanding? I was conscious then, and that is why I made the enquiry. That means, even before I gain a clear knowledge about something, consciousness was existing in me. In other words, it is the consciousness that existed even before knowing the present object that functionally assumed the form of the present knowledge of the object.

This is true not only with the individuated consciousness that experiences the world. Concerning the universal Consciousness, of which the world is the manifest form, also the same is true. What existed before the multifarious world or rather worlds came into being as a known reality? The Consciousness to which the existence of the world became an experience must have existed even before the experience took shape. This Consciousness is termed *cid-vastu* in Vedānta, *cit* meaning "Consciousness," and *vastu*, "Substance." It is not merely *cid-vastu*; it is also *sad-vastu* (the really Existing Substance). That means, more than being the Consciousness that experiences the world, it also is the causal Substance that assumed the form of the world, or rather worlds, thus experienced.

The world-experience could well be compared to ornament forms; then what existed in the place of gold is Consciousness alone. Gold must have undoubtedly existed before the emerging of ornament forms. Similarly, Consciousness must have existed as the causal Substance, even before the emerging of world-experience.

Without Consciousness Existing Nothing Can Have Being

Gold, in order to become an ornament, requires the artful work of an imaginative goldsmith; but it is not so with Consciousness to appear as the world. Unlike gold, Consciousness is life itself, is imaginatively creative on Its own. Its creative urge finding self-actualization is what we call the creation of the world. Infinitely extensive is the artwork of creation which thus finds expression, and our place in it is like that of a pigment-particle of the paint used in some remote corner of that art work.

The point that Consciousness, as a cause, has no *pradhvaṁsa-abhāva* (posterior non-existence), was given stress to in the last verse. The present verse, in its turn, teaches that knowledge (a functional mode of the one Consciousness) has no *prāg-abhāva* either. Before becoming a pot, clay has inherent in it the potential to become that pot. In this sense, the Nyāya Philosophy holds, clay has in it the *prāg-abhāva* of the pot. *Prāg-abhāva,* translated as "anterior non-existence" implies that, a cause, before becoming an effect, has inherent in it the "non-existence" of the effect. The prefix *prāk* means, "anterior to something." But in the case of Consciousness, though a cause in which are inhering infinite potentials of effects, it has no *prāg-abhāva,* for Consciousness was existing before knowing also. In other words, being a cause that has no anterior state in which the effects were non-existent, the idea of *prāg-abhāva* is of no relevance in the case of Consciousness.

In short, no sort of *abhāva* or non-existence is predicable of Consciousness as a cause. It always has *bhāva* or existence alone. The non-non-existent Consciousness assuming manifest form (*bhāva*s) is what we, in our conscious experiences, think of as the existence (*bhāva*) of the world.

How Can the Unknowable Have Bounds?

Consciousness, thus, has no state of being non-existent (*abhāva*). Consciousness has neither the state in which it remains having no *bhāva* or manifest form, another sense in which the word *abhāva* (*a+bhāva*), meaning "*bhāva*-less," is to be understood. Consciousness is the one omnipresent Reality. Its facets of self-manifestation are infinite, indescribable, unknowable. The infinitely expanding universe, that modern astro-physics is familiar with, is merely a minute part of the self-unfoldment of Consciousness. We, the beings that form part of that universe, the life principle in us, our freely imagining mind, the creative faculty in us, our free will, our thinking faculty, the decisive decisions taken by us, the final conclusion we arrive at, our value notions and evaluations — all such are part of the mystery of the multifarious self-manifestations of the one Consciousness that has no state of *abhāva* (the state of being non-existent as well as the state of not self-manifesting).

For example, we sow a seed and within a few days a sprout appears from it and it grows into a plant or tree that yields enjoyable fruits or vegetable. We do not see any mystery in it. But do we know how the plant or tree grows from the tiny seed? No. That this process requires the support of earth, water, air, manures and the like, is what we know about it. How the actual growth happens remains unknown. We simply say, it happens as part of nature or *prakṛti*.

What do we know of this nature? What we do know about it is very little, and what we do not know is endless. Therefore, when we say it happens as part of *prakṛti,* we only mean, we are ignorant about it. "Nature" or *prakṛti,* in this context, is a scientific term to signify our scientific ignorance of what really happens in and around us. The phenomenon of a seed growing into a plant or tree and then yielding some nourishing fruits, is not treated as a mystery by us just because we see such phenomena all around us. As what we do not know about nature is far more than what we really know, it is possible that we may encounter some phenomena quite unfamiliar to us. On seeing such, we simply think of it as a miracle or even godly, as if other phenomena are not so. For example, we may happen to see a person who can produce something out of empty space. Do we know all the laws of nature so that we may determine that such a phenomenon is not possible? No. Nature always remains a mystery to us. As part of that mystery many things could happen not yet known to us. The above-mentioned uncommon person is only one among such.

On encountering something uncommon like that, what we should become aware of is how ignorant we are about nature. Removing our ignorance is the proper remedy for this, but we are tempted instead, again owing to our ignorance, to worship the uncommon phenomenon as well as the person instrumental to it, treating both as godly. Such is the nature of our ignorance. Freedom from this ignorance constitutes real wisdom. On the dawning of this wisdom one realizes that everything in nature is a mystery. The greatest of all mysteries is the Consciousness that mysteriously unfolds, from Itself, everything in nature, both common and uncommon, both known and unknown, both here and hereafter. This mysterious Reality does not restrict Itself within the bounds of human understanding, for the human mind is simply a minute part of the mysterious self-unfoldment of that very same Reality. That Reality therefore is boundless, and what is boundless always remains a mystery.

The Reality or Consciousness that has no non-existence (*abhāva*) of any kind at any time, and of which the apparent manifest forms (*bhāvas*) are mysteriously numerous and extensive, is thus naturally boundless. Everything bounded is a manifest form (*bhāva*) appearing and disappearing in the boundless Reality. All the specific and distinct knowledges about everything are merely wavelike phenomena in the ocean-like Consciousness. Being thus boundless, Consciousness has to be unknowable as well.

Consciousness Alone is All That is

It is when we become enlightened as to the unknown and boundless Consciousness which alone truly exists, we start thinking about the reality of everything that we have so far been thinking of as real. We become convinced then that the various manifest forms (*bhāvas*) of that Reality, Itself having no *abhāva* (state of being non-existent), were only incorrectly being thought of by us as real on their own. On intuitively perceiving that one Reality, all that appeared as real disappears in the being of the Real and then the Real Consciousness alone is perceived in everything. One who knows the secret of the gold-ornament relationship sees gold alone in all ornament forms. Similarly, on realizing that one unknowable and boundless Consciousness alone is Real, one begins to visualize all the apparent forms of the world as filled with the being of that unknowable Reality. Thus one sees that Reality alone in everything. Therefore, if asked, "Have you seen that Consciousness-Reality?," the only answer would be, "I don't see anything other than Consciousness." The very same Consciousness, in religions, is termed God. Many who are antipathic to religions, ask the question, "Have you ever seen the God you are talking about?" The only answer would be, "I see nothing other than God everywhere."

Verse 7

aṛiyunnuṇṭ illenniṅṅ-
aṛiyunnīl eṭil et eẓunnīṭum?
aṛiyappeṭum-enkilum-all-
aṛivall-enniṅṅu namme nokkīṭil ।

Being is always known.
Non-being is also (ascertained by knowing),
Not by not-knowing.
Then, which arises in which?
(Does knowledge of nothingness arise from existing Consciousness,
Or does consciousness arise from nothingness?)
Even when objects (that appear to be other than Consciousness) become known,
Such objects are never really non-Consciousness in essence,
As is evident from our subjecting ourselves
To our own knowing.

Expansion:

> We always have the experience of knowing one object after another. Even "I do not know" is an experience arising in consciousness; it never is mere absence of knowing. Then, does non-knowledge arise in knowledge or consciousness, or does knowledge just arise from nothingness? The truth is that non-knowledge arises out of consciousness. We usually become aware of various objects as if we are knowing something other than consciousness. But, that the essential content of the object or what is non-knowledge, is also none other than consciousness, becomes evident to us only when we make ourselves the object of our knowledge.

We know certain things. Certain other things we do not know. "I know that" is the feeling we have about all the things we are familiar with. In my knowledge about myself as well as in my knowledge about the world, my experience is of "knowing" and not "not-knowing."

There is no one who knows everything. Asked about anything we do not know, we simply respond, "I don't know that." To say "I do not know that" also expresses a knowledge. To say, "I do not know," still falls within the range of knowledge. I can as well say, "I know that I don't know." But saying, "I do not know that I do not know" makes no sense. That means, just as "knowing" is a state of functional consciousness, so is "not-knowing."

Then the question arises, "Does not-knowing emerge from the being of consciousness, or does consciousness or knowledge emerge from nothingness?" "Knowing" and "not-knowing" are both experiences welling up from one and the same consciousness. Therefore we have to admit that the absence of knowledge also has its source in the being of consciousness.

As we have already seen, consciousness has no state of non-existence (*abhāva*). Then, "knowing" and "not-knowing" are *bhāva*s (manifest forms) assumed by the one Consciousness that has no *abhāva*. That means, these apparent manifest forms arise from that which has no *abhāva* (non-existence). The *abhāva*-experience, "I do not know" also thus arises as a *bhāva* (manifest form) of the one unmanifest Consciousness. In short, from the Consciousness that has no non-existence arises the experience of non-existence. On the other hand, the statement, "The event of knowing happens in the non-existent consciousness" is self-contradictory, and such an event is impossible.

Even when Objects Become Known

That which is known is called an object, the Sanskrit equivalent being *viṣaya*. Our concept is that mind or consciousness knows external objects. One of the implications of this concept is the notion that the known object is different from the knowing mind or consciousness. The question, both in philosophy and science, "How do the objects that are merely inert matter, find unity with mind resulting in our objective knowledge?" remains still unanswered. This question is an offshoot of the above-mentioned preconceived notion of the separateness of mind and matter.

Never Non-Consciousness in Essence

Every object is something that becomes known to a knowing mind. Are such objects non-consciousness (non-self) in essential content? That these objects also are different facets of the self-manifestation of the one Consciousness (*cit*) is the basic stance of Vedānta. Such a perspective is not known to most of us simply because our minds are conditioned by modern education that created the notion of the separateness of mind and matter in our minds. We need to give up all such prejudices, which, we are not sure, are scientifically admissible or not, and start our thinking anew. Such a search for Reality leads us to the basic understanding that what appear as inert matter and thinking mind are but different transient forms assumed by the one unconditioned Consciousness that alone has real existence. Mind and matter, thus, find unity and become lost in the being of the unconditioned Consciousness, referred to as *tat* (That) in the Upaniṣads.

Subjecting Ourselves to Our Own Knowing

There is a context in which it becomes revealed that what appears as object is also pure Consciousness in content. It is when we make ourselves the object of our knowledge. That means, when I know myself. Then the object to be known is "I." This "I" is neither the physical body, senses, mind, intellect nor anything that could be thought of as "mine," but is the possessor of all such. That this "I" is merely a subjective experience of luminous existence is evident to all of us. Now, who is the subject or the one who knows? That also is "I." Are there two "I"-s then, — one, the subject and the other, the object? As we are quite sure, no such two "I"-s exist. That means, when I know myself, one and the same "I" or consciousness assumes the role of the subject on the one side, and of the object on the other. That one consciousness that can assume these two roles when I know myself, can also do the same when I know other objects also. And really that is what happens.

A Vedāntin's perception of a subject knowing an object is not as the coming together and becoming one of two entities of entirely opposite natures. Really the union is between the one manifest form called subject and the other manifest form called object, of one and the same Consciousness or *Ātmā*. The real event in the union of the two is simply the two realizing their intrinsic oneness. This momentary realization of the non-dual *Ātmā* is what we in our transaction refer to as a specific knowledge.

Water assumes the form of the pot or pan it is poured into. This change of form in the water is caused by its contact with the respective conditioning factors, i.e., with pots, pans and the like. Similar is the difference between subject and object; both are different apparent forms assumed by one Consciousness, because of its contact with two different conditioning factors (*upādhis*). Such conditioning factors are also forms assumed by the one Reality owing to its own mysterious creative power. The union of the two results in Consciousness actualizing and experiencing Its actual oneness, by forgoing the two conditioning factors and thus transcending the subject-object duality. The event of giving up the conditioning factors is counted in modern thought as the union of subject and object. The enlightened ones alone perceive this as a momentary sparking of non-dual experience that goes on incessantly; others consider it as a subject gaining the knowledge of an object. This latter perception only takes us back to the already-mentioned unanswerable question.

The entire perceptible world, though considered an object of knowledge, thus in essential content, is Consciousness alone.

Verse 8

aṛiv-enn anney itum uṇṭ-
aṛiv-uṇṭ ennāl it-eṅṅu ninnīṭum?
aṛiv-onn-eṇṇam ver-ill-
aṛiv-allātenkil entirikkunnu?

As long as Consciousness exists, "this" (the world) also appears to be.
If Consciousness alone is,
Then, where else can "this" have being?
Pure Consciousness is one alone;
Then, nothing else exists as countable.
Then, what is it that has real being?
(It is not "this," the world that has real being,
One Consciousness alone has being.)

Expansion:

As long as Consciousness or *Ātmā* exists, so exists the object of which one becomes conscious also. We refer to each such object as "this" and the aggregate of all "this" constitutes the world. The visible world, thus, exists as long as the ultimate Reality or *Ātmā* exists. Though "the known" apparently exists along with the knowing mind, the real existence, as we have already seen clearly, is that of Consciousness or *Ātmā* alone. On becoming enlightened of this, the existence of "this," the object of knowledge or the world, would be found to be nowhere else than in that Consciousness. Consciousness is not only the ultimate Reality, but is also one in number. That means, nothing that could be considered as "other than consciousness" exists. What absolutely exists thus is one Consciousness alone. How then does what we call the world apparently exist side by side with consciousness? The world does not really exist parallel with consciousness. What really exists and appears as the world, is nothing other than the one and only Consciousness.

As Long as Consciousness Exists, "This" also Appears to be

When did the world come into being? When will it cease to be? These questions, though basic, are answered differently by scientists and religionists. Two different human disciplines may offer different theories or explanations concerning one and the same reality or phenomenon. Such theories make no difference in the real being of what is thus theorized about or explained. It continues to exist as it is taking no notice of such theories and explanations developed about it. That means, reality does not vary in accordance with the theories science develops, and reality need not necessarily be as we theorize.

Many could be the human opinions about the real. But we are concerned here not with such opinions, not with explanations, scientific or otherwise, given to it, but with the Reality that remains unaffected by such theories and opinions.

How is this Reality related to the world? As long as the Consciousness that really has no beginning and end, exists, the world that could be referred to as "this" also exists. Such is the way the two are related. The world also appears to be as long as Consciousness or *Ātmā* exists. That means, the appearance of the world, or rather worlds, also is beginningless and endless as is *Ātmā*. The world did not, really, originate from *Ātmā* at any particular time, but has existed beginninglessly and endlessly along with *Ātmā*. That the knowing consciousness exists means "the known" also necessarily exists. Otherwise, the consciousness loses its status of being "the knower" or "the witness." If a witness has to exist, then there should be something to be witnessed. Without the one the other is meaningless. The same is true with the relationship between *Ātmā* and the world appearance.

This could easily be understood with the help of the gold-ornament analogy we are familiar with. The substance called gold does not perish. This imperishable gold exists always in some form, and all such forms are perishable. That is to say, the indestructible gold cannot exist without having some destructible form. Likewise, a non-existing gold never assumes the form of ornaments. The transient appearance of the ornaments thus implies the existence of the eternal gold. Thus, without the one the other becomes meaningless. Really, the eternal gold and the transient ornament forms do not ever remain separate. What exists is the non-duality wherein the gold substance and ornament forms remain inseparable. This non-dual reality, when seen from the indestructible substance or existence (*sat*) aspect, is called gold, and when perceived from the point of view of the destructible form (*bhāva*) aspect, it is called ornament. Calling it differently does not make it really two. The existence of the one implies the other.

This is the way Consciousness or *Ātmā* and the apparent world are related. One existing means the other also exists. To say that the eternal Consciousness exists without assuming the transient world-form, and that the transient world appears to be with no eternal causal Consciousness existing, are both equally meaningless. What really exists is the one and non-dual Reality. Seen from the point of view of the eternal Substance it is called Consciousness or *Ātmā*, and seen from the perspective of the transient appearance, the same is called the world. Calling it differently does not make the Reality two.

The same vital philosophical point of non-duality is clarified in the *Bhagavad-Gītā* when it says:

nāsato vidyate bhāvo nābhāvo vidyate sataḥ ।
ubhayor api dṛṣto 'ntas tvanayos tattva-darśibhiḥ ॥
— II.16

The unreal does not manifest itself, the real never remains with no manifest form either. The secret in between these two is perceived only by real philosophers.

The Guru himself, while portraying Consciousness as the causal Substance of the world-appearance, in chapter IV of the *Darśana Māla*, says:

yacca nābhāti tad asat
yad asat tan na bhāti ca — II.8

That which does not manifest as the world is unreal. That which is unreal cannot manifest as the world either.

Consciousness (*cit*) is what really exists; thus it is *sat* (Existence) as well. Such a *cit* is sentient or lively (*cetanā*) also by nature. That which is sentient or active remains always with functions. That means, Consciousness always functions; it never remains idle and inert. When being functional, the aspects such as "the knower" and "the known" emerge ceaselessly in it.

If Consciousness Alone is, Then, Where Else Can "This" Have Being?

As long as the knowing consciousness exists, as we have just seen, the known objects also exist. At the same time, we understood earlier in this work that Consciousness alone has real existence. Then what is the status of existence of the known objects, and where do they exist? Their existence really is in the one Consciousness as Its own manifest self-expressions. It is only that the one Consciousness that alone exists, as part of Its infinite possibilities of creative self-unfoldment, appears as the existence of objects. It is comparable to the phenomenon of gold appearing as the existence of ornaments. That means, while the known objects exist always along with the knowing consciousness, their existence is in the being of Consciousness itself, like the existence of ornaments in the being of gold.

Consciousness is One Alone

We saw clearly in verse 4 and the comments on it, the nature of the all-inclusive plenitude of the unconditioned Consciousness. It alone has fullness; Its being fills the fullness of the eternally and endlessly existing infinitude. Such an eternal and endless existence can never be more than one in number. Therefore, the Consciousness-Reality we are concerned with, numerically has to be one.

Nothing Other Than Consciousness Exists as Countable

Counting things becomes necessary only when they are treatable as one different from another. When one alone is perceived, no counting would be felt to be of any value; all countable apparent entities are merely different manifest forms of the one and only Reality, the one Consciousness. Therefore, counting and separating out non-consciousness from consciousness, as well as one consciousness or knowledge from another, is meaningless. Nothing to count exists because nothing other than Consciousness exists as countable.

Then What is it That has Real Being?

When examined thus, does this world we perceive by counting and measuring have an existence of its own? No; all this is nothing more than the divine sport of the one Consciousness, the one *Ātmā*.

Verse 9

aṛivinn iṭam onn-uṇṭ-ill-
aṛiyappeṭum-ennatinnu veṛāyī
aṛiv-ennāl aṅn-et-īy-

aṛiyappeṭum ennat eṛum eṇṇīṭil?

Pure Consciousness has being of its own.
No object of knowledge has separate beingness.
Then, how can consciousness, when keenly observed,
Reach out and grasp an object (as if it were something else)?

Expansion:

> The one Reality is Consciousness or *cit*. It alone has being of its own, and room for existence; and that room is also one. No other room, therefore, exists for what we call the objects of knowledge to be. Being so, how can consciousness reach towards the objects as if they exist somewhere outside, in order to know them? Thus it becomes clear, when closely examined, that to conceive of the knower's consciousness or mind going out to grasp external objects is totally wrong.

How do we know an object? Our senses come into contact with their respective objects, and we recognize each of them. Such is the context in which we gain perceptual knowledge. This is explained in one way as the event in which the knower's mind or consciousness proceeds towards the object perceived and attains a sort of identity with it. This concept mainly belongs to the classical Eastern idea of perception. Perception, according to modern science, on the other hand, occurs when the externally existing objects come into contact with sense organs and create a bio-chemical impulse in the sense organ, which then is transformed into an electrical impulse that is conveyed through neurons to the concerned area of the brain, where it again is transformed into a bio-chemical effect that can produce a sort of side effect which we experience as sense-perception. Put otherwise, the modern scientific concept of knowing an object is that the external object, through sense contact, enters the mind and creates the experience of perceiving the object as a sort of reflection of it in the mind. Either way, the idea is that one proceeds to the other and enters it which creates the perceptual experience. It is this idea that the Guru corrects here.

Consciousness Alone has Being of its Own

We have seen in our previous considerations that Consciousness alone has real existence and that It must be one in number. Whatever has being, has to have some room for existing. If Consciousness alone exists, then the same Consciousness alone has room for being. That means, nothing other has room to exist. It was also seen that what is usually thought of as "the other" is nothing but a mode of appearance of the one Consciousness. Therefore "the other" should also exist within the being of Consciousness. In short, the object known has room to exist only in Consciousness, which Itself is one alone.

How can Consciousness Reach Out and Grasp an Object?

If the object of knowledge has its being in the room that is Consciousness Itself, then how is it to be understood that the knowing consciousness leaves its own room of existence and reaches out to the object in order to know it? No such reaching out can happen.

To think that the event of knowing an object takes place as the object outside enters the being of the knowing mind, is equally wrong. How can an object that has no being other than in consciousness enter the very same consciousness to be known by it?

We thus conclude, objective knowledge occurs, not when the knowing mind enters the known object, nor when the known object enters the knowing mind.

How does the apparent event of having perceptual knowledge occur? Any attempt to arrive at a logically laudable answer to this question ends up only in an infinite tangle of arguments and theorizations that always can be countered. We saw earlier that all that exists in the objects known is but one Consciousness alone.

This implies also that the potential to manifest as all the objects is in the very same Consciousness-Reality. Then the question, "How does objective knowledge occur?" does not arise for a *jñānin*. He or she is aware the same Consciousness-Reality has inherent in It the infinite possibility to assume the form of all conditioning factors that make Itself appear as numerous objects, numerous subjects and numerous knowledges.

The reality in numerous ornament forms is one gold. Along with this awareness one should know also that gold has in it the potential to assume an infinite variety of ornament forms. It is therefore natural with gold to assume all such forms. In the case of gold, it needs the help of a goldsmith to make it appear in various forms. That is not the case with Consciousness or *Ātmā*. There is no need of any such efficient cause. Its own mysteriously creative urge incessantly creates out of Itself numerous forms, ranging from the most subtle mind to the grossest matter. Nothing is impossible with Consciousness or *Ātmā*. The same stated in religious terms would be, "Nothing is impossible with God." We need not therefore throw ourselves into the impossible task of ascertaining with certitude what are those numerous possibilities. The attempt to arrive at such an understanding is made by our faculty called the intellect. This very intellect, it is to be remembered, is nothing more than an infinitesimally minute particle of the Consciousness-Reality unfolding Itself. With such a particle as an instrument, to measure the infinitude of its own Source-Reality is impossible. It is like trying to measure the ocean using a drop as the standard for measurment.

Therefore it is best for us to realize the one mysterious Consciousness, and to perceive ourselves and our mind as inseparably one with It. The efforts made by the mind to know the objective world, as well as Itself, are also to be seen as that one Consciousness functioning.

The myteriousness of the Consciousness-Reality is portrayed by the Guru in the next verse.

Verse 10

aṛiyunnīl ann onn īy-
aṛiyappeṭum ennat uṇṭu poyīṭum
aṛivil it et aṛiyunnīl-
aṛiv-ennāl eṅṅuninnu vannīṭum?

Consciousness does not know (any object as something else).
The moment this realization dawns
Everything converges to absolute oneness.
What were till then counted as objects,
Just becomes devoured (by the one Consciousness).
And within Consciousness (that functions)
What could there be that remains not known?
Where, then, is the origin of every specific knowledge we have?
(Within one Consciousness alone do
Emerge all specific knowledges.)

Expansion:

Consciousness does not go somewhere and grasp something that is not consciousness. This truth becoming revealed means the revelation of the oneness of Reality also. These are not two revelations. On this realization, the objects that were previously thought of as existing separate from consciousness or mind, become engulfed by the one Consciousness that alone ultimately exists. This existence is a creatively functional one. As it functions so, is it impossible for that Consciousness to formulate any kind of specific knowledge within Its own being? No.

When knowing the world and ourselves, we have the notion that the knowing mind and the known objects are separately existing entities. But the meditations we have made so far have made it sufficiently clear that the one reality that exists is Consciousness alone. Therefore, the question of the knowing consciousness reaching out to an object and knowing it, or a known object entering the knowing mind through some means, does not arise at all. That means, the experience of having a specific knowledge of something does not necessarily mean that a mind is knowing an object external to itself.

Everything Converges to Absolute Oneness

Normally the above-mentioned knowledge never occurs to us. This new awareness reveals also that there exists no more than one reality. Really, the knowledge that Reality is one alone and that subject and object do not have separate existencies are not two understandings. The two are simply different ways in which one and the same revelation is expressed.

What were Counted as Objects Become Devoured

As it becomes evident that one Reality alone exists, any enquiry into the existence of objects turns out to be futile, for their existence by then would have been engulfed by the Consciousness that alone really exists. Put otherwise, the objects known would no longer be seen as separate from Consciousness.

Within Consciousness What could There be That Remains not Known?

No one knows what potentials of which nature and extent hide within the one Consciousness, to become unfolded into various manifestations. For this reason, to predict what kind of experiences we could expect in life, and what are the types of experiences we would not have, is impossible. One and the same Consciousness or *Ātmā* creatively unfolds Itself as the subject, as the object and as the event of knowing, popularly known as *tripuṭi* in Vedānta. This creative urge of *Ātmā* is such that no possibility, no matter whether worldly or unworldly, could be ruled out.

Why does Consciousness unfold from Itself all such manifest forms? Consciousness or *cit*, being creative and dynamic, has in It the inner urge to see for Itself the nature of the infinite potentials hidden within Itself. In order to actualize this urge, It brings out from Itself all such potentials and enjoys doing so. This enjoyment, not depending on anything external, is in effect the realization of the *ānanda* content of Itself. This could be compared to small children who in order to enjoy bringing out the potentials within themselves, create many things with whatever is handy, and immediately destroy them to give shape to something else. The Guru himself, in his *Ātmopadeśa Śatakam*, makes this point clear as follows:

> Pure Consciousness (*Ātmā*),
> In order to actualize the potentials hidden within,
> Transforms Itself assuming the forms
> Of various specific manifestations such as the earth,
> And moves spiralling up and down and back and forth,
> Making many apparent forms emerge,
> Like the glowing figures of a spiralling fire stick. — v. 33

The appearing to be, of everything that is known, is, as is held traditionally in Vedānta, like that of the glowing figures we see when a burning fire-stick is spiralled. The apparent circling fire-line has no being, what really exists is one tip of the burning fire-stick alone. Similarly, one Consciousness alone is real in all that is apparent, forming the objects of knowledge, emerging as if in a cyclic order. Being Consciousness, It is fully conscious of whatever takes place in Itself including Its own knowing functions. In this sense, It is the Consciousness that knows consciousness, or Knowledge that knows knowledge. The same Reality is designated as *Ātmā* and *Brahman* in the Upaniṣads. As the all-pervading substance, (*ātata*), it is termed *Ātmā* or *Ātman*; and as the Reality that grows endlessly (*bṛmhati*) as everything, It is called *Brahman*. Comparable to a grand magic show is the way in which *Ātmā*, in an inexplicable way, unfolds Itself as all the countless apparent forms and the corresponding names, as also the mental faculties and senses that are instrumental in knowing everything, as the doer of actions, and as the actions themselves, as is made clear by the Guru himself when he defines *Ātmā* as of the essence of Consciousness. He says:

> That which is conscious of itself
> Even when in darkness, is the *Ātmā*.
> It is pure, unconditioned Consciousness.
> And it manifests as all names and forms.
> As all mental faculties and senses.
> As all actions and their doers.
> Lo and behold,
> What a Grand Magic all this is! — *Ātmopadeśa Śatakam*, v. 27

Where is the Origin of Every Specific Knowledge?

Seen from the perspective of the ultimate Reality, from where do arise all the specific items of knowledge that we experience one after another endlessly? These cannot come from anywhere else than from the one ultimate Reality, the unconditioned Consciousness that is conscious of Itself. All specific instances of knowledge are wave-like forms that emerge and merge back in the ocean-like being of Consciousness.

Verse 11

aṛivinn aṛivāy ninn-et-
aṛiyikkunn-iṅṅu nām atāyīṭum
aṛivet inam eṅṅaney-īy-
aṛiyappeṭum ennat et it otīṭil ।

The Consciousness that makes known of all specific
knowledge —
We, in essence, are that.
Upon becoming enlightened thus,
How could then arise such questions as
"Of what category is the phenomenon called knowledge?"
"How does it know?"

"What is it that we call the objects of knowledge?"

Expansion :

> One Consciousness is conscious of all the specific items of knowledge, and It makes us constantly know of all such instances of knowledge. We are really that Consciousness Itself. Or, one can say that the Consciousness that remains as the brightness-experience "I" in all of us Itself is the *Ātmā*. When this non-dual secret becomes revealed to us, no doubt of any kind remains in us to be cleared.
>
> Of what category is the phenomenon of mind or consciousness? How does each specific knowledge get formulated in the mind? Of what sort are the objects of knowledge that form part of the world? Such are some of those doubts.

This composition of fifteen verses began with explicating the philosophical stand that "The known 'this' is no other," because what is referred to as "this" or the objective world is also Consciousness in essence. Therefore, nothing other than one Consciousness ever has real existence anywhere. This general perception is maintained throughout the work.

The next verse counters the ordinary argument that the known object can exist even without the knowing consciousness existing. It is asked, "Which is the consciousness to which the knowledge occurs that the object can exist without a knowing subject?"

This is what verse 3 shows: the one Consciousness shines but is not measurable by any of the valid means of knowledge (*pramāṇas*). All the measurable items of knowledge, i.e., all the knowledge that could be ascertained to be right or wrong with the help of *pramāṇas*, have their being only in the one Consciousness that is not measurable. It is similar to all dream-visions having existence only in the dreaming mind. Thus the existence of everything measurable is in the one immeasurable Consciousness.

Consciousness alone is the all-inclusive plenitude. If something is outside the bounds of knowledge, this fact is also a knowledge, and thus is not outside the bounds of consciousness. That consciousness, in its turn, is not something knowable as an object that exists apart from the knowing mind. The boundlessness of the one Consciousness is the point stressed in verse 4.

This Consciousness-Reality never gives up Its status of being Consciousness to descend to be something else, i.e., in order to become the world. We do not see, in the usual course, that what appears as the world is pure Consciousness alone. When realized thus, the Consciousness thus known and the world-appearance cease to be two. Consciousness does not cease to be Consciousness in order to appear as the world. When the oneness of the two is realized, what ceases to be is the world, and not Consciousness. This point is stressed in verse 5.

Verse 6 underscores that what existed before the event of knowing something, is Consciousness alone. Being such, Consciousness is not knowable as an object of knowledge, and thus is boundless as well. When this one Consciousness is realized to be the being in oneself, all that appears to exist as "the other" ceases to be. In short, what exists before and after knowing is Consciousness alone.

We have the experience of knowing something. Not knowing something is not mere absence of knowledge, but is also a sort of knowledge, because we are aware of being ignorant. Now the question arises: does ignorance arise from knowledge or knowledge from not-knowledge? This point was clarified in verse 7, where it was demonstrated that ignorance also arises within Consciousness.

Consciousness-Reality, and the object of knowledge in the form of which It manifests Itself, always co-exist. One cannot exist functionally without the other. Really, Consciousness alone has real being, and the objects do not have separate being. That means, the one Reality or Consciousness functionally appears as the objects of knowledge as well. This aspect of perceiving Consciousness was brought into relief in verse 8.

Verse 9 underscored that, one Consciousness alone having room to exist, the objects known do not have any room of their own to exist. Then, how is it possible to think that the knowing mind reaches out to an object in order to know it? To think that the object enters the knowing consciousness when the event of knowing takes place is also equally baseless because no object exists outside Consciousness.

Consciousness, in the event of knowing, does not really go out and grasp something which is non-consciousness. Upon realizing the real oneness, one finds that what was thought of as the external object is devoured by the one Consciousness. Furthermore, with regard to this Consciousness, nothing is impossible for It. No knowledge originates from outside Consciousness; all knowledge originates from and occurs within the one Consciousness that alone has real existence. This aspect is portrayed in verse 10.

Thus, after reflecting on the main philosophical issues related to Consciousness and its functions, and resolving all of them in view of the above-mentioned basic stand of Vedānta, it was concluded in verse 10 that no knowledge emerges other than from the one Consciousness-Reality. The problems raised thus and the resolutions of the same were philosophically all of a generic nature.

Now from verse 11 onwards, we leave behind the generic nature and turn to the realm of the experience of a realized individual. So far we were perceiving that, whatever be the problems that rise up, everything distinct that is causal to the emerging of the problem, becomes sublimated as the one Consciousness. From now onwards we see the reverse side of the way of approach — that of perceiving how the one Consciousness, when functioning, becomes unravelled as all that we specifically know. The former approach adopts a way of thinking that ascends from the many to the one, and the latter descends from the one to the many. The first ten verses can be seen as following a synthetic line of thought, and the rest of the verses resort rather to an analytic perspective. A careful observation of all such subtle methodological and structural details alone reveals the originality and beauty of the present work from the pen of the Guru.

We are That

The sum and substance of what we have known clearly from the reflections we made so far is that one Consciousness that is conscious of all the knowledge we happen to have, alone and nothing else, has real existence. This truth has to become a real experience for each of us in the form, "I am that Consciousness." To put it in terms of the gold-ornament analogy, the truth that one gold alone exists in all the ornaments is realized by each individual ornament as "I am that gold." It is the one Consciousness that knows everything and makes me know of everything, that remains in me making me know "I am."

As we have seen, one Consciousness alone has existence and room for existing. Then what about "me" who understands this truth? Is it that "I" also do not have being? No one can deny one's own existence, and the experience "I am" is with all of us. Only that my existence really is the existence of that Consciousness. Moreover, that Consciousness becomes directly known to "me" only in the form of the knowledge "I," or in the form of self-knowledge. This is the reason in Vedānta for considering knowing "myself" or self-knowledge as the best and most direct way to realize *Brahman*. That means, that Consciousness and the I-consciousness in "me" are one in essential content. The cryptical statement "We are that" here could be considered as another version of the famous *mahāvākya* (great dictum) *tat tvam asi* (That thou art) of the *Chāndogya Upaniṣad*.

This one Consciousness, as the all-pervading and ever-growing Substance, is termed *Brahman* as was seen earlier, and as the Substance in the being of oneself, as *Ātmā*. Then the present sentence could be interpreted as a variant version of yet another *mahāvākya, ayam ātmā brahma* (This self is the Absolute) of the *Māṇḍūkya Upaniṣad.*

On Becoming Enlightened about This

Our philosophical understanding has to become transformed into experiential awareness. It is here that we need the graceful guidance of an enlightened *guru*. Any intelligent scholar may be capable of expounding the basic philosophical principles of a generic nature. But such scholars are not *gurus*, nor even necessarily *jñānins*. We come across numerous scholars who are well versed in the philosophical teachings of the basic textbooks of Vedānta, like the Upaniṣads, *Bhagavad-Gītā* and *Brahma-Sūtras*. They may be quite capable of expounding such teachings appealingly as well. But they do not live as *jñānins*. They are *ajñānins* not because of any lack of knowledge of the Vedānta philosophy. What is lacking in them is the transformation of such philosophical truths into the experiential truth, and living every moment of their actual life actualizing that philosophic truth. It is here that one needs the guidance of a *guru*.

What is rendered here as "On becoming enlightened about this," literally means "on having undergone teaching and learning under a *guru*, culminating in attaining the final certitude." *Oathu* is a technical term used in the Malayalam language to signify "reading, learning, teaching, and becoming enlightened" in the Vedic and Vedāntic contexts, and is the word used by the *guru* here. A *guru*'s teaching need not necessarily be verbal; it could even be in the form of a silence brimming with meaning. A disciple, having thus been imparted the non-dualistic secret from the *guru*, feels to have become free of all doubts, resulting in the experience of absolute Peace.

Of What Category is Knowledge?

We feel that we have known something clearly only when we get definite answers to the questions like, "What is it?," "Of what category is it?," "How was it originated?, "What are the factors involved in its being?" As long as we do not get clear answers to such questions, we feel something is still vague about it. But no such questions have any place in the case of knowledge knowing itself, or consciousness becoming conscious of itself. If you insist on getting answers to such questions in this case, you are, according to the *Bhagavad-Gītā* (IV.40), a *samśayātmā* (one of doubting mind). You are destined to perish in the spiritual sense then, with no definiteness having been arrived at.

The final certitude about Consciousness, on the other hand, is marked by the conviction that It alone exists, that It alone has room to exist, and that I am that Consciousness in essential content. Neither doubts nor unanswerable questions torment a person of this certitude, and such a person experiences absolute Peace in life.

We categorize things when there are many things to know and where differentiating one from another becomes necessary. In the case of Consciousness, as It alone exists, differentiating It from another thing that exists along with It, is not a necessity. It, on the other hand, is a catagory in itself, that is inclusive of everything categorizable. Therefore, thinking of Consciousness as belonging to any discernible category is of no relevance.

Likewise irrelevant is the question, "How was consciousness originated?" We try to understand something by asking ourselves or someone else, the questions like, "What was the causal substance from which it originated or was created?," "How did it originate as an effect from such a cause?," "Who was the efficient cause for its emergence?," "What was the purpose, if any, of its origination?," "To whom is it useful?" Consciousness, as we have already seen clearly, was never originated, has always been existing, is the causal substance as well as the efficient cause for the origin of everything that has come into being in all the worlds, and gives room for existence to everything, by being the Reality that alone has room to exist. To ask how did that Consciousness originate makes no sense.

The questions, "What are all these that we encounter as objects of knowledge?," is similarly irrelevant. By now we have understood that the existence of all the objects is only in the being of the one Consciousness, and that these objects appear to be distinct only as the manifest forms of that Consciousness, without which forms It never exists.

How Does it Know?

The question how does consciousness or mind know objects, also does not arise. Because, what appears as objects is Consciousness Itself. Thus, consciousness knowing objects means, Consciousness knowing Itself. Being Consciousness, It cannot remain without knowing Itself either.

I became aware also that I am that Consciousness Itself. That means, what appears as objects of knowledge to me is myself. The being of such objects, in other words, is in myself. I exist and in my being the objects also exist. Stated though in many such ways, the real oneness of Consciousness is ineffable, but directly experienceable.

Such is the secret we should experientially realize with the graceful instruction of a *guru*. What the Guru ultimately teaches is given in the next verse.

Verse 12

aṛiv ennatu nīy atu ninn-
aṛiv-iṭṭ aṛiyappeṭunnat ennāyī
aṛiyappeṭum itu ranṭ onn-
aṛiyunnunṭennum onn-at-illennum ।

What that one Consciousness is, even That you are.
That Consciousness, being such,
By subjecting Itself (to self-unfoldment),
Assumes the appearance of "the known."
"The known" thus emerged is of two categories:
One that makes you feel,
"I am well aware of it,"
And the other that makes you feel, "It is beyond my ken."

Expansion:

The one pure Consciousness that is conscious of all knowledge, and that makes you know of everything, Itself is your essential content. That Consciousness which is yourself creatively unfolds Itself and assumes the form of the objects known. Such knowable objects are of two kinds: one, the objects that arouse in you the feeling, "I know it," and the other that arouse in you the feeling, "I do not know that," or "It is beyond the bounds of my knowledge."

That One Consciousness — Even That You are

The awareness we have clearly gained as of now is that the one ultimate Reality, that alone has existence of its own, is pure, unconditioned Consciousness. One Consciousness alone is what exists in the ultimate sense. At the same time, our own existence as individuals is undeniable to each of us. How is this contradiction to be understood? It means only that this existence of ours is not really ours but is of the one Consciousness. In other words, it is the being of the one Consciousness that is felt as the being of ourselves. Mostly we remain completely oblivious of this truth, and hence our thinking, "I have my own existence." It was to highlight this aspect that it was stated in the previous verse, "The Consciousness that makes us know of all specific knowledges — we in essence are That."

It is those who are unaware of this Reality that need the instruction of a *guru*. The essential content of the instruction thus given by a *guru* would be somewhat like this: "The Consciousness you are in search of is what sits here before me in your form. I am also so. Therefore, perceive that Consciousness as yourself."

This becomes all the more clear if we take the example of gold and ornaments. A piece of ornament makes the enquiry as to the reality in all the ornaments. That reality is gold. But the ornament is unaware of the truth that the same gold is what appears there assuming its own (the ornament's) form. Therefore, another ornament that knows the truth, tells this piece of ornament, "The very same gold you are in search of is what appears here in your own form. Therefore the best way for you to know gold is to know yourself. You are that gold."

By Subjecting Itself to Self-unfoldment, It Assumes the Appearance of "The Known"

It is natural with gold to assume some form of ornaments, coins, etc. Though gold is indestructible, all the forms in which it appears are destructible. Looked at in this perspective, the process by which gold assumes the appearance of ornaments, is a sort of coming down from its being the indestructible substance (*sat*) to the destructible apparent forms (*bhāvas*), to borrow the terms used in the *Bhagavad-Gītā* (II.16 already quoted). The same is true in the case of the one Consciousness-Reality as well. It also never exists without assuming some fleeting apparent form. One such form is that of the object of knowledge. That means, one of the transient forms into which the eternal Consciousness comes down is what we call an object.

This basic principle becomes experiential in the life of each, not as some unfamiliar Consciousness-Reality assuming the form of some objects yet to be known, but as oneself assuming the form of one's own objects of knowledge, whereby the person concerned realizes the one Consciousness-Reality as the substance in his or her own being. The *guru* therefore tells the disciple, "You yourself appear as the objects you know." The statements, "The one Consciousness appears as the objects of knowledge," "You appear yourself as the objects of knowledge," "Your consciousness assumes itself the form of the objects of knowledge," and "I appear myself as my objects of knowledge," thus mean the same.

Such phenomenal objects of knowledge are of two types:

ONE THAT MAKES YOU FEEL, "I AM WELL AWARE OF IT"

One category of the objects of knowledge consists of those about which one feels, "I know this," "This is such and such," "It is made of such and such," "It is good for such and such," "I like it or dislike it," and the like. That means, these are objects that are within the bounds of information one has acquired in life. The peculiarity of this sort of objects is that each is recognized by us. Being numerous, diverse in nature, various in kinds, and contradictory or non-contradictory, also mark such objects. Each such object is a distinct one.

THE OTHER MAKES ONE FEEL, "IT IS BEYOND MY KEN"

There is yet another category of objects. It is anything about which we can make a statement like, "I know nothing about it." This means that such a category is beyond the bounds of any specific knowledge. This category would even include objects which no one knows of. This means, we also admit there are objects beyond the bounds of any-one's knowledge. All such unknowables cannot strictly be treated as non-objects. Such unknowables could apply to virtual or actual objects on the one side, and to the Absoulte on the other.

Verse 13

aṛivum atin-vaṇṇam cenn-
aṛiyunnavanil pakarnnu pinnīṭum
aṛiyappeṭum itil onn īy-
aṛivin pori vīṇu cīntiy añcāyī ǀ

Pure and unconditioned Consciousness,
Likewise, assumed the form of "the knower."

Again, of the two kinds of "knowns,"
The one (i.e., "the known" that is knowable)
Became split up into the five (sense-objects),
As the sparks of the knower-consciousness fell on it.
(In the meanwhile, the knower-consciousness also became split up into five senses.)

Expansion:

The one unconditioned Consciousness, as it creatively unfolds Itself as the objects, does so as the knowing subject also. Such is the way the emergence of "the knower" and "the known" could be understood as taking place in the one Consciousness. We already know, as was shown in the last verse, that the "the known" is of two kinds. One of these two, i.e., the objects that are knowable, sparked by the knower's consciousness, becomes separated out as the five sense objects, i.e., sound, touch, form, taste and smell. Along with it, on the side of the knower, the Consciousness becomes broken up as the five respective senses also.

The Consciousness that each of us experiences directly without the mediation of anything like the senses, becomes subjected to self-unfoldment impelled by Its own creative urge and thus assumes the form of the objects, i.e., the objective world. Consciousness thus having assumed the form of the objects is often referred to as *idanta*, meaning "this-sense" or "this-ness." Along with it there will be the corresponding subjective aspect called *ahanta* (I-sense or I-ness). This latter aspect is also nothing other than yet another form in which Consciousness manifests Itself. That means, the one Consciousness, as part of Its creative self-unfoldment, appears as the objects on the one side and as the knowing subject on the other. Such objects are referred to variously depending on the epistemological context dealt with, as *viṣaya* (object of knowledge), *jñeya* (that which is to be known), or *prameya* (that which is to be measured). Correspondingly, the subject is also referred to as *viṣayin* (the subject of knowledge), *jñātā* (one who knows), or *pramātā* (one who measures).

Having a specific knowledge of anything happens apparently as a result of the contact between the subject and object. Both the subject and object are merely two different manifestations of one and the same Consciousness. The event of knowing also is a functional expression of Consciousness. That means, the subject, the object and the event of knowing, popularly known in Vedānta as *tripuṭi*, the tribasic factors, are simply three manifest aspects of the one Consciousness. These three seem to be three only because of the contact that Consciousness has with self-created conditioning factors called *upādhi*s. The Consciousness foregoing these three conditioning factors and achieving Its intrinsic oneness is thus what we term as the event of acquiring a specific knowledge, though we normally remain unaware of this. As every specific knowledge gets formulated in us, we remain unaware of ourselves actually being the knowers of the seemingly external known objects, and of a specific knowledge occurring. On the other hand, the clarity of the specific knowledge-experience alone shines at that moment. We simply thus remain oblivious of the truth that that event is one in which we realize, at least momentarily, the real oneness of the Consciousness-Reality — indeed a momentary ineffable realization of the non-duality of the Real. Instead, we think, we are knowing and enjoying certain objects existing externally.

To be vibrant is natural for Consciousness. As part of it, when It assumes the form of the objects, It always yearns for becoming united with the subject; and as It appears as the subject, always in search of objects. All these self-activations ultimately aim at actualizing the non-dual experience in the above-mentioned manner.

Of the Two kinds of "Known," the One

Let us now go back to the last verse where it was stated that "the known" has two apparent modes. One of these two, i.e., "the known" that is actually knowable, alone has multiplicity of numbers and variety of kinds and the like. It alone constitutes the world of everything we can know clearly and distinctly. It, in other words, is the totality of objects that we can hear, touch, see, taste, smell and also think of.

Consciousness is like a burning fire. It never ceases to flame. When It flames as the knower, Its sparks fall on the world of objects or rather as the world of objects, and split into five, thus making distinct the sense objects.

Along with the object becoming divided thus into five, the corresponding senses that form part of the knower become differentiated also. Distinct objective knowledges become actualized as an outcome of this systematic self-unfoldment to which Consciousness subjects Itself in order to see for Itself what are the potentials hidden within Itself.

Such is the way the one Consciousness or *Ātmā* unfolds Itself as the changeful apparent world, where the the knower, the known and the events of knowing are distinctly discernible.

It is with a one-to-one correspondence that the one Consciousness finds self-expression both subjectively and objectively. That means, every apparent aspect on the objective side will have a corresponding aspect on the subjective side. The mutual matching of these two manifest forms of Consciousness is the theme pondered on in the next two verses.

Eight constituent factors are pointed out there by the Guru on both sides. These numbers may vary according to the epistemological background in which we set the scene. For example, just now we saw five each on both sides. All such enumerations of constituent factors are relevant only when we become interested in analytically understanding the functional states of Consciousness. Otherwise, what exists is one Consciousness alone, always realizing Its own inner nature on Its own, and actualizing all Its inherent potentials. In such a tone the work ends.

Verse 14

aṛiyunnavan enn aṛiyām
aṛivenn aṛiyunnavannum ennākil
aṛiv onn aṛiyunnavan onn-
aṛiyunnatil āṛit-eṭṭum āyīṭum ।

Everyone always knows, "I am the one who knows."
This happens even in the case of
One who knows, "Everything is one Consciousness alone."
Thus, this knowledge one,
The knower another,
And the six "knowns" (the five knowable sense-objects and the one unknowable)
Together make it thus eightfold
(Seen thus from the side of "the knower").

Expansion:

The notion "I am the one who knows" is always there as we happen to know each object. This knowledge is there even in the one who is well aware that everything is but one Consciousness alone. Eight distinct factors thus become discernible in the Consciousness as It becomes manifest as the subject or *ahanta*. These eight are: the knower, the knower's knowledge of being the knower, and the knowledge of the six "knowns" (the five knowable objects and the one unknowable).

Everyone Knows, "I am the One who Knows"

As we know each object, we have also the awareness "I understand it," "It is clear to me now," or "It is not yet clear to me." Without knowing oneself as the knower, no such statements would be possible. This knowledge of being the knower need not necessarily always be explicit. It does not usually come to the fore when one's interest is mainly in the object known and its utility. But the same knowledge becomes pronounced when one's interest turns subjectively toward oneself; for example, when one asks oneself,

"Is it clear to me?" In short, knowledge and the knower remain as if the two are separate in each and every context of knowing an object.

Even in the Case of One Who Knows, "Everything is One Consciousness Alone"

This knowledge of oneself being the knower prevails, not only in the case of knowing worldly affairs and objects. The basic truth we have realized by now is that ultimately one Consciousness alone exists. Even in the case of this knowledge, the sense of oneself being its knower may loom large in us. But the truth is that, when one Consciousness alone has existence, the existence of "I" as the knower can never be a separate one. It must be inseparably one with the Consciousness which alone really exists. Still, until the real non-duality becomes experientially real, the sense "I am the knower" is felt even in the case of this ultimate knowledge. Until then, the differentiation between Consciousness and I who knows the Consciousness, or between knowledge and its knower, is felt by the knower. Without such a differentiation, admitedly, no analytical knowledge of the situation would be possible either.

These Together Make it Thus Eightfold

Now let us pass on to the case of knowledge concerning objects. That objects of knowledge are of two kinds was seen earlier in verse 12. One kind is the actually knowable objects, and the other is the object that is not knowable or known. Of these two types, the former becomes diversified as five separate sense objects. The knowledge about these is what we call sense perception, as was stated in verse 13.

"Knowing" may be of various kinds, but "not knowing" cannot be so; it is just "not knowing" and is not further categorizable. Only among the known objects is felt the need of differentiating one from another. In the case of the object not known, no such differentiation is necessary nor is it possible. Therefore the sense of not knowing is always one.

Numerous are the objects that we do not know. How is it that all such are to be categorizable as one? This doubt is but natural. But all that is beyond the bounds of knowledge become categorizably differentiated only when they become known. As long as such remain beyond our ken, they belong to the single category of the unknowable or the unknown. Really, it is to be remembered, what we are concerned with here is not the objects by themselves, but with the knowledge of such objects.

That which is beyond the bounds of knowledge could also be understood as that Reality which never becomes an object of knowledge. It is the one unthinkable and ineffable Reality, and was referred to as "That Consciousness which makes us know all specific knowledge" (v. 11). In traditional Vedānta it is known as *Brahman* or *Ātman*. That Reality is one alone.

Thus our knowledge about the objects in total consists of five sense perceptions of worldly objects and the one about the "not known," or that which transcends all knowledge. Thus our objective knowledge has six apparent facets.

To these six objective knowledges are to be added the two subjective knowledges, i.e., knowledge and the knowledge of being the knower. These together constitute the one Consciousness having become subjectively manifest with eight functional facets.

Verse 15

aṛiyappeṭum itin-ottīy-
aṛiv-eẓonn iṅṅu tānum eṭṭāyī
aṛiv-iṅṅane vevveṛāy-
aṛiyappeṭum ennatum viṭurttīṭil ।

As related to objects also,
Consciousness appears eightfold —
The seven along with oneself as the eighth.
(Five sense objects, the one unknown and knowledge itself
as an object form the seven.)

Pure Consciousness thus appears
As variously understandable
Only when subjected to analysis.
(Otherwise It remains pure and unconditioned.)

Expansion:

Now let us see how the one Consciousness unfolds itself as the objective side. Five sense objects and the one unknowable together constitute six objects of knowledge. In the statement "This is knowledge," knowledge itself becomes the object. Thus the number of objects of knowledge rises to seven. When "I" is also added, the number becomes eight.

Consciousness thus creatively unfolds Itself as having a parity between the subjective and objective sides. But all such classifications and systematizations become meaningful only when you subject the functional states of the one Consciousness (the ultimate Reality or *Ātmā*) to an analytical study. Otherwise, as pure experience, It remains always non-dual.

In the last verse, we saw what were the forms in which the one Consciousness manifested Itself on the subjective side. That side could be called that of *ahanta*. Now we come to the other side *idanta* or the objective side of a knowledge situation. In other words, we now examine what are the forms in which the same Reality finds creative self-expression as the objects of knowledge in the broadest sense.

The Seven Objects

The objects of knowledge, basically and comprehensively seen, are seven in number, all being forms assumed by the one Consciousness. Sound, touch, form, taste, and smell, are the objects perceived by our sense organs, and the entire objective world is an aggregate of such objects. That which is beyond the bounds of knowledge was also seen earlier as an unclassifiable object. As we experience every such perception, we feel, "This is a knowledge." In this experience there is also an object, which is none other than "knowledge." Adding this "knowledge," the number of objects increases to seven.

Oneself as the Eighth

When I feel, "I am knowing this now," I am, consciously or unconsciously, aware, "I am the knower." Thus the knowing "I" also becomes an object, though at a subtle level. The objects of thought altogether now, thus come to eight.

There is always thus a parity between the subjective and objective sides of every context of knowing. If an object is out there, a corresponding idea is formed in the mind subjectively. It is meaningless, therefore, to argue for the prominence of the subjective side (idealism) or of the objective side (materialism). Both the idealistic and materialistic or rather realistic aspects are merely two mutually matching self-manifestations of one non-dual Consciousness, which alone is ultimately Real. Though called Consciousness in the epistemological frame of reference, the same is called *Ātmā* or *Brahman* in the metaphysical context.

Only When Subjected to Analysis

The ideas we gather as we hear the words "gold" and "ornaments" are different. It is one entity existing alone that we call "gold" by looking at it from one point of view, and "ornaments" from another. Though thus *understood* as two, the reality understood always *remains* one, inseparable as gold and ornaments. The differentiation is only in the ideas we create in our mind about it. The same is true with the Consciousness-Reality. It is when we look for the factors involved in some act of knowing, by making use of our own intellect as a tool, that we differentiate the subject and the object and the constituent elements of each. Only in the realm of our intellectual understanding do all such make any sense. Though *understood* thus differently, what really *exists* is one Consciousness or *Ātmā* alone. Our intellect really is a momentary spark that emerges from the very Consciousness that is attempted to be measured. Such an intellect is the measuring rod we make use of to evaluate that one Consciousness. No wonder that this attempt fails. On the other hand, when the intellect makes the attempt with a clear awareness of its own nature, content and status, of being a spark of the one Consciousness, then the result will be comparable to the experience of the salt-doll that goes deep into the ocean in order to measure its depth; to use an analogy very dear to Sri Ramakrishna. Ultimately there is no differentiation between the measurer and the measured. The end result of this process is the non-dual experience of oneself becoming merged and lost in the one Consciousness or *Ātmā*, and That alone remaining.

Auṁ

Part IV

Homa-mantram

(Chants for Oblation in Fire)

Introduction

NARAYANA Guru has composed many works in the Sanskrit, Malayalam and Tamil languages, in both poetry and prose. Differing from his other works, Guru wrote the *Homa-mantram*, as a *mantra* (a chant aimed at salvation) to be recited at a fire-sacrifice. Composing this one *mantra* gave him the status of being a *ṛṣi* in the traditional view, that a *ṛṣi* is one who composes *mantras*; though even otherwise he is a *ṛṣi* as revealed in all his other works. This *mantra* could at first sight be mistaken for a part of some ancient Vedic text because of the idiom it uses.

The fire-sacrifice really forms part of the *karma-kāṇḍa*, the section of the Vedas dealing with rituals. The *jñāna-kāṇḍa* or the section that expounds wisdom, known as the Upaniṣads, ignores the value of rituals because of their lower and relativistic nature, and in its stead, teaches the absolutist higher wisdom, known as Vedānta.

A few of the Upaniṣads, instead of just invalidating ritualism, show how the very same ritualistic concepts could well be sublimated and elevated to a higher level of wisdom-significance. In the context of the history of cultures, this way of correcting a prevailing cultural trend of narrow vision and lesser value, by letting it be eclipsed by the brilliance of a higher understanding, higher value and broader vision of life, is sometimes called a "dialectical revaluation." The *Bhagavad-Gītā* compares this revaluation, which contrasts Vedism with Vedānta, to small pools being submerged by flood waters inundating everything. Vedism, thus, loses its meaning and value as Vedāntic wisdom outshines it. The *Chāndogya Upaniṣad* is one glaring example of this kind of cultural revaluation.

Instead of ruling out ritualism altogether in the present *mantra*, which is to be chanted while performing the fire-sacrifice, Narayana Guru admits it and shows us how each element of the ritual helps lead us to the highest realm of non-dual wisdom. This perception is not merely a philosophical or theoretical one, but it also reveals how a philosophical understanding of life and day-to-day life-values become inseparably one. A close examination of this *mantra* followed by proper cogitation (*manana*), along with a detailed study of the *Chāndogya Upaniṣad*, reveals how this *mantra* condenses the entire wisdom message spread over the eight lengthy chapters of the Upaniṣad.

The ritualistic tradition of Vedism holds that each Vedic *mantra* has its own *ṛṣi* (the seer who conceived and composed it), *devatā* (the deity praised) and *chandas* (the prosodic metre in which it is composed). In the case of the present *homa-mantra*, the *ṛṣi* is Narayana Guru himself and the *devatā* is Fire or *Agni*, because apparently the *mantra* is addressed to Fire. All the Vedic *mantra*s are not necessarily composed in the format of metres, particularly the *mantra*s of the *Yajurveda*, the most ritualistic of all the Vedas. Narayana Guru also, following this Yajurvedic tradition, composed this *mantra* adhering to no prosodic rules. Still it lends itself to being beautifully chanted.

If we closely examine its content, we will see that Narayana Guru, the *ṛṣi* of this *mantra*, is not acting as a proponent of a particular school of thought. On the other hand, he reveals himself as a real visualizer (*ṛṣi*) of what ultimately exists and the meaning of life. This short *mantra* contains the essentials of the entire gamut of the Upaniṣadic wisdom. For this reason, it is an invaluable gem in the treasure-chest of India's wisdom heritage and is to be kept well preserved while being made available to all.

The present commentary attempted serves merely to reveal in a summary fashion the denotations and connotations hidden in the words of this *mantra*. Going into all the details with sidelights into the ideas and suggestions each word of this *mantra* contains, would assume the size of a large volume that encompasses all the aspects of the spiritual tradition of India. Without entering into such a task, we here attempt to simply clarify the direct meanings of the words and their first-hand suggestions, in view of the overall message the *mantra* gives.

Fire Sacrifice as a Symbol

The Indian culture has its roots in the Vedas. One of the most important symbols very dear to Vedism is the fire sacrifice and is known as *yajña* or *homa*. Almost all the world religions, in one form or another, can be seen to incorporate this symbol. Abraham and Moses, for example, of the Jewish and Christian culture, can be seen in the Old Testament of the Bible, performing fire sacrifices.

The most apparent characteristics of fire is brightness, while its flames move upward. These peculiarities might have made humans take fire to represent their aspiration for attaining the brighter world of higher wisdom and realizing higher values in life. The fire sacrifice can thus be seen as a symbol representing the human willingness to sacrifice all that is of lower value for the sake of attaining higher value and wisdom.

Performing rituals is a sort of action, and therefore rituals, in general, are known as *karma*s (actions). Human actions can be categorized into two: actions performed for direct worldly benefits, called *laukika karma*s, and symbolic actions that represent certain ideas or ideals, called *vaidika karma*s. The word *laukika* means "related to the world" and *vaidika* "related to knowledge." Though breathing, blood circulation, and digestion of food are all actions that take place within one's being, in the usual course these are not treated as *karma*s, as they take place involuntarily as biological functions. But philosophically looked at, all these are also *karma*s, only that these are a part of nature appearing in individual beings. Deliberately performed actions alone are usually treated as *karma*s, and all such are aimed at attaining certain goals. Such *karma*s have behind them what is known as *kartr̥tva-bodha*, one's sense of being the doer of actions. Those who perform such *karmas* would also be mentally attached to what they do and to the end-results of each action. This attachment is known as *karma-bandha.*

Ritualistic actions or *vaidika karmas* are very different from such worldly actions. (The word *vaidika* means both "related to knowledge," and "related to the Vedas," for the word *veda,* though it refers to the most ancient scriptures of India, literally means "knowledge".) Though rituals are also performed deliberately with specific ends in view, the actual ritual part has only a symbolic significance, because the goal aimed at is not a natural outcome of those actions. As symbols, these rituals signify something, and it is this significance that makes one expect the future attainment of certain results. That means, the attainment of a ritual's goal depends on the completeness of the knowledge the performer has of the symbolic meaning and their probable benefits. The fire sacrifice (*agni-hotra*) is such a symbol, and now we have to consider what it signifies.

Humans perform both worldly and symbolic actions planned with specific ends in view. While performing such deeds they maintain the sense of being the doers of those actions. Upon performing each action they often become anxious about its outcome. As though to overcome this anxiety and in order to make the results of *karmas* favourable, people become tempted to pray to God or the unseen element (*adṛṣṭa*) that makes actions fruitful. Even this does not completely relieve the anxiety. Its full relief happens only when one's sense of being the doer of actions is relinquished. In truth, one's ability to do something is merely a part of the creative urge of the total nature of which we are all integral parts. In fact, no one has any creative ability of one's own making. When we do something with the sense, "I am doing this," we are actually attributing to ourselves the doerhood that really belongs to the total nature. This creative urge in individuals assumes the form of imagining and willing (*icchā-śakti*), the ability to do something physically (*kriyā-śakti*), or the ability to know (*jñāna-śakti*). Offering back to nature what was wrongly appropriated as ours, is what the fire sacrifice signifies. In this case, fire stands for the total creative urge of nature.

Veda and Vedānta

Yajña, though conceived by the *ṛṣi*s to be understood symbolically, began to be considered a religious ritual to be actually performed, from the period even before the Vedas were codified into four by Vyāsa. This is evident from the Vedic hymns themselves. *Svarga* (heaven) might have been originally conceived as the Supreme Happiness we can attain through wisdom that allows us to offer ourselves and our being the doers of actions, into the blazing fire of the total nature or the Absolute (*Brahman*). Many Upaniṣadic citations indicate this. One example is *mantra* 34 of the *Kena Upaniṣad*. But in the course of time, *svarga* began to be taken as a high world filled with maximum pleasures. This idea leads to the notion that humans have to make constant efforts in this world to reach heaven after death. Heaven is supposedly inhabited by gods (*devas*), and pleasing them with the offering of oblations in the sacrificial fires began to be thought of as the way to ensure happiness both here and hereafter. The oblations offered are believed to be carried by fire to heaven which becomes the food of the gods, and for this reason fire is also called *huta-vaha*, the carrier of oblations. Because of the development of these religious concepts, Jaimini, the author of the *Pūrva-Mīmāṁsā-Sūtras*, happened to say, *svarga-kāmī brāhmaṇo yajeta* (Let a brāhmaṇa desirous of reaching heaven perform fire-sacrifices). Furthermore, the gods such as Indra, Varuṇa and Mitra, are implored in different contexts of the Vedas to grant the favour of having many children along with possessing much wealth. All this indicates how Vedism, originally symbolic in significance, degenerated into a pleasure-seeking religious trend. Indicating all this, the *Bhagavad-Gītā* says:

> *yām imāṁ puṣpitāṁ vācaṁ pravadanty avipaścitaḥ* ।
> *veda-vāda-ratāḥ pārtha nānyad astīti vādinaḥ* ॥

kāmātmānaḥ svarga-parā janma-karma-phala-pradām |
krīyāviśeṣa-bahulāṁ bhogaiśvarya-gatiṁ prati || — II.42, 43

The undiscerning, delighting in the letter of the Vedas, and professing, O Pārtha, that nothing else aspirable exists, discourse about it in such flowery words;

Saturated with desires, with heaven for their goal; those words of theirs proclaim repeating births and *karma* as final rewards, and prescribe various specific rites with a view to ensuring worldly enjoyments.

Elsewhere the *Gītā* says:

traiguṇya-viṣayā vedā, nistraiguṇyo bhavārjuna || — II.45

The realm of the three *guṇa*s is the Vedas' concern. Go beyond these three *guṇa*s, O Arjuna.

These words also underscore the narrow-minded and relativistic value concepts of Vedic ritualism, and also of the necessity of freeing ourselves from them. Mending the shortcomings of one's narrow-minded and relativistic value notions can never be accomplished by resorting to means of the same nature. Only the fully open, broad-minded, all-encompassing and absolutist wisdom (*jñāna*) can liberate man thus. What is wrong with Vedism can be overcome only when it becomes outshone by the full brightness of wisdom. The nature of this wisdom is what Vedānta proclaims.

Indian spirituality has been growing in two directions known as *karma-mārga* (the path of actions) and *jñāna-mārga* (the path of wisdom). The path of actions means the way of following ritualistic actions. Meritorious actions of public benefit, known as *pūrta-karma*s, are connected to such rituals, for example, digging public wells and tanks, planting shade trees, and building camp sheds for travellers. Pure Vedic rituals are known as *iṣṭa-karma*s and these two together *iṣṭā-pūrta-karma*s. As for a *jñānin*, whether he performs *karma*s or not, he always remains liberated of all bondage caused by *karma*s. The *Gītā* again says,

brahmaṇy ādhāya karmāṇi saṅgaṁ tyaktvā karoti yaḥ ।
lipyate na sa pāpena padmapatram ivāmbhasā ॥
— V.10

Placing all *karmas* in *Brahman*, with attachments given up, he who acts is untouched by sin, as is a lotus leaf by water.

How the all inclusiveness of the path of wisdom indicated by Vedānta engulfs and makes insignificant the path of rituals in the Vedas, is poignantly portrayed in the *Gīta* as follows:

yāvān artha udapāne sarvataḥ samplutodake ।
tāvān sarveṣu vedeṣu brāhmaṇasya vijānataḥ ॥
— II.46

All the Vedas are of no more use to an enlightened brāhmaṇa than is a small pool in a place flooded everywhere.

The analogy of the pool and flooding water makes clear how the scope and value of Vedism is very limited, and how that of the wisdom of Vedānta is all-inclusive and of the highest value in life. The analogy also shows how without rejecting Vedism, it is admitted into the fold of Vedānta but made insignificant in the latter's all-shining broad daylight.

This is a method all the seers have been making use of from time immenorial. The *Chāndogya Upaniṣad*, for example, re-visualizes and re-values the rite called *Udgītha-upāsanā* of the grand ritual *Somayāga*, by attributing to it the meaning signified by the sacred syllable *AUṀ*. Then the *Somayāga* itself and finally all *yajñas* in general are re-visualized likewise as given a new wisdom-significance. This series of revaluations finally reaches the stage of perceiving the entire world and the phenomenon of life as a sort of *yajña* or fire-sacrifice.

Uprooting some cultural strand that has become an inseparable part of people's view of life is impossible. The best way to correct anomalies in such outlooks would be to absorb them into the fold of a more correct perspective and thus to submerge their value into the flooding values of the later development. This method enables people to uplift themselves to the higher levels of wisdom without cutting off their cultural leanings and the values of the ideas and ideals they already uphold. The words of Jesus, "I did not come to destroy but to fulfil" (Matthew, 5.17) are to be understood as related to such a cultural exigency.

People around Narayana Guru were of the culture of temple worship. Guru showed how this culture could be instrumental in leading them to higher wisdom through his installation of new temples along with the writing of new hymns to praise the newly installed deities. These hymns show how the new deity is to be seen as signifying higher wisdom. How to effect a similar kind of re-visualization and revaluation of the very ancient ritual of fire sacrifice, which forms part of the Vedic culture, is exemplified by Narayana Guru in the present *Homa-mantram* that reads as follows:

Text, Translation and Commentary

ॐ अग्ने तव यत्तेजस्तद् ब्राह्मं
अतस्त्वं प्रत्यक्षं ब्रह्मासि ।
त्वदीया इन्द्रियाणि मनोबुद्धिरिति सप्तजिह्वाः
त्वयि विषया इति समिधो जुहोमि ।
अहमित्याज्यं जुहोमि ।
त्वं नः प्रसीद प्रसीद
श्रेयश्च प्रेयश्च प्रयच्छ स्वाहा ॥
ॐ शान्तिः शान्तिः शान्तिः ॥

aum̐ agne tava yat tejas tad brāhmam̐
atas tvam̐ pratyakṣam̐ brahmāsi ।
tvadīyā indriyāni mano-buddhir iti sapta-jihvāḥ
tvayi viṣayā iti samidho juhomi ।
aham ity ājyam juhomi ।
tvam̐ naḥ prasīda prasīda
śreyaś ca preyaś ca prayaccha svāhā ॥
aum̐ śāntiḥ śāntiḥ śāntiḥ ॥

AUM̐ O Fire, this brightness of yours pertains to
Brahman.
Therefore you are the perceptible *Brahman*.
You have the (five) sense organs, mind
And intellect for your seven tongues (*sapta-jīhvāḥ*).
Into you (being such) I offer the objects
(Of sense organs, mind and intellect)
As sacrificial fire-wood.
And into you I offer myself
In the form of clarified butter.

You be pleased with us, be pleased with us !
Please confer on us the higher values
As well as the worldly values. *Svāhā*.
AUṀ Peace ! Peace ! Peace !

O Fire, This Brightness of Yours Pertains to Brahman

This *mantra* is meant to be recited on kindling the sacrificial fire, and is addressed to the fire thus kindled. Fire, as was stated earlier, is the deity (*devatā*) of the present *mantra*. This deity is praised, not as the carrier of oblations as is held by the Vedic custom, but as the one having brightness, symbolizing *Brahman*, as its defining characteristic. The suggestion is that the fire and its brightness together could be made use of as a means to attain *Brahman*-wisdom.

In essential content, *Brahman* is unconditioned Consciousness (*cit*), an experience of pure brightness. The main defining characteristic of fire is also brightness. Consciousness, being brightness in essence, illumines itself as well as everything else. So does fire also. Fire and *Brahman* thus have common features in these respects.

Fire always flames upwards. Knowledge also leads man upwards in life. Another characteristic of fire is that it is all-pervasive. For example, a piece of firewood, when ignited, blazes. The initial ignition simply makes the fire that was already hiding in the fire-wood become visibly apparent. Likewise, fire remains invisibly inherent in everything physical. Water is not an exception in this respect. All the rains that pour over the earth's surface flow towards the oceans, and this goes on unceasingly. Still the ocean does not overflow. An Indian poetic concept is that this is so because a great fire called *baḍavāgni* hides within the ocean and constantly consumes all of the extra water that reaches the ocean.

Brahman also is all-pervasive in nature. With regard to all-pervasiveness also, thus, fire and *Brahman* are similar. What is dissimilar in them is that fire is visible to the eyes, whereas *Brahman* is visible only to the intuitive eye of a contemplative. The visible fire, therefore, is made use of as a tool to help one to know or rather to realize the invisible *Brahman*.

Therefore You are the Perceptible Brahman

We have already seen the similarity as well as the dissimilarity of fire and *Brahman* or Consciousness, particularly that fire is visible and *Brahman* is invisible. A seeker in search of *Brahman*-wisdom called *jijñāsu,* is the one who is to make use of this similarity and dissimilarity to attain wisdom. In order to attain this goal, the flaming fire is here considered the visible *Brahman.* This imagining is just like when a teacher in an algebra class asks the students to suppose a certain unknown value as "x." That supposition is to be given up on finding the real value of "x." Likewise, upon realizing *Brahman,* having used the supposition (that fire is visible *Brahman*) as an aid, the supposition is to be discarded.

You have Sense Organs . . . for Your Seven Tongues

In the Vedic context, fire is known also as *sapta-jihvā* (the one having seven tongues). This concept is conveniently made use of here to help the seeker experience his or her own mergence in the being of Consciousness, the essential content of *Brahman.* The seven tongues of fire, as named in the *Muṇḍaka Upaniṣad* (1.2.4) are *Kāli, Karāli, Manojavā, Sulohitā, Sudhūmravarṇā, Sphuliṅginī* and *Viśvarucī.*

Sapta means "seven," and *jihvā,* "tongue or flame." The seven tongues do not necessarily denote the number of flames in a burning fire, but are the names of seven primary ways in which fire flames, symbolizing the ways in which the Absolute manifests. The word *Kāli* means "the black one," and as the name of a flame it indicates that the fire burns with a blackish smoke. *Karāli* means "the dreadful one" and the fire that flames in such a manner could be designated *Karāli. Manojavā* means "quicker than thought." A fire that spreads unbelievably fast could be called by this name. *Sulohitā* means "that which is beautifully red in colour." The copper-coloured flame of fire is designated as *Sudhūmrạvarṇā*. *Sphuliṅginī* is the sparking fire. *Viśvarucī* means "that which tastes everything." A fire that guts everything could thus be called *Viśvarucī*. Whichever be the form in which it flames, the fire in all such is one alone. The difference in appearence depends mainly on the nature of the fuel consumed and the circumstances involved. Similarly, though we gain various kinds of knowledge through the functions of the five sense organs, mind and intellect, the consciousness that unfolds itself as all these knowledges is one and the same. Though *manas* (mind), *buddhi* (intellect), *citta* (store-house of memory), and *ahaṁkāra* (I-sense of the knower) are considered the basic mental faculties by Vedāntic psychologists, these four in the present *mantra* are represented by *manas* and *buddhi* alone.

Here also we see a similarity in fire and consciousness — both have seven tongues. The functions of consciousness through the sense organs and mental faculties are imagined here as the seven tongues of consciousness that is represented visibly by fire. Hence the fire is addressed, "You have the five sense organs, mind and intellect for your seven tongues."

Into You I Offer the Objects

Though the presence of fire, as held by the philosophical tradition of India, is everywhere, it is felt directly only when it burns. The unmanifest fire that becomes manifest requires the coming together of fuel and fire. Put otherwise, fire becomes visible when fuel is sacrificed in the fire. Making use of this as a convenient analogy whereby the *mantra* can reveal the secret of the nature of Consciousness or *Ātmā*.

It is the one unmanifest Consciousness that becomes manifest as our experiences of hearing, touching, seeing, tasting, smelling, imagining and thinking. But that causal Consciousness as such has no mode of appearance of Its own. At the same time, It becomes manifest as the experience of seeing when a visible form as an object is sacrificed in the fire of the sense organ eye. Similarly, when the object sound is offered into the fire of the sense organ ear, the same Consciousness becomes apparent as the experience of hearing. Such is the case with each of the sense experiences. The causal Consciousness could thus be intuitively visualized as underlying all the specific experiences we have in life. Conceived thus, it could well be said, visualizing the one all-underlying Reality or Consciousness in all the specific life experiences, is like one fire manifesting in its seven various ways. Rather than as an event of pleasure-giving sense perception, the contact between the senses and their respective objects could thus be seen as an occasion for Consciousness to become manifest in a specific way, and thus to realize the grandeur of *Ātmā*, the ultimate Reality.

The natural outcome of the contact of a sense organ with its object, when taken as resulting in sense perception, is to like it (*iṣṭa*), dislike it (*aniṣṭa*) or to feel indifference (*udāsīna*). Such feelings create a sort of ongoing turbulence within. How such feelings of likes and dislikes eventually result in our own perishing is graphically portrayed in the *Bhagavad-Gītā* as follows:

> Man, brooding on objects of pleasure, develops attachment towards them; from attachment arises desire; from desire springs anger.
>
> Anger makes him deluded; from delusion arises lapse of memory; because of memory-lapse is lost proper understanding; lack of understanding results in perishing. — II. 62, 63

It is for this reason that our ancient Masters have forewarned us of the necessity of having a sense of detachment towards pleasurable objects, in order to ensure real and lasting happiness in life through Self-knowledge. On the other hand, perceiving each sense-experience as a new facet of the manifestation of Consciousness or *Ātmā*, makes the very same sense perception a helpful means for realizing *Ātmā*. This perception, instead of creating attachment towards sense-objects, enables us to make our entire life an unceasing experience of directly visualizing *Ātmā* in everything. Then the contact of the senses with their objects causes no attachment, with the understanding that *guṇa*s are just acting upon *guṇa*s (*guṇā guṇeṣa vartanta*) as the *Bhagavad-Gītā* puts it again.

> But he who knows the basic truth about the distinction between *guṇa*s and *karma*s, O Mighty Armed, remains unattached, knowing that (*karma*s are) just *guṇa*s acting upon *guṇa*s.
>
> — III.28

This perception is a sort of sacrificing of all the pleasurable objects that create attachments into the fire of *Ātmā* or Consciousness to make It shine bright.

Into You I Offer Myself

Everything in all the worlds is an object of perception. On having sacrificed all such objects into the fire of *Brahman,* the only thing that remains unoffered is the offerer or the subject himself or herself. The subject or I-sense, represented by clarified butter, is also now offered into the fire of *Brahman*.

Be Pleased with Us ! Be Pleased with Us!

Sacrificial fire-wood and clarified butter (*ghee*), signifying all the perceptible objects in all the worlds and the perceiving subject, have now been offered as an oblation into the fire of *Brahman* or *Ātmā*. This offering symbolizes a special kind of perception. It is the perception in which all the worlds and their perceivers are seen to be inseparably one with *Brahman,* or as *Brahman* Itself become manifest. Now what remains is the fire alone, *Brahman* alone. The Guru himself in another context says, "All the worlds become sublimated and attain the status of being pure Consciousness." (*Ātmopadeśa Śatakam*, v. 50)

Do we and the world we perceive really become non-existent upon realizing this oneness? Do all the pains and pleasure just vanish on attaining this realization? No. The Guru answers the question thus:

> Everything is existent indeed.
> Only those of philosophical vision perceive all these as one.
> — *Ātmopadeśa Śatakam*, v. 88

The world does not really cease to exist on realizing that *Brahman* alone has existence. On the other hand, both the objects and the subject, the worlds and we who perceive them, are all thereafter seen as having being as various manifest forms of the one Consciousness. We do continue to have pleasurable and painful experiences in life. Such experiences are then seen as the Reality's graceful offering back (*prasāda*). It is in this sense that it is prayed, "Be pleased with us ! Be pleased with us !" (*tvam naḥ prasīda prasīda*). Though in the form of a prayer, these words really indicate our understanding that all the joys and pains in actual life are the graceful offerings (*prasāda*) we get back from *Brahman* upon offering ourselves and the world into It. This offering back, in the context of fire-sacrifice, is known as *yajña-śiṣṭa* (remnants of offerings).

Please Confer on Us Higher Values as well as Worldly Values

The values aspired to by humans in life are classified as *śreyas* (higher values) and *preyas* (worldly values) by the *Kaṭha Upaniṣad* in its *mantra* II.1. The latter makes life in this world physically comfortable. The former, on the other hand, are values aspired to, for their own sake, by humans everywhere and the highest of them is marked by attaining immortality, or realizing Supreme Happiness. The Nyāya system of Indian Philosophy calls the former *niḥśreyas* and the latter *abhyudaya*. Though thus classified, experiencing each happens only within Consciousness. Put otherwise, it is Consciousness that actualizes both the realms of values in actual life. Hence the same Consciousness is prayed to for the actualization of both in life. Aspiring to the one at the cost of the other is not the way recommended here, and to do so is not possible in actual life, as is admitted by many of the Upaniṣads. The *Taittirīya Upaniṣad*, for example, says,

> He who knows this becomes well-founded. He becomes the possessor of food and the eater of food. He becomes great with progeny, with cattle (wealth) and with the splendour of sacred wisdom; great in fame. —III.6.1

This Upaniṣadic passage says that both kinds of values become well-founded in the one who knows the Reality expounded therein. Along these lines, the Guru also prays for the possession of both kinds of values.

Svāhā

According to the Vedic tradition the recital of all the *mantra*s addressed to gods (*deva*s) as part of a fire-sacrifice, should end with the sound *svāhā,* and those addressed to manes (*pitṛ*s) with the sound *svadhā*. The present *mantra,* though of wisdom-significance, acknowledges this tradition because it is conceived as pertaining to a ritualistic context. No special meaning, it seems, is attributed to this sound. If we ignore the strict grammatical rules of the Sanskrit language, as is often done by admitting poetic freedom or the freedom of the Vedic usage, the word *svāhā,* could be taken to mean, "Thus it has been said well." Indian mythology holds that *svāhā* is the name of the wife of the Fire god (*Agni*).

Integration of *Jñāna* and *Karma*

It is to be noticed here that this fire-sacrifice, though in external appearance acknowledges all the ritualistic custom, is much different in nature from the fire-sacrifices the Vedas ordain. Though this is a ritual in external appearance, it is purely of wisdom-significance. Therefore, to say whether this pertains to the context of *karma* or *jñāna* would be somewhat difficult. *Karma* becoming transformed as a means of *jñāna,* or *jñāna* becoming actualized through *karma,* is witnessed here. It could therefore be rightly said that the integration (*samanvaya*) of *jñāna* and *karma* is effectively accomplished by this fire-sacrifice conceived by Narayana Guru.

Śaṅkara repeatedly warns seekers of the danger of mixing up *jñāna* and *karma* as spiritual disciplines. He considers doing so a fallacy called *jñāna-karma-samuccaya-doṣa* (the fallacy of mixing up *jñāna* and *karma*). The reason for Śaṅkara thinking so is that the result attained by means of *karma* is transient, whereas that of *jñāna* is eternal. A seeker in search of eternal Happiness, therefore, has to ignore the path of *karma* or rituals and should resort to the path of wisdom.

Is it possible for us, having active physical bodies, to live without doing any *karma*? No. As long as confined to the body, one has to do *karma*s. The *Bhagavad-Gītā* categorically says, "Even bodily existence would be rendered impossible by your remaining actionless." (III.8). For this reason, the best way recommended by the *Gītā* is renouncing the fruits of action.

How and where are those fruits of action to be renounced? All the *karma*s, whether in the universe as a whole, or in an individual being, take place really as part of the creativity of total nature or *prakṛti*, as part of the ever-flowing cosmic system. Each individual has to know that his or her voluntary and involuntary actions are really part of the total system of life. The ability to do deeds in each individual is part of nature's creativity. That means, individuals do not have *karma*s of their own. Nature's *karma* is wrongly taken to be an individual's own. This enlightenment, in effect, is the renouncing of all actions and their fruits into the total Reality. *Karma,* thus, instead of being something opposed to *jñāna,* turns out to be a dependable means of attaining *jñāna.* Such an integration (*samanvaya*) of *karma* and *jñāna* is one of the basic teachings of the *Bhagavad-Gītā*. Resuscitating that wisdom teaching is what Narayana Guru does through composing this new sacred chant for a formal fire-sacrifice. As was stated earlier, this chant condenses into one short *mantra* the entire teaching of the *Chāndogya Upaniṣad*.

Part V

Daivadaśakam

(Ten Verses Addressed to God)

— Universal Prayer —

Introduction

MANY are the philosophically rich poems we are blessed with from the peerless pen of Narayana Guru. Of these, *Daivadaśakam* could be considered among the simplest. In those days, a few children lived at the *āśrama* founded by the Guru at Sivagiri. He felt the need of having a universal prayer meant to be recited by these children at their evening prayer sessions that formed part of the daily routine of the *āśrama*. The present prayer is the outcome of it.

Though written in the format of a prayer, the Guru could contain his entire philosophical vision within its ten verses. It may be that seers like him can write only in such a manner. Their creative minds always remain in the fullness of the intuitive vision of the ultimate Reality. Whatever pours out of them will be part of their replete inner content.

The present commentary attempts to delve into the depths of the philosophical vision that fills these seemingly simple verses.

A Religious Observance

Praying is a religious observance, and it has found its place in one way or another in all religions. It prevails even in religions that avowedly do not admit the existence of a God or souls. Even down-right nihilists and atheists seem to have some sort of prayer-like observance. Instead of being a prayer addressed to God, a prayer may don the garb of a hopeful wish. Even those who do not pray, at least greet each other wishing the best. Such best wishes also imply a sort of prayer. In short, prayer is a psychological phenomenon that manifests in all humans, the religious as well as the non-religious. Even people wishing "Good luck" to each other is a kind of prayer and is therefore a sort of religious ritual. All ceremonies, by nature, have religious elements in them and no human does away completely with ceremonies. In short, religion is a mood that creeps into the minds of all humans, even if they do not like to think of themselves as religious. The unbelievers consider the people who wish the best and observe other such ceremonies as good-natured ideal humans; the believers, on the other hand, consider such ceremonial words of masters as their blessings. Humans, by their very nature, consciously or unconsciously, accommodate religion within their minds. That means, religion has a place we are not usually aware of, in our life. What is the nature of the religion's place in us ?

Religion in Human Life

Why can't we live without religion? Religion, in modern times, has been thought of even as "the opium that blinds the minds of men." What really then is the role of religion in human life?

Of all living beings humans alone have some role for religion in their lives. That means, to have religion is one of the features that differentiate humans from other living beings. The main feature among such is the thinking habit of man. The popular scientific definition of the human is as a thinking animal. Other beings do not have schools, do not have books, do not have libraries, and do not have conferences. All these form part of human life as a sort of extension of the thinking habit in man. Having religion is yet another peculiarity of the same nature.

One feature, again originating from the thinking habit of man, differentiates human life from the life of other beings: all other beings simply live, whereas humans lead their lives.

Freedom

Two things have to be very clear in our minds in order to lead our lives forward: we should be well aware of the goal we should reach, and then we should know clearly how to achieve that goal. The former could be called ends-awareness, and the latter means-awareness.

When two friends meet each other, the first thing they ask will be, "How are you?" These words of greeting are aroused actually by the above-mentioned two awarenesses. If what happens in life becomes conducive to the attainment of one's already-determined-goal-of-life, and if the efforts made to achieve those goals really help achieve them, then we would say, "I am fine." Mostly it does not happen like this. There is a big question mark about it. That is the reason why greeting each other with such questions became part of the social life of men.

Each human being has, or should have, in his or her mind, consciously or unconsciously, a notion about his or her goal in life, as well as of the means of achieving it. Always accompanying this awareness is the freedom to choose one's goal as well as the means of attaining it. If this freedom is denied, life becomes meaningless. This sense of freedom in human life is fundamental. Many admittedly are not capable of taking a proper decision about such a goal and the means of attaining it. In such a case, many seek the advice of those who are thought of as more knowledgeable. Still no one gives up one's freedom to abide by such advices or not to. It is when this sense of freedom is always present in life that life is felt to be meaningful. Whether one misconceives of one's freedom in life and the meaning of life, is yet another matter. The spiritual dimension of freedom is also not reckoned here.

Total Dependence

To be fully free to choose what the good of life should be, and how to achieve it, is only one side of the picture of human life. Yet another side, that of complete dependence, also exists. Man is bound to live with a full sense of freedom in a world not at all in his control, but as part of a boundless universe which has an order of its own, complete in itself. Humankind has not been able to discover all the laws that govern this nature, nor we have any hope that one day we will get a complete picture of all nature's laws. This universe is so vast and complex. Humankind has, of course, found out certain laws of nature, but their meaningfulness is confined to an extremely limited sphere of the universe. Neither is it certain that these are the only laws that govern nature. The concern of most modern scientists and technologists is limited to making use of the laws of nature discovered so far to help render human life more effortless and pleasurable. Bringing those laws of nature into human control is never thought of, nor is it possible. Man is capable to live only by abiding by the exigencies of nature that takes into account no one's interest in particular. That means, to live as part of the whole, with no freedom to choose, but by complying with whatever nature demands, is human destiny. Human life, in this respect, is not at all free, but is fully dependent on the unpredictable vagaries of nature.

The Oscillation of Life

Life is a sort of progression from the past to the future. In this process, it becomes inevitable for human beings to reckon with the unbridled sense of freedom on the one side and total dependence on nature on the other, and to reconcile these two extreme poles. Put otherwise, the advancement of human life oscillates between these two opposite poles. Man here finds himself helpless, unable to bring together the course of personal life and its goals, with the course of the eternal flow of nature.

Religion Comes to the Rescue

In this context, religions promise that people can reconcile their personal freedom with the overall flow of nature which seems to care for nothing. Religion prepares us to perceive these two facets as pertaining to a neutral overall Reality and Its scheme of life. On its own, that Reality transcends the above-mentioned dual poles. Nothing outside this one Reality happens in either the "free" personal life or the total nature. Religion thus shows us how to unite ourselves with the total Reality rather than with either of the opposite poles, thereby enabling us to fill our lives with peace and sense of fulfilment.

This one ultimate Reality is conceived of differently by different religions. Indian Philosophy thinks of It as *Brahman*, the all-underlying Substance. The prophetic religions like Judaism, Christianity and Islam, on the other hand, think of that Reality as Jehovah, God, the Heavenly Father or Allah. Without His knowledge, outside His reign, nothing happens anywhere in the world, either in the personal life of humans or in the total flow of nature. Humanity's being free on the one hand and dependent on nature on the other, was also decreed by God. Therefore, to live in compliance with the commandments of God is the best way open for humans to be happy in life. Such commandments reach humans through the messengers of God, known as prophets. Obeying these commandments enables one to live a free life while being part of the total flow of nature.

Religions like Buddhism and Jainism do not believe in the existence of a God. Such religions do admit *dharma* as a fundamental factor that unifies the life of each individual with that of the total. The rolling on of the wheel of *dharma* (*dharma-cakra-pravartana*) here assumes the position of God's will in the prophetic religions. This basic factor concerning religion could be seen even in modern ideologies like Marxism that do not claim to be religions, or rather are anti-religious. The only difference with such ideologies is that "the total nature" is replaced by the "total human society." There the seat of God is occupied by the State that supposedly is bound to ensure the happiness of individuals as well as of the society. Instead of individuals subjugating themselves to the will of God, people are asked to obey the commandments of the State. In both cases, what psychologically takes place — bringing the individual's will and the will of nature under the control of a third factor — is one and the same. The State functioning as the third factor most likely would be beset with one danger: the State is run always by wilful politicians who are power-mongers. The goal achieved by their efforts is liklely to be vitiated by their depraved personal motives. Such a defect does not vitiate religion, although priestcraft has always been the bane of religions.

Vedānta, that admits *Brahman* or *Ātman* as the ultimate Reality, asks individuals to realize their identity with *Brahman*, as an ornament finds its identity with gold. The total nature, no doubt, is already in full identity with *Brahman*. Thus, the individual finding his identity with *Brahman* results in the vanishing of the problem of bringing together the individual's will and the will of nature. This realization of oneness ensures everlasting peace in life as well as immortality, for the ultimate Reality is immortal.

The Hope Given by Religions

Unifying the will of individuals and the will of the total nature could be thought of as possible in two ways. One, to bring down the will of nature in conformity with the individual's will. This evidently is not possible for the simple reason that the will of the total nature works in a way quite incomprehensible to human minds. What is then possible is the second alternative — that of raising the individual's will up to agree with the will of the total or the will of God. To comply with God's will means to leave the will of the individual so flexible as to be in tune with the unpredictable and unthinkable will of God. That means, to make God's unforeseeable will one's own, or to remain fully satisfied with what nature confers upon us. Dependence on nature then becomes transformed as being one with nature. This sense of oneness with the whole renders life filled with the feeling of blissfulness and fulfilment. Life then is felt as being lived meaningfully. Such is the hope all the religions promise to mankind.

Prayer (*prārthanā*)

Prayer in this sense is the incessant effort made by people to keep their will always attuned to the will of God. And for this reason, it has purely a personal significance, not a social one. This is quite evident in the words of Jesus, "When you pray, go into your room, and when you have shut your door, pray to your Father who is in the secret place; and your Father who sees in secret will reward you openly" (Matthew 6.6). Still, prayer, as a ritual in Christianity, has taken the shape of a sort of tool for maintaining the institutionalized integrity of that religion. Prayer, as conceived by all the prophets and *gurus*, is not an institutionalized ritual, but is an individual's attempt to relate his or her existence as one with the existence of the total or of God, and thus is purely a personal affair.

Hugo, in his classic novel *Les Miserables*, spends a whole chapter going into the depths of the psychological and philosophical implications of prayer. He thinks of the one who prays as a small "I" and God to whom prayers are addressed as a big "I." Prayer, then, is the intense and innate effort the small "I" makes to attain his or her full identity with the big "I." Thinking of God as the big "I" implies considering the whole world as a single unit, and God as the Consciousness that pervades all through its being, as the personal consciousness fills the whole being of an individual. The study made by Hugo accords fully with the spirit of all religions, and thus his theory of prayer cannot be repugnant to any of them.

The place prayer has in the philosophical vision of Narayana Guru also is of the same nature, as is made clear by him in the concluding verse of the *Daivadaśakam* as follows:

> In the deep ocean of your Glory
> Let us all become immersed
> There to dwell, dwell for ever
> In Felicity Supreme !

The Guru, addressing Śiva, sang in another context as follows:

> O God, please keep in mind
> That this humble one has no other desire
> Than attaining to the state of You
> And I being one, at this very moment.
>
> — *Sadāśiva-darśanam*, v. 5

The "us all" in the former citation is to be understood rather as referring to the collection of individuals than to society in general. Thus it is evident from all this, how personal is the value of prayer in human life.

What to Pray for?

The Sanskrit word for prayers of petition is *prārthanā* (*pra+arthanā*). *Arthanā* means, "to earnestly ask for something," and the prefix *pra* stands for *prakarṣeṇa*, "properly." All prayers of petition ask for some favour. What would make such a favour "proper?" Oblivious of the already-mentioned subtle principles implied in prayer, many blunder. Caught as they are in the mire of their personal, relativistic problems and worries, they often become tempted to ask for the favours of alleviating their personal worries such as their children getting cured of their illnesses or getting solutions to family financial problems. "May I have prosperity," "May I have good offspring," "Let my enemies perish," are some other favours asked for. Even as we pray for all such personal favours, unwittingly we make the big mistake of taking the decisions in life and entreating God to work them out. Many are even willing to make monetary offerings to God to get their personal prayers granted. A more philosophically correct attitude on our part, on the other hand, should naturally be, let God take decisions in life and that we may abide by such decisions.

A song or poem addressed to God or to some deity, that simply glorifies God or a deity with nothing prayed for, does not constitute a *prārthanā* (prayer of petition); such works are termed hymns or *stotra*s or *stuti*s.

We should remember that money is simply a man-made device, not God-made. Therefore, God, most probably, is not familiar with it. When asked for money, for this reason, God may simply say, "I don't know what it is. I know rice, wheat, fruits, vegetables and many natural products good for human consumption. Only if you ask for such, might I be glad to grant it."

This unprincipled trend in prayer is not a new phenomenon. It has always existed ever since the practice of praying came into vogue. A philosophically sound prayer need not be expected of those who are not familiar with the basic principles of life. Unprincipled prayer prevailed even in the very ancient Vedic literature of India. If such failings are to be expected of the Vedic *ṛṣis*, what would then be the case with ordinary supplicants? The 'Śrī Rudra' part of the *Yajurveda*, for example, says:

adhyavocad adhivaktā
prathamo divyo bhiṣak
ahīṃś ca sarvān jambhayan
sarvāṃś ca yātu dhānyaḥ — I.6

Let Rudra, the first amongst all, the one who is a physician even to gods, the one who argues for one's own dear supplicants, become one who argues for me. Let him exterminate all enemies like snakes. Let him exterminate all the invisible enemies.

The above-said prayer apparently emerged from the life-perception of an ordinary human being who treated snakes and like beings as enemies. Suppose snakes also make similar prayers to Rudra. It would naturally be in the form, "O Rudra, please exterminate these people who are after us with long sticks to beat us to death!" Though snakes, scorpions, and ferocious animals like leopards and tigers are all often inimical to humans, they too were created by God, and they never transgress what is naturally rightful to them. Humans alone, though endowed with the understanding of what is rightfully allotted to them and what is not, often tempted by greed, violate the laws of nature as well as the overall natural system of life, and do things detrimental to the interests of other beings and eventually to themselves. Given all this, it is to be doubted whether Rudra would really heed the above Yajurvedic prayer. The Vedic culture was basically one of performing fire-sacrifices to propitiate gods for personal benefits and for the conveniences of humans. Almost the same prayer-culture could be considered to have continued unchanged in India even until now. All the later transformations in the vision of life and in the profound philosophical speculations that emerged as part of the Upaniṣadic culture, apparently did not strike roots in the mindset of the general public.

Whose is the Prayer?

Admittedly, the relevance of prayer is in the heart of each individual. Still the prayer each one makes should not be for the fulfilment of personal interests. Rather it should be for the fulfilment of that which is aspired to by all humans in general. Then alone the interests of the individual and the interests of the total nature find a common ground. Then, "my prayer" gets transformed as "our prayer." With this in mind, let us examine whose prayer Narayana Guru conceived the *Daivadaśakam* to be.

The First verse says, "O God, keep watch on *us* here."

Verse 3 says,

> Food and clothes and such other daily needs,
> Providing *us* ever with no lapse,
> You make *our* lives generously blessed;
> You alone are *our* sole Master !

Again verse 4 says,

> Like ocean, waves, wind and depth,
> Are *ourselves*, *māyā*, your glory and you.

Verse 8 says,

> That state *we* hail.
> O God, success be yours !

And finally verse 10 says,

> In the deep ocean of your Glory
> Let *us all* become immersed;
> There to dwell, dwell for ever
> In Felicity Supreme !

The italicized words in these quotes clearly show that this prayer is not made by an individual in view of his or her personal motives, but is conceived as made by all humans together for the good of all in general. This, in other words, is a universal prayer. If other living beings practice praying, this could be found acceptable to them also.

What Should We Pray for?

Let us look at the text now with a view to see what favours are asked for in this universal prayer. It is but natural to expect that favours of universal value alone are asked for. The prayer in the first verse is, "O God, keep watch on us here." The favour asked for in verse 2 is, "Let this mind attain rest pulsationless in you." Though verse 3 sounds like asking for our daily needs, it really makes no request as such; instead it admits only that God already provides us with everything we need with no lapse. Verse 4 makes the request for granting a clear understanding of a philosophical truth. The prayer in the final verse, as we know, is to dwell for ever in the Glory of God in Felicity Supreme. All these evidently are prayers for something of higher, universal values. Each request, when closely examined, would be seen to lead in succession to the sublime heights of non-dualism, finally resulting in the supplicant becoming lost in the Glory of God.

A Philosophically Sound Prayer

This text was composed by an avowed *advaitin* (non-dualist). An *advaitin* really needs no prayer, for in his perception there is no duality between the supplicant and God. But a non-dualist may feel that those who follow him, aspiring for the perfection of wisdom, need a prayer. Such a prayer should be a means for them to attain the heights of non-dualistic perception. The present prayer is a perfect example of such, as will become evident as we go through its lines.

India, as is well known, is a land of spiritual wisdom. A major part of its spiritual literature is in the form of hymns and prayers, in which *bhakti* or devotion always plays an important role. All these undoubtedly centre around one God, variously named by many poetically-minded seers. *Ekam sad viprāḥ bahudhā vadanti* (The ultimate Reality is one alone, but scholars speak of it in various ways.) is one of the Vedic dicta. Conceived by many in various ways, the one and only Reality is variously named as well, each such conceived form being known as a deity (*devatā*). Praising these deities gained a religious momentum, and as a result almost all the prayers composed by the great Masters of India happened to be in the form of praising one or another of these deities. The necessity of praying to the one God, in the meanwhile, has almost gone into oblivion. Thus Indian spirituality began to be dubbed as polytheism or at least henotheism (the worship of a particular god without disbelieving in the existence of other gods).

Though almost all the available prayers and hymns composed by our Masters are philosophically profound, such an one addressed to the one God and not to any particular deity like Śiva, Viṣṇu, Brahmā, Subrahmaṇya, Gaṇapati or Devī, can hardly be found. This cuts a poor figure of Indian spirituality altogether. Even the well-known hymns composed by the great Śaṅkara are no exception. Of course, the *Īśa Upaniṣad* begins with the word *Īśa* meaning "the one God," but as it ends *Īśa* gives place to the deities like Pūṣā (Sun) and Agni (Fire). Looked from this perspective, we see in the vast panorama of the spiritual literature of India, from the most ancient times to the most modern age, it was the pen of Narayana Guru, though in the Malayalam language, that blessed us with a philosophically profound prayer addressed to the one God, acceptable not only to Indian spiritual tradition in general, but to all the religions of the world as well. How philosophically sound this prayer is, will become clear as we proceed.

God — Reality or Illusion?

The word *daivadaśakam* means, "ten verses on God." The name of this work takes for granted God as a reality. The beginning word of the prayer is itself *daivame,* meaning "O God!" This prayer was composed by the Guru with his close devotees and disciples kept in mind. The Guru, in the meanwhile, had also disciples who were atheists. That the existence of God was admitted by the Guru is evident also from his most famous dictum *oru jāti, oru matam, oru daivam, manuṣyanu* (of one kind or caste, of one faith or religion, of one God is man). The question of *jāti* (caste) is not of any relevance here. We have already discussed in detail the role of religion in human life. Now the question remains as to the existence of God.

All dictionaries of all languages have in them a word that signifies "God." Even the person who denies the existence of God, has to make use of the word "God" to do so. That means, as long as languages exist, the word "God" or its equivalent, and the concept it signifies, will persist.

Someone denying the existence of God implies, the concept of God is already in his mind. Denying something categorically requires a clear knowledge of what is being denied. That means, the concept of God is already in the mind of an atheist also. Believers too only assert the existence of a God according to their own understanding.

Both believers and non-believers use the word "God." But do both have the same idea in their minds when they use the word? Though there is no foolproof method to check this, one thing is definite: one's idea is of something existing, while the other thinks of something not existing. Clearly the two do not mean the same though both use the same word. It is to be conceded then that the two do not argue for or against one and the same thing, but they use one word to mean two ideas. The only available way to find out how the two differ is by both defining what they mean by God. It would then be found to our great surprise that the two give different definitions. That means, what one asserts is not what the other denies. This puts an end to their arguments also.

A definition of God exists in the minds of both believers and non-believers. That means, God does exist by definition. There is, thus, God-consciousness in both. Something that exists in consciousness has necessarily to be consciousness in essence. The God asserted by believers also is consciousness in essence. Both thus come to an agreement in this respect.

Suppose a non-believer denies God with no clear idea in his mind as to what he denies; this makes no sense because denying something with definiteness means, the person who denies knows what he denies. Similarly, asserting something also presupposes the knowledge of what is being asserted. An interesting fact in this respect about God is that both believers and non-believers have no clear idea as to what God is. The believers openly hold that God is an unknowable Reality, whereas non-believers acknowledge that they are not quite sure what they are denying. It thus becomes all the more clear that, more important than arguing for or against the existence of God, is knowing clearly what is meant by God. Once clearly known, the arguments, for as well as against, becomes irrelevant, for something clearly known needs no asserting and can never be denied.

Therefore let us also try to comprehend what is to be understood by God, using Narayana Guru's *Daivadaśakam* as a handy means.

Text, Translation and Commentary

Verse 1

daivame kāttukolkaṅṅu
kai viṭāt-iṅṅu ñaṅṅale ।
nāvikan nī bhavābhikk-
orāvi-van-toṇi nin padam ॥

O God, caringly protect us here
From over there, never
Letting loose your hold.
You are the navigator
In this ocean of becoming,
And the mighty steamer is
None other than your feet (word).

THE present poem is meant to be a universal prayer, that is to say, a prayer that leans towards no particular religion. Guru composed this prayer at a stage in his life in which he had become famous as the proponent of the well-known motto "Of one kind, of one faith, of one God is man." Only a universal prayer could be expected of his pen in such a mature stage. And this writing was occasioned by the feeling he had for the need of a new prayer text to be chanted by the children living with him in the *āśrama* at Śivagiri, during their daily evening prayer gathering. Although meant directly for those children, it is of great benefit for all who are child-like in respect of wisdom. Leading the child-like ignorant, who are immersed in the miseries of worldly life, to the enlightenment of wisdom and to the ultimate Happiness that wisdom results in, with the formal prayer as a means, is what the present work accomplishes.

There is no being in this world that does not seek happiness. The ultimate goal of a spiritual seeker is also none other than experiencing supreme Happiness in life. Happiness, thus, is the one goal for everyone, irrespective of being ignorant or enlightened. For this reason, Happiness — Felicity Supreme — (*sukham*) is the word with which this prayer ends.

Thus, attaining happiness in actual life is the one goal aimed at by all of us when we make any sort of effort. Still we are well aware that attaining happiness is not completely in our control. On becoming aware of this, we search for some other source of happiness, and finally we arrive at the idea that some unknown Reality controls everything.

Just as ordinary happiness is not in the control of worldly minded people, so is the case regarding the Supreme Happiness sought by spiritual seekers. In both cases, they perecive the intervention of a third, unknown factor, a chance element, which is called "God" (*daivam*) here. Therefore, this prayer begins with the word *daivame* (O God), and ends with *sukham* (Felicity Supreme). Both ends put together, it becomes "*daivame sukham*" (O God, Happiness).

O God! (*daivame*!)

The word used by Guru here to denote God, as is common usage in the Malayālam language, is *daivam.* In the Sanskrit language from which the word was adopted into Malayālam, it means, "fate, destiny, luck, fortune." But in Malayālam, it gained the meaning "God." In Guru's vision here, "God," rather a religious term, stands for the more philosphical terms, *Brahman*, *Ātman* and *aṛivu*

(Consciousness) which he prefers in his other philosophical works. And addressing the Supreme Reality as "God" naturally fits within the context of a prayer.

Literally, the word *daivam* means that which is related to *devas* (gods, the inhabitants of the Vedic heaven). *Deva, devī, devatā* and all such terms have one common source — the verb root *div*, meaning "to shine." The inhabitants of heaven are called *devas* because they supposedly are shining ones by nature. *Brahman* also, pure Consciousness (*cit*) in essence, could equally be conceived as *daivam* (God) because Consciousness experientially is pure Effulgence. In the Sanskrit language, the word usually used to denote God is *Īśa* or *Īśvara*, literally, "one who controls."

We all know that God, also called *daivam* or *Īśa*, signifies that which creates, sustains and destroys everything and everyone. Hence God is conceived as the all-controller. This idea is present even in the minds of atheists, for denying the existence of God also presupposes the idea of God in the mind of the one who denies. The existence of all ideas, we know, is in everyone's mind or consciousness. This consciousness is merely an experience of effulgence within our being, and every idea that becomes formulated in it is some specifiable experience of brightness. In short, God, as an idea as well as the all-underlying Substance, and even of all specific ideas, is Effulgence in essence, as is well acknowledged in the other philosophical poems of Guru, which thus could be termed *daivam* also.

This *daivam*, as we have just noticed, is to be understood as the meaning of *Īśa* in the Sanskrit language, as well as in Vedānta. Therefore, knowing the meaning of the word *Īśa* also would be relevant here. It is a word derived from the verb root *īś*, meaning "to be in total control" (*īś aiśvarye*). *Īśa*, thus, is the one Reality in total control of all the worlds. Such a controlling Reality has naturally to be that of a knowledge or consciousness, which can be considered as confined to an individuated body or as existing as an abstract Reality.

This effulgence of consciousness being Its essential content, *Īśa* is *daivam* as well.

Caringly Protect us (*kāttukolka*)

As everyone looks at their own lives, they realize that their own birth, existence and death, as well as the actualization of their happiness, are all beyond the bounds of their control. They finally decide that God's hand works in everything. Those who come to such a conclusion take refuge in that God, and become willing to make their own desires, which are in their control, to abide by the unknown will of God. So they always pray to God for Its caring protection all through their lives.

A Link Connecting Religions

This prayer begins with asking for the caring protection of God from above, as indicated by the original word *aṅṅu* which means "over there," as well as "you." The former sense stands out when it is related to the other word *iṅṅu,* meaning "here" referring to the supplicant living in this world.

To think of God as seated on high, overseeing all the worlds and all human affairs, is more familiar to the Semitic religions which could also be called the prophetic religions, than to the religions of the East, especially to the philosophical vision of Vedānta. The latter's perception of God is as the one all-pervading Reality. Of these two slightly different God-concepts, which one is meant by Guru in the present prayer?

We get an answer to this question when we contrast the first and last verses of this prayer. The last verse reads as follows:

> In the deep ocean of your Glory
> Let all of us become immersed,
> There to dwell, dwell for ever
> In Felicity Supreme!

The Glory of God is not perceived there as pertaining to the most high, but is compared to the vast ocean here and now. That means, the significance of God's existence is to be felt by each of us here and now like the presence of a boundless ocean. Thus it could well be said that this prayer begins with a tone familiar to the prophetic religions and ends with echoes of the ideas of the non-prophetic religions of the East. This prayer, thus, serves as a sort of link connecting the two main religious trends. The Guru in this way keeps his perfect neutrality.

Two God-Concepts

It might seem the above-said two God-concepts — one as the all-pervading Reality and the other as the overlord of everything, who sits in the most high heaven — are mutually exclusive.

Children, in the usual course, grow up hearing from their parents and teachers that God is seated high in heaven. They would naturally point their finger upwards to show where that heaven is. Reaching that abode of God after death is the hope that many religions give to believers. If heaven as God's abode is above this world, is it possible to reach there by flying in a spacecraft that never stops going upward? The above-said children as well as the priests who preach of God, will not agree to such an idea. Both will simply say, God's abode is not in a heaven reachable by an ordinary spacecraft, but can be reached by the spacecraft of our imagination, or only after death in the form of our spirit.

That means, the abode of God, the most high heaven that the Semitic religions conceive of, is located not in any outer space, but in a mental space. This latter kind of space, in Vedānta, is known as *cidākāśa* (conscicusness-space).

Vedāntins teach that God or *Brahman* is the all-pervading Substance. That Substance also is nothing but pure Consciousness in essence. That means, God's existence, according to them, is in conciousness, as Conscionsness (*cit*). We thus find that the two religious trends find a common ground in Consciousness. The words of Jesus, "The kingdom of God is within thyself" could be recalled in this context.

Then, does that consciousness within us have an above and a below? This above and below really pertain to the context of our value sense, and is not of any spatial significance. For example, suppose you see a pebble on the floor of your drawing room. You pick it up immediately and throw away. Suppose on picking it up you find it to be a gemstone, then you keep it securely. It both cases you make an assessment of the value of the stone. Not only in this case, but in the case of every act of knowing, you consciously or unconsciously make an evaluation of the object known by relating it to your likes and dislikes. This is something natural with the knowing function of consciousness. The Vedāntic explanation of this phenomenon is that *cit* (Consciousness) is also *ānanda* (Value sense) in essential content.

Along with this evaluation, you assign a proper place to the object thus known, in your world of values. Certain things thus known are just ignored by you as of no value, assigning them a very low position, and certain other things are given some place of high value in your understanding, and even in life. Assigning a lower or higher place to what you happen to know is part of human nature, and could be evidenced on some occasions of your social life. If it so happens that an honourable person arrives at a formal gathering, you naturally hurry to offer him or her a higher seat, called *agrāsana* (the topmost seat). Why is it so? How are the respect we feel towards the person and the seat offered being high or low related? We just do not know. Why can't we offer him or her a seat in a lower row? We have no answer except that we cannot do otherwise. The only answer is that human nature is such. Something considered to be of great value is given a high position, and everything of lower value, lower positions. In other words, all our considerations are graded value-wise, as if belonging to a vertically arrangeable series. Such values, of course, are felt by you nowhere else than in your own consciousness.

Of all such knowledges, that of the highest value is of God, which really is unknowable. Therefore, the position assignable to God in our world of understanding also has to be the highest one. This explains why God is always thought of as seated in the most high. This value-world being within our understanding, the kingdom of God could equally be thought of as within ourselves.

The difference between the God-concepts of two religious trends could thus be seen to be abating until finally to vanish altogether. The kingdom of God thus is in heaven, it is with yourself, and it is all-pervading. These different concepts of the one and only God are arrived at when perceived from slightly varying angles. Such different perspectives of God really in no way alter the real being of God.

Here (*iṅṅu*)

When God is thought of as occupying the highest pole in the vertical heirarchy of values, we the supplicants are to be given a position at the lowest pole here and now. Those who pray to God consider themselves to be immersed in an ocean of sufferings here, and so they look to God to save them from it. In another context also, where he prays to God, assuming it as of the form of Devī (Mother Goddess), the Guru says,

> Call me who salutes you,
> To your abode there
> From here where, rowing in the ocean,
> No help excepting you
> Is forthcoming for me.
>
> — *Devistavam*, v. 8

The difference between "there" (*aṅṅu*) and "here" (*iṅṅu*) as two extreme poles of a vertically conceived axis, is sharply noticeable in this context also.

Bhagavān

When God and the supplicant are thus seen to form the opposite poles of a vertically conceived situation, in India, the higher pole is called *Bhagavān* and the lower pole *bhakta*. The one endowed with the qualities called *bhaga*s is named *Bhagavān*. Śaṅkara in the "Introduction" to his commentary on the *Bhagavad-Gītā* defines *Bhagavān* thus: *bhagavān jñāna-aiśvarya-śakti-bala-vīrya-tejobhiḥ sadā sampannaḥ* (*Bhagavān* is always rich in wisdom, power, controlling power, vitality, strength, and brilliance). According to another version, *Bhagavān* is the one who is well aware of everything concerning *utpatti* (origin), *vipatti* (destruction), *āgati* (comings), *gati* (goings), *vidyā* (knowledge), and *avidyā* (ignorance) of all beings. Mankind feels the imperfection of all such qualities in them, while God is conceived as the abode of their perfection. Therefore they look towards God for succour. This idea of *Bhagavān* appears in this prayer in verse 8, to be discussed later.

A *bhakta* is "one who does service, performs worship or meditates upon." The verb-root *bhaj* from which the word is derived means also "to know, to respect, to select, to acquire."

Such are the connotations of the two Malayālam words *aṅṅu* and *iṅṅu* meaning "over there" and "here." The word *aṅṅu,* which means also "you," could be taken in the sense of addressing God. Only that, in that case, it loses the charm of considering God as the other pole of the supplicant here.

Never Lose Your Hold (*kaiviṭāte*)

Everyone who prays seeks God's succour, particularly in difficult situations in life. As we have noticed, God could be conceived either as seated in heaven or as the Reality in one's own being, that is to say, in one's own heart. In either case, how can we expect God's helping hand to extend towards us — in the former case, heaven is too far away to have God's protecting hand reach us, and in the latter, God is already within us, meaning, there is no need to extend Its hand.

We have just noticed also that the reality of the kingdom of God is within oneself. Given that God is the Reality in one's own being, Its protective hands are felt insofar as one is well aware of God being the Reality in oneself. That God being Consciousness (*cit*) in essence, Its protection also is availed to the extent we remain conscious of being God in essential content. Put otherwise, experiencing God's caring protection is a double faceted one — God being Consciousness in essence and we being conscious of ourselves to be God in essential content. In short, to not ignore God at any moment of our life comprises the feeling that God extends his protecting hands. In other words, experiencing God as the Reality in everything, as well as in oneself, is felt as the incessant protection of God.

Us (*ñaṅṅale*)

This prayer, as was seen earlier, is meant to be a universal one, not for an individual person, nor for any personal favour. It could thus be considered the prayer of the entire human race, or even of all living beings, as suggested by the word *ñaṅṅale* (us). For this reason, the only favour asked of God is also of the most universal nature — ensuring the happiness of us all.

Ocean of Becoming (*bhavābdhi*)

Are we then not happy now? No, everyone complains of life being full of miseries. Difficult situations arise in worldly existence and transactions with others, untoword events and natural calamities happen, having to face diseases and even death, relationships with those who are very close become tense — all such are enough to cause pepole feel life to be full of sorrows. For this reason, life is treated by many as an incessant stream of worries, or even as an ocean of sufferings. The never ending process of birth and death that is always full of anxieties and worries, the uncertainty concerning what happens after death, and other such fundamental problems, also cause agonies in life. Many feel, they are lost in an ocean of sufferings caused by the incessant flow of events in nature. This flow of events, in Vedānta, is known as *bhava* meaning "becoming." The ocean of sufferings is therefore called *bhavābdhi* (*bhava* + *abdhi*), *abdhi* meaning "ocean." This is yet another word for *saṁsāra-sāgara* (*saṁsāra* + *sāgara*). *Saṁsāra* means "that which is in a constant state of change," and *sāgara* "ocean." The religiously minded, particularly of India, think that souls repeatedly assume new bodies and discard old ones, and it is this that constitutes the essential content of *saṁsāra*. Those who perceive life thus, therefore, think, getting out of this ocean of sufferings, or reaching its other shore, is what one ultimately should aspire to in life.

Suppose the entire nature stands still with no change taking place in it. No misery will be felt in such a world; neither will be life in it. That means, life demands that constant changes take place, and that every change entails the disappearance of one state of existence and the appearance of another — the death of one state and the birth of another. Human existence is no exception to this rule. Life thus naturally presupposes birth and death. Pleasures and pains always go with this phenomenon. Understanding life thuswise itself is the only way to save ourselves from *saṁsāra.*

The prayer made here has to help the supplicant cross this ocean, for which the mighty ship that comes across is thought of as God's own feet or word, and the navigator of the ship, God Itself.

The poetic beauty and the philosophical profundity of this imagery stands out all the more when contrasted with another ocean Guru mentions at the concluding verse of this prayer. It is the ocean of God's Glory as against the ocean of *saṁsāra* or *bhava.* On finding oneself in such an ocean, what one feels like praying for would be to dwell forever in Its Felicity Supreme, instead of crossing to Its other shore. This ocean of God's Glory, in his more strictly philosophical poems, is called by Guru *saṁvit sāgara* (the ocean of Consciousness) or *saṁvit-kaṭal*, meaning the same, or the ocean of *Ātmā* or *Brahman.*

What really is the nature of the ocean of becoming or *bhava*, from which we wish to be rescued? It is nothing but the Glory of God, the Glory of the Absolute, finding self-expression. Ignorant of this, we count it as the ocean of sufferings, forgetful that happiness and suffering are part of that self-unfoldment of the Glory of God. The alternation between happiness and suffering is part and parcel of life. It is what makes life really meaningful, because with no suffering felt, happiness would become meaningless. Perceiving life as well as the total nature as part of the God's Glory become manifest, is the essential content of Vedāntic wisdom, and to this enlightenment it is that the present prayer leads the supplicant. The eight verses between the first and the last could well be considered as philosophically unfolding the proper path towards this enlightenment. The attainment of this wisdom results in the realization that what was initially thought of as the *saṁsāra-sāgara,* is no longer so, but is the ocean of God's Glory from which one does not wish to get out, but instead to become immersed in and to dwell in forever.

You Are the Navigator (*nāvikan nī*)

If one were to fall overboard in mid-ocean, the only hope for him or her would be a ship happening to cross by in the vicinity, and the captain noticing the helpless castaway. The same is true with one lost in the *bhavābdhi* or *saṁsāra sāgara*. A *guru,* enlightened, capable and willing to show such a person the true nature of life and the Reality underlying it, might happen to come across a real person's life, or else a person might happen to meet such a *guru* by chance. Just as a ship comes to pass through the area where the person is in distress by chance, so too is the case of a true seeker meeting a true *guru*. This Chance-element, with a capital "C," could be called God. That means, both occur as willed by God. Therefore God and *guru* are here suggested to be synonymous. In the days when Guru penned these verses, steamships were the primary means of transport across by sea, hence the imagery of the steamer.

God and *Guru*

The only way to cross the ocean of *bhava* is becoming enlightened of the Reality and the true nature of life. And this enlightenment is to be attained with the guidance of a *guru* unless the seekers are mature and intuitive enough to attain this goal on their own through self-disciplines involving a sort of self-heating up, known in India as *tapas*. Such a *guru*'s place is given to God here. Keeping aside the chance element already mentioned, is it proper to equate a *guru* — a living human being — with God? Though such a question is pertinent from a rational point of view, it is familiar to the spiritual tradition of India, to treat a *guru* as equal to God. One of the well-known praises of *guru* runs as follows:

> *gurur brahmā gurur viṣṇuḥ*
> *gurur devo maheśvaraḥ* ।
> *guruḥ sākṣāt param brahma*
> *tasmai śrī gurave namaḥ* ॥

> Guru is Brahmā the Creator: Guru is Viṣṇu the Sustainer; Guru is the effulgent great god, the Destroyer (Śiva): Guru is even the transcendental *Brahman* become perceptible. Salutations to such a Guru.

The creation, sustenance, and dissolution of everything in all the worlds is a systematized one. All systematization requires a knowledge or consciousness functioning behind it. When considering the ultimate Reality, the Absolute or *Brahman*, in which all these take place, Itself being Consciousness in essence, it is but natural to think of that Consciousness as the Creator, Sustainer and Dissolver of the world. This Consciousness Itself, as we have already seen, is the essential content of God (*daivaṁ*). How the word *daivam* means "that which is effulgence in essence" we have also already noticed.

Now what is the meaning of the word *guru*? Of its two syllables, *gu* stands for darkness, and *ru* for obstructing it. The word *guru* thus means "one who dispels darkness, the darkness of ignorance." As we are well aware, only brightness can put an end to darkness. In short, the two words *daivam* and *guru* signify one and the same.

The Mighty Steamer is none Other Than Your Feet/Your Word

The original words *nin padam* mean "your feet" as well as "your word." Both meanings are relevant in this context. Let us consider the two separately.

Your Feet

Anthropomorphism is natural to the Indian spiritual tradition, though *Brahman* (the Absolute) is accepted as formless. Different deities are attributed different forms. Though both the feet and the face of a deity are poetically likened to a lotus flower in Indian tradition, *bhakta*s are always described as taking refuge at their feet. This feature has bearing in regard to the basic understanding of life. All the phenomenal appearances of life have a firm existential ground. Always relying on that Reality, rather than on fleeting phenomenal appearances, is but natural with those who discriminate between appearance and reality, because such a reliance alone rescues us from the occan of *saṁsāra*. Our understanding of life also gains steadiness then. The necessity of this firmness is indicated by the supplicant, though unknowingly, by worshipping the feet of God, because feet are the organs with which we stand firmly. In the context of strict philosophy, these feet of God stand for the ontological (*sat*) aspect of the Absolute. Put otherwise, it is the expression of the supplicant's desire to perceive their own existence firmly founded on the Existence aspect of God. Attaining such an existential identity with God is itself the ultimate goal any supplicant can aspire to.

As related to the *guru* concept also, the very same practice of adoring the feet is of great significance. It is customary in India to pay obeisance to a *guru* by first touching his or her feet, and then saluting with folded hands. Feet are the organs with which we walk also. The path on which a *guru* walks is that of Reality. Student seekers touching the feet of a *guru* indicates their willingness to tread along the same path, and for this reason, they are called *brahmacārin*s (those who walk on the path of *Brahman*).

Taking refuge at the feet of God could be considered merely as a sign of one's dependence on God. The practice of taking refuge at the feet of a *guru* is more than this: it also marks a contract entered into by a disciple with his or her *guru.* By this contract, it is as if the disciple surrenders his or her personal freedom before his or her *guru.* By doing so, what one could expect to gain in life is owning the absolute Freedom the *guru* always enjoys. A *guru* lives as that Freedom become embodied. A disciple aims at becoming so.

Your Word

A disciple, seeking wisdom, takes refuge at the feet of a *guru.* This wisdom is no ordinary knowledge; it is the knowledge of the Reality in the being of oneself as well as of everything; it is the knowledge by which the knower becomes merged and lost in the known; it is the knowledge of the Reality that finds expression as all ordinary knowledges. That Reality being what unfolds Itself even as words articulated, no word expresses what It is. This Knowledge of all knowledges, in India, is linguistically symbolized by the sign ॐ (AUM) pronounced "om." It virtually is not a word. Becoming enlightened of the secret symbolized by this sign is considered the ultimate goal of any seeker. Expounding its importance, the *Kaṭha Upaniṣad* says:

sarve vedā yat padam āmananti
tapāṁsi sarvāṇi ca yad vadanti
yad icchanto brahmacaryam caranti

tat te padam saṁgraheṇa bravīmi
oṁ ity etat — I. 15

The word that all the Vedas declare, that all the austere enquiries proclaim (as goal), aimed at which *brahmacarya* is practised in life — that word I shall tell you in a nutshell: It is Aum.

This sign is known also as *praṇava,* literally "that which is ever new" (*pra + nava*), *pra* standing for "properly" and *nava* for "new." It is called so because the Reality it symbolizes never loses novelty. The Ṛṣi Patañjali, in his *Yoga-Sūtras,* says about it:

tasya vācakaḥ praṇavaṇ — 1.27

He — God — is given expression as *praṇava.*

Expounding the hidden meanings of this cryptical and mystical symbol is what the *Māṇḍūkya Upaniṣad* accomplishes. We do not intend to make a detailed examination of it here as our elaborate commentary on this Upaniṣad is already available in print (a DK Printworld publication).

Becoming enlightened on the secret of the wisdom, embodied by this monosyllable, is what helps one cross the *bhavābdhi* or *saṁsāra sāgara.*

The next verse takes us right through the essential content of this wisdom.

Verse 2

onn onnāy eṇṇiy eṇṇit to-
ṭṭeṇṇum poruḷ oṭuṅṅiyāl ।
ninniṭum dṛkku pol uḷḷam
ninnil aspandam ākaṇam ॥

Counting all the countables
One after another, and when
Everything is reckoned and finished with,
Thereafter continues
To exist the perceiving mind.
In like manner, let this mind
Attain rest pulsationless in you.

The most fundamental problem that all philosophizing tries to solve is, how to relate systematically and understandably, the world we perceive, the perceiver or the knowing mind and the one ultimate Reality, as belonging to a functional whole. This means, a clarification of the ultimate nature of Reality is attempted in all such philosophizing. How these are to be intuitively pereceived as essentially one, and how one is to arrive at this perception, are summarily portrayed by Guru in the four lines of this second verse.

The ultimate Reality, called *Brahman* in Vedānta, as already seen under verse 1, is what is thought of as God in this prayer. That this *Brahman* is pure Consciousness in essence also is a basic tenet of Vedānta. The Vedāntic explanation of the appearance of the world is that it is *Brahman* manifesting Itself, while also undergoing no intrinsic change. It is often compared to the gold that assumes the form of various ornaments while remaining as gold. That means, the essential content of all that appears to be is nothing other than *Brahman* or pure Consciousness.

We have already examined in our comments on verse 1 of *Aṛivu,* how all that is visible or knowable, in essential content, is unconditioned Consciousness alone. This Consciouness, felt by the person who perceives as the knowing mind, is called *dṛk* in Vedānta, literally "the eye," and signifying the knowing subject. Then the object known is called *dṛśya* (the visible, the knowable).

An introductory textbook on Vedānta called *Dr̥g-dr̥śya-viveka* (Discriminating the Knower and the Known), attributed to the well-known Śaṅkara, deals with this topic. "The countables" referred to in the present verse are equivalent to what Śaṅkara means by *dr̥śya* in that work.

Śaṅkara says, if an object seen is *dr̥śya,* then the eye that sees it is the *dr̥k.* Such objects could be countless, but the eye or *dr̥k* remains one alone. This eye may have its varying conditions, like having good sight, bad sight or no sight at all. All such conditions are known to the mind (*manas*) that functions from behind. Thus, if the eye is a *dr̥śya,* then *manas* is its *dr̥k.* The *manas* may have its own altering states and functions, like desiring, imagining, loving, hating, doubting, being faithful or unfaithful, fearing and so on. All such altering states of mind are known to the consciousness behind it. Thus, mind, in this context, becomes *dr̥śya* and consciousness its *dr̥k*. But there is no *dr̥k* that makes this consciousness its *dr̥śya*. It is both *dr̥k* and *dr̥śya* at the same time when it is aware of itself. This consciousness, therefore, sometimes is called *sākṣī-caitanya* (witnessing consciouness) or *pratyag-ātmā* (the self behind which no one can go on in search of). Nothing exists outside the amplitude of this witnessing consciousness. Thus, all that is observable, whether gross or subtle, physical or mental, seem to converge to one point-like consciousness — the consciousness of the individual observer, here rendered as "the perceiving mind" (*dr̥k*). This is how the observed world and the observing mind are related in Vedāntic perception.

This intuitive perceptual process is not meant to terminate with the convergence of the observables into the knowing consciousness. What really is the individual consciousness? It is just a minute functional fragment of the one all-inclusive Consciousness — the Consciousness that finds expression as all the knowing minds as well as all the knowables. That all-inclusive Consciousness is what we call God here. The knowing mind, if it intends to know itself, should find its oneness with, and merge with, God.

This final merger completes a full circle. First, the universally observed objects merge in the being of the individual's knowing consciounsness. Then, this individuals' consciousness finally merges "pulsationless" in the being of the universal Consciousness or God. This God is what assumes the form of all that was first universally seen as the the observables. Though presented here as a process of one stage following another, in actual experience, no such is relevant. Describing this experiential vision as a step by step process, really, is part of the limitations of verbal expression. Its real meaning is something a true seeker has to experience in himself or herself.

Such is the manner in which Guru experientially perceives, or intends the supplicant to perceive, the first mentioned three basic facets of Reality in a dynamic non-dual vision, rather than merely as a static concept. Pure Consciousness in essence, the three cannot remain distinct realities either.

The very same experiential vision of a full circle formed of all that is observable in all the worlds, the individual self and *Bhagavān* (as Universal Being or Consciousness), is depicted as follows in the *Bhagavad-Gītā*.

yajjñātvā na punar moham
evam yāsyasi pāṇḍava ।
yena bhūtāny aśeṣeṇa
drakṣyasy ātmany atho mayi ॥ — II.35

By knowing that, you will not get into confusion any more. You will then see everything that has come into being in yourself, and yourself in Me.

As is evident from this quotation, the Guru considers this verse to present the core of *jñāna* or wisdom.

The glimpse of the core of wisdom seen here thus could be considered as forming the topmost rung in the heirarchy of values. After indicating this pole, the Guru in the next verse takes us to the other pole, the lowest one, where we value our daily bread, clothing, and possessing a shelter and other worldly needs. All other human values could then be given their respective positions somewhere between these poles.

Verse 3

anna-vastrādi muṭṭāte
tannu rakṣiccu ñaṅṅale ।
dhanyar ākkunna nīy onnu
tanne ñaṅṅaḷkku tampurān ॥

Food and clothes and all such,
Providing us ever with no lapse,
You make our lives generously blessed;
You are alone our sole Master.

The one Absolute or God unfolds Itself as the world, as we have already noticed and which will be stated directly in verses 4 and 5. We are all beings that have emerged as a result of it. And as part of this unfoldment, there appears everything that beings are in need of. Such is the way the Absolute systematizes Its own self-manifestation. It could therefore be said, God or the Absolute is always mindful of all our worldly needs like food and clothing, and It thus makes our lives generously blessed.

The creation-story that appears in the first section of the *Aitareya Upaniṣad* comes near to the idea presented here. *Ātmā*, which alone existed in the beginning, created out of Itself all the worlds and the beings in them. Then It entered all those beings in the form of hunger. And Itself then assumed the form of all edibles needed to satisfy that hunger. Finally, *Ātmā* looks back at both (the hungry beings and the edibles). It then sees Itself alone in both.

The hungry beings feed themselves on the edibles, resulting in their satisfaction. This experience, in fact, is nothing other than the *ānanda* (Happiness or Value-sense) content of *Ātmā* actualized. This *ānanda,* along with *sat* (Existence) and *cit* (Consciousness) forms the real essential content of *Ātmā*. Put otherwise, the self-unfoldment of the one ultimate Reality, called God here, as the enjoyer and the enjoyed, happens in such a way that it enables each living being to actualize its own *ānanda* content.

No Asking for Food and Clothes

It is usual among people, as some religions might also teach them, to ask God for our daily needs such as food and clothing. No such request is present in this prayer. On the other hand, it is admitted that God already provides us with all such needs. How this is done by God we have just seen. The only favours asked for in this prayer are for God's caring protection and the happiness of all. This happiness, in its turn, as seen in the concluding verse, is that of experiencing oneself merged in the Glory of God. This mergence is attained through wisdom, which also is prayed for. The prayer makes no mention of anything about the details of what makes us happy otherwise. It could thus be said that the Guru, through this text, teaches us an ideal way of praying to God.

Who Produces?

Most of the food items, clothes and other such necessities of life are produced by human efforts. A farmer, when he produces something from his land, thinks "All this is the result of my toil."

What does a farmer really do when farming? He simply sows some seeds in the soil along with manuring it properly. In time it is also watered. The seed, water, manure and all such are simply products of nature; they were not created by the farmer. After sowing, the seed sprouts, it grows up, and then in due course it yields a crop. All this happens only by the mysterious creative potential within nature, not by any effort of the farmer. Then, who really is the producer? It is nature, not the farmar. The latter is incapable even of creating a grain of wheat or paddy.

When we say all this happens because of the power of nature, it is as if we feel that we have understood something by saying so. Really we understand nothing. What happens remains a mystery, though the word "nature" sounds like a scientific word. This nature unfolds itself as animals and humans and as their ability to toil, as the unknown power of the seed to grow a hundredfold, as the satisfaction that the consumption of such a yield gives, as well as everything else. The Consciousness that functions in all these together is thought of here as God, and is termed "our sole Master." The original Malayālam word is *tampurān,* a variant form of the Tamil word *tampirān* meaning "our Master."

Generously Blessed (*dhanyar*)

Dhanyar, in Malayālam, is the plural form of *dhanya,* meaning one who has the sense of fulfilment throughout life. It is rendered here as "generously blessed," and is a derivative of the word *dhana* meaning "wealth." It etymologically means, "that which yields fruits" (*dhana dhānye*). The best of all such fruits is the satisfaction we feel in life. This is yielded not by money, but by the enjoyable produces of nature. Ranging from the fulfilment of bodily needs like food and clothing to that of the highest wisdom — everything ensures happiness and thus is wealth (*dhana*). All that is necessary to ensure our sense of fulfilment is provided by nature, provided that we use these in a just way by using our intelligence, yet another natural gift.

If nature provides us all with everything we need, why do people starve in some parts of the world, whereas in some other parts food is wantonly wasted? It is so because what nature produces is not intelligently utilized. People are tempted to make use of their nature-given intelligence to satisfy their greed and make personal gains, rather than for the sake of understanding their oneness with nature, and thus with the entire human race. They claim nature's produces in one region as their own, and thus deny the right to enjoy the same to others in some different region. These regions are divided with artificial lines drawn on a map, though they are never seen on the earth's surface. Such lines divide the world into many countries. This artificial and unintelligent division of the world causes not only the starvation of people in some parts of the world, but is also the root cause of most problems and wars of today's world. Such a wrong use of human intelligence, in Vedānta is known as *avidyā*.

The next verse indicates how we should properly understand all that is. That is, eveything together forms a structurally perfect, functioning system.

Verse 4

āẓiyum tirayum kārrum
āẓavum pole ñaṅṅaḷum ।
māyayum nin mahimayum
nīyum enn uḷḷil-ākaṇam ॥

Like ocean, waves, wind and depth
Are ourselves, *māyā,* your glory and you.
Let us inwardly have
Such an awareness (of life's scheme).

The appeal made to God in this verse is that we should have a clear understanding of the total system of life and the world. We saw in verse 2, how the three aspects — the totality of the world, the knowing mind and the all-inclusive Reality or God — are to be seen as one, which pertains to the context of pure wisdom; and in verse 3, how the beings in the world depend on God for their daily needs. How all these are to be intuitively perceived as belonging to a single functional system is portrayed here in verse 4 with the help of the ocean analogy. "We" (*ñaṅṅaḷ*) or the world, *māyā,* "your glory" (*nin mahimā*) and "you" (*nī*) or God, are the fundamental categories to be seen related.

What is to be Prayed For?

It is a comprehensive understanding, not any personal favour, that is appealed for. This understanding, though not aspired for by all, is aspirable by all, and thus has a universal dimension. It finally results in the Supreme Felicity prayed for in the concluding verse. Such is the way the format of this prayer-text is structured. God always remains generous enough to grant us this vision, but we need to keep our inner eye wide open and ready to imbibe that wisdom.

As for a prayer that is simply aimed at gaining a few personal favours, a supplicant could feel that such an appeal is not needed because God, being omniscient, knows the needs of all Its creations. God should therefore fulfil all such needs unasked for.

God in this verse is likened to the depth in an ocean. The way to secure the Grace of God is to perceive It as the depth principle in our own being. How this is to be accomplished is delineated in this verse with the help of an ocean analogy. The fundamental aspects to be correlated in a systematic way in arriving at an intuitive perception of the ultimate Reality is compared here to the ocean and its different aspects.

Ourselves Like the Ocean

"Ourselves" (*ñaṅṅaḷ*) here stands for the totality of individual beings including the supplicant. This totality is otherwise called "the world" or "the cosmos." This "world" is not to be understood as it means in modern science. This science treats the observable aspect of the world alone as worth considering as existent, and ignores the place of the existence of the knowing mind. It treats mind merely as a side-effect of certain chemical actions that take place in the physical object called brain. The spiritual sciences like Vedānta, on the other hand, consider both as relevant, and as both together to constitute the world (*prapañca*). So also the individual and the universal aspects are covered by the one word *prapañca*.

The real content in the ocean and the waves is water, and in it the individual and the universal always find unity. How does this one reality emerge as waves? How does the one all-underlying Reality appear as everything that forms the world? When encountering such basic problems, we feel that all this happens as part of an overall system of existence always beyond our understanding. Then a sort of urge wells up in us to ask, "Who am I that forms part of this system?" and then, "How and wherefrom did this world in which I am a part, originate?" The answer to these questions, though not immediately apparent, is implicit in this verse. But seeing it clearly requires us to ready ourselves with a penetrative, intuitive mind accompanied by an intense yearning to have the above-said questions answered. This involves a sort of self-heating known as *tapas* in India.

Māyā like the Waves

Guru's basic philosophical stand is that one ultimate Reality alone exists. The world, all the individual entities in it and even the most insignificant of their qualities, appear in this one Reality and disappear into It, just as waves appear and disappear in the ocean. This Reality, in this prayer generally, is conceived as God, though the Upaniṣads prefer to call It *Ātmā* or *Brahman*. Each of the individual entities that emerges in It, taken separately, has a beginning and an end. The state in between the two is called its lifespan. The emerging and disappearing of such entities continue endlessly, and no one knows when and where this process began. The totality of this continual flow, in which individual entities emerge and disappear, is what we call the world.

Even when individual entities appear to exist as one separate from another, the real content in all of them is one Reality alone, just as all the waves are water in essential content. The apparent entities do not have their own existence. What appears as the birth, life and death of individual beings is nothing more than a fragment of the beginningless and endless self-unfoldment of the one ultimate Reality or *Ātmā*. We are that immortal Reality even when living as individuals; we were that Reality before assuming the present form, and we will continue to be that Reality after the dissolution of the present form as well. This is how the lives of individual beings are seen by Guru as related to the Real in all his philosophical works as well as in this prayer.

Guru, in the chapter *Māyā-Darśanam* (Vision by *Māyā*) of his *Darśana-Mālā* (Garland of Visions) defines *māyā* as "that which does not exist" (*na vidyate yā sā māyā* — IV.1). The very same non-existent *māyā*, mysteriously enough, is then stated as manifesting as *vidyā* and *avidyā* (science and nescience); *parā* and *aparā* (the transcendental and the non-transcendental), *tamas* (darkness), *pradhāna* (the inherent potential), *prakṛti* (nature) and all else. Such manifestations, in the present verse, are compared to waves in the ocean. Waves do not exist apart from the ocean, and in this sense are non-existent. Likewise, the infinite and insurmountable potential to unfold as all that was stated above is inherent in the one *Ātmā*. This potential is what Guru calls *māyā*, as is evident in verses 53 to 60 of his *Ātmopadeśa Śatakam* (One Hundred Verses of Self-Instruction). Not existing apart from *Ātmā*, the only existent Reality, this *māyā* is to be counted as non-existent.

Yet it remains an undeniable fact that manifest forms beginninglessly and endlessly do appear. Also we cannot deny that the way the one Reality unfolds thus is ultimately a mystery. That all such manifest forms are felt by all as real is equally true. Taking into account this mystery, Guru on many occasions compares the emergence of the apparent world from the one invisible *Ātmā*, to a great magic show (*mahendra-jāla*). The Sanskrit as well as Malayālam term for magician is *mayāvin* which equally means "a wielder of *māyā*." A magician's performance includes creation, the temporary existence and disappearance of some fleeting phenomena. Likewise, the effects of *māyā* include what is known as creation (*sṛṣṭi*), existence (*sthiti*) and dissolution (*saṁhāra*) of all individually existing entities.

The non-existence of *māyā* in *Ātmā*, in Vedānta, is termed *prāg-abhāva*. *Prāk* means "anterior," and *abhāva*, "non-existence." The analogy used to make the nature of this anterior non-existence is that of the clay and the pot. The potential to assume the form of a pot is already hiding in clay, though a pot has no existence in clay. Such non-existence of potential effects in their causes is counted as the anterior non-existence (*prāg-abhāva*). Thus it is said, the *prāg-*

abhāva of a pot exists in the clay. Resorting to the same kind of reasoning, it is said, the *prāg-abhāva* of *māyā* exists in *Ātmā.*

The analogy of the ocean and its waves, in the usual course, is used by Guru to show how the one reality and countless apparent forms, or how the universal and the particular, do not exist separately; their existence is non-dual. But here it is used in a slightly different epistemological context. Individual entities appear in the universal existence as an effect of *māyā.* How this *māyā*'s existence is inseparably one with *Ātmā* and how it is indefinable, i.e., how it is difficult to say whether it is or it is not — these must have been the problems in the mind of Guru when he compared *māyā* to the waves of the ocean.

Every wave, superficially seen, has its own existence, as well as an emergence and a disappearance. But seen from the point of view of the ocean, it alone exists, and waves do not exist apart from it. Likewise, when the ultimate Reality and the apparent world are seen as one and non-dual, *māyā* has no existence or relevance. But perceiving these two as two or as cause and effect, allows for the question to arise, how the effect originates from the causal Reality. *Māyā* is then admitted as that cause. Guru draws a clearer picture of *māyā* thus in his *Ātmopadeśa Śatakam:*

Within the waveless ocean
(That the primeval Consciousness is),
There is the subtle yet
Infinitely potent trait called *māyā.*
It manifests Itself endlessly
Assuming the apparent perishable forms
Such as of water with its quality taste.
It forms the many enduring manifest worlds

— v. 57

Another mysterious aspect of *māyā* is its veiling power. When we see a pot we forget to treat it as clay; on seeing an ornament, that it is gold alone remains somehow unnoticed by us. So too, by seeing the world, its essence as *Ātmā* alone remains hidden from our view. It is as if the clay's assumption of the form of a pot itself functions as a sort of veil over the clay-reality, thereby rendering it unnoticeable. Likewise, *māyā* and its effects together work as a kind of veil over the *Ātmā* that render It invisible, and the effects of the unreal *māyā* — the appearance of the world, the appearance of the duality of cause and effect — visible. Even in this veiling power of *māyā,* Śaṅkara differentiates its two aspects — one that of *āvaraṇa* (veiling) and the other of *vikṣepa* (projecting). Not only is the Real veiled by *māyā,* but the unreal world is projected onto the Real. The former is called the *āvaraṇa-śakti* (veiling power) of *māyā* and the latter *vikṣepa-śakti* (projecting power). These two effects and their cause *māyā* are inclusively covered by the *māyā,* here compared to waves.

Your Glory Like the Wind

How do waves emerge in the ocean? There is no apparent reason seen. The unseen presence of wind is finally found to be that cause. Likewise, there has to be an unseen cause for the emergence of effects from their causes, for the emergence of the apparent world from the one *Ātmā.* This unseen cause is seen here as nothing other than the Glory of God (*nin mahimā*), and is therefore compared to the wind-factor in the ocean.

The waves that emerge because of the presence of wind, range from tiny ripples to tidal waves that can even overturn mighty ships. Likewise, all that emerge from the one causal Reality range in one respect from the most subtle mind-factor to the gross and ever expanding universe; and in another respect, from the extremely minute energy-particles to the unthinkably and infinitely expanding interstellar bodies.

The appearance of the waves, even as they do not exist apart from the ocean, is made possible by the unseen wind. Similarly, we could naturally ask, what makes *māyā* and its effects remain always inseparable from the one ultimate Reality. Presuming no other cause than the Glory of God or the Absolute is possible. For these reasons, this Glory is likened to the wind-aspect in the ocean. Śaṅkara, in his *Vivekacūḍāmaṇi* (Crest-Jewel of Discrimination) calls this Glory, *parameśa-śakti* (the power of the Supreme God) (v. 110).

This Glory of God is admissible not only to spiritual traditions and religions; the modern science also acknowledges that there is a mystery-factor. According to this science, the utimate reality is energy. How does this non-material energy assume the gross form of the inert soil, as all the minerals and metals that can assume many shapes by being subjected to other forms of energy like heat and pressure? How does it assume the form of all the living organisms, as all the animals and human beings, as the human brains that are capable of thinking, imagining, loving, hating, philosophizing, creating poetry and all other art? Science gives no answer except that energy inheres in it all such possibilities. Whether thought as of energy or of God, a glory or mysteriousness is undeniable. This mystery-factor, as is natural to the context of a prayer, is here admitted to be God's Glory, and is compared to the wind-factor in the ocean.

You are Like the Depth

The original word for "depth" here is *āẓam,* the one used to mean "ocean" is *āẓi.* That which has *āẓam* (depth) is *āẓi* (ocean). This latter word also means "that in which things immerse." Though all of us think we are familiar with it, the place of the depth in the ocean is a peculiar one. Despite the fact that we often measure it, the depth of the ocean remains an invisible principle inseparable in the ocean's being. While the ocean extends horizontally and boundlessly, depth in it is a vertical principle. So too, the being of God can be considered the vertical principle in the horizontally spread-out world.

The first-hand impression we have is that depth is something measurable, and is therefore visible. Really the water alone is visible. When water exists, its presence alone is felt by us, and not the depth. When no water is present, the existence of depth does not become relevant either. For example, suppose one dries out a pool in order to know its depth. Then no depth would be there to measure. Likewise, when the world exists, we perceive it alone, and do not notice the depth-like principle of God in it. In the absence of a world, the existence of a God as its Creator, Sustainer and Destroyer, also becomes of no relevance, and there would also be no one to think of God's existence. In this context, in which God is said to be that Creator of the world and of humans, it could be equally contended that humans themselves created God as their Creator. Then who created whom? Human beings created God as their Creator and God created humans. Really one is meaningless without the other. Their mutual relationship is as between the depth and the ocean.

Suppose someone tries to measure the depth of an ocean. This can be done by dropping a long line into the ocean with a weight tied at the end. As the weight touches the bed, the line is pulled back and its length is then measured. But what is actually observed and measured is the line alone, not the depth as such. The latter simply is understood from the length of the line measured. So too God's presence in the world can be understood, but never can be observed or measured. No ocean exists without depth, so too no world exists without God.

Being compared to the depth of the ocean in no way compromises God's status as the Substance in the being of everything, mentioned earlier in our comments on the first verse and yet to be explicitly stated in the next.

How God is the principle of depth and the Substance in everything simultaneously, is not logically demonstrable. It can only be known by the seeker in the course of his or her *manana* (meditative cogitation).

A Structurally Perfect Whole

In this verse, the four elements associated with the ocean are compared, one by one, to four factors associated with the Real. More than understanding each pair separately, their unitive existence that forms a structurally perfect and functional whole has to be taken into account. These factors — ocean, waves, wind and depth — exist together, one inseparable from the other. So too, we, *māyā,* God's Glory, and God are inseparably one. Other such discernible universals could also be correlated likewise. Their co-existence also is to be intuitively perceived here. According to the Upaniṣads, such a structural perfection of the world already existed as a potential in the primeval desire *Ātmā* had for Its own unfoldment into the many. This truth is openly stated in the *Īśa Upaniṣad* as follows:

kavir manīṣī paribhūḥ svayambhūḥ ।
yāthātathyatho 'rthān vyadadhāt śāśvatībhyaḥ samābhyaḥ

— v. 8

He, the seer, thinker, all-pervading, self-existent, has duly distributed through endless years the objects according to their natures.

Narayana Guru's choice of four elements alone is also similar to the four states of consciousness inherent in *Ātmā* in the *Māṇḍūkya Upaniṣad* which says,

> *so 'yam ātmā catuṣpāt* — v. 2
>
> *Ātmā,* being such, has in It four quarters.

What these four quarters are and how they remain correlated are discussed in detail in our commentary on that Upaniṣad. (A DK Printworld publication).

The essence of the prayer made in this verse is, let us have an intuitive awareness of the coherent unity of the four fundamental factors mentioned here, comparable to four factors in the ocean.

The next verse considers how God relates to Its creation.

Verse 5

nīyallo sṛṣṭiyum sraṣṭāv-
āyatum sṛṣṭi-jālavum ।
nīyallo daivame sṛṣṭikk
uḷḷa sāmagriy-āyatum ॥

You are the creation, the creator too,
As also the myriads of created things.
You again, O God, are the Substance
Of which all creation is made.

The four factors examined in the last verse belong to the Real, considered from Its overall structure. Another set of four, in the present verse, are equated to God; these four are those involved in the context of creation. The Creator, the Substance for creation, the act of creation and the created things constitute these factors. All these four are seen here as inseparable from God. Of the basic problems common to philosophy, one is, "From where did this world originate?" Almost all the schools of thought give their own answers. Modern science counts this world merely in material terms, and concludes that it originated with an enormous explosion known as "the big-bang," and most probably will cease with an opposite implosion named in advance as "the big crunch." Nothing existed before the big-bang — no energy, no matter, no time, no space, nothing whatsoever. If nothing existed before, then what was it that exploded? If no time existed before, "when" did the explosion take place? Scientists keep mum on this issue or rather they choose not to ask.

Similar to the scientists' way of thinking, the prophetic religions hold that the world was created by God from nothing. How is it possible to create something from nothing? The answer is: with God nothing is impossible; He can create the world even from nothing.

The spiritual traditions of the East are not satisfied with such a stand. They admit an ever existing indistinct Reality; this Reality constantly assumes all distinct forms; such forms range from the minutest energy particles to the largest inter-stellar bodies, from the subtlest of minds to the grossest physical bodies. The constant flow of such fleeting forms aggregates into what appears to us as the world, in which the observer forms a part. An indication of how this creation occurs was seen in the last verse in reference to the *māyā* principle. The present verse goes into the more specific details of it.

The Upaniṣads are the most basic source books from which Vedāntins developed their line of thought. There are many contexts in which the Upaniṣads sketch a clear picture variously of creation. The *Aitareya Upaniṣad,* for example, begins with these words: *ātmā vā idam eka evāgra āsīt, nānyat kiñcana miṣat* (*Ātmā* alone existed here in the beginning; nothing else was present even to pulsate). This *Ātmā* brooded upon Itself as if a bird sits on its egg, with the desire to create the world. Just as a chick emerges in due time from a hatched egg, so the world emanated from the *Ātmā*. The universal and the particular aspects of what appears to be, the senses and their objects, hunger and edibles — all took shape in a proper order. Finally, *Ātmā* looks at everything thus created and sees Itself in all of these.

Ātmā thus is the material cause in the creation of all the worlds; *Ātmā* is Itself also the incidental cause of this creation; the essential content in everything thus created is *Ātmā*. Creations are also nothing but *Ātmā*. The act of creation took place, or rather takes place, constantly in *Ātmā*. This overall picture is portrayed in the present verse in the format of a praise to God.

Even when assuming the forms that appear in the ever flowing world, *Ātmā* alone is the real content in them all. Thus, *Ātmā* alone existed before creation, *Ātmā* alone exists in all the creations, *Ātmā* alone will contiune to exist forever. Thus, nothing new was really created, and virtually no creation took place. Only *Ātmā* exists, with all Its creativity. The perception of Vedāntins, therefore, with regard to creation is that no creation at all really happens. This theory is known as *ajāta-vāda* (the theory of no-birth). This theory implies that death also is unreal. If birth and death are unreal, to speak of a lifespan also is meaningless. Narayana Guru admits this stand when he says as follows in verse 78 of *Ātmopadeśa Śatakam*:

> No death is real,
> No birth is real,
> Nor is any lifespan real.
> No human and no god is real
> All these are but names

And corresponding forms.
Their beingness is an illusory phenomenon,
Like the flowing water seen
In the mirages of the desert lands.
They have no being of their own
This is always to be kept in mind.

Even as *Ātma* remains birthless and deathless, the appearance of phenomena that constitutes the world goes on within Itself, while It undergoes no intrinsic change. This kind of appearance where effects are seen within a cause, with no intrinsic change taking place in it, is known as *vivarta.* A piece of rope wrongly seen in a snake, is an example of *vivarta.* So too, the arising of waves in the ocean-water. Likewise, the existence of the world is an illusion seen in the one *Ātmā.* The creation of the world itself is then an illusory vision. Considering creation according to this perspective is known as *vivarta-vādā* (the theory of illusory appearance). A vivid picture of such a world-appearance is portrayed by Guru in his *Ātmopadeśa Śatakam* thus:

Individuated forms, like waves in the ocean,
Emerge in sequence, and so do they merge.
When will this process come to an end?
Oh! this is nothing but the action going on in
The ocean of primal Consciousness. — v. 56

A serious student should not miss noting the following points in this picture:

(1) The appearance of specific forms takes place in the one ever-existing ocean of Consciousness (*saṁvit-kaṭal*) which is no other than *Ātmā.*

(2) This emergence and re-mergence of individuated forms is comparable to the emergence and remergence of waves in an ocean. That means, these emerging forms have no being apart from the ocean of Consciousness.

(3) Such emergence and re-mergence does not cause any intrinsic change to the water-content. So too, the arising of beings in It does not change *Ātmā* into non-*Ātmā*.

(4) Such emergence and re-mergence is an endless process.

(5) There is an element of mystery in this as indicated by the exclamation *hanta*! (oh!).

(6) This happens in *Ātmā* as the creative urge, called *karma* by the *Bhagavad-Gītā* (VIII.3) as what is inherent in It, finds expression. All the wave-like individual beings, as part of the one ocean of Consciousness, are filled with this urge and so find expression as their *karma*s. Such *karma*s really belong to the one *Ātmā* as Narayana Guru explicitly states himself in the chapter *Karma-Darśana* (Vision by *karma*) of the *Darśana-Mālā*.

In the *Daivadaśakam*, the supplicant praying to God is related to *Ātmā* in the way a wave is related to the ocean. He or she looks around and sees the endless rows of waves similar to himself or herself. Inspired by one of the aspects (the self-enquiry aspect) of the *karma*-urge within, he or she thinks of the creation of all these waves, himself or herself not excluded. This enquiry ends upon perceiving God (*Ātmā* or the ocean of Consciousness) alone in everything and existing everywhere. The supplicant then says, with folded hands and a bowed head, as if addressing a person, "O God, you are the act of creation, you are the Creator, you are the myriads of creations, you are the Substance of which all these are created."

Cause and Effect

Created things are thought of as an effect (*kārya*). An effect should originate from a cause (*kāraṇa*). Trying to find out the cause of something observed is the job of almost all branches of modern science. All logical thinking is also founded on the cause-effect relationship. The concept of this relationship is known as the theory of causation.

According to this theory, no effect emerges without a cause. For example, a pot is a creation and therefore is an effect. The causes behind the emergence of this effect are the raw material clay and the potter as the creator. In Indian philosophy, the former is known as *upādāna kāraṇa* (material cause) and the latter *nimitta kāraṇa* (efficient cause). Without these two the pot cannot come into being. Though Western Philosophy, from the time of Aristotle, admits two more causes, namely the formal cause and the final cause, these two are seen as inclusively covered by the *nimitta kāraṇa* by Indian Philosophy, because both are ideas in the mind of the creator. Likewise, if the apparent world is an effect, it should have its causes.

Abhinna-nimitta-upādāna-kāraṇa

There is one ultimate Reality and It alone has its own being. This, as has already been made clear, is the basic stand of Vedānta. Narayana Guru, a confirmed Vedāntin, also admits the same stand, and that Reality is called God here, as well as *Ātmā, Brahman* or *Aṛivu* (unconditioned Consciousness) in his other works. This Reality, being the one all-underlying Substance, is termed *sat* (Existence) in Vedānta in general, and is referred to as *satyam* (Reality) in verse 7 of this prayer. God thus is admitted to be the material cause (*upādāna-kāraṇa*) of all creations.

Who or what, then, is the efficient cause? Having admitted that no other reality than God exists, the act of creation cannot be attributed to any other agency. Therefore, the efficient cause, in this case, also has to be God. This idea is seen admitted by the Upaniṣads when referring to the originally existing *Ātmā*, for example,

so 'kamāyata bahuḥ syām prajāyeya
— *Taittirīya Upaniṣad*, 2.6.1

It desired, let me be born as many.

Thus, in the case of the world's creation both the material cause (*upādāna-kāraṇa*) and the efficient cause (*nimitta-kāraṇa*) are seen as God or *Ātmā* in Vedānta. In this sense *Ātmā* is considered the *abhinna-nimitta-upādāna-kāraṇa* (the material cause and efficient cause in one) of the world. The words, "You are the Creator" and "You are the Subtance of which all creation is made" of this verse, put together, reflect this position of Vedānta.

You Are the Creation

The act of creation itself or the emanation of the effect from its cause is another factor that forms part of this creation context. How an effect emanates from a cause, or how the cause-effect relationship is to be understood in a logically tenable way, has always been a perplexing problem for almost all philosophers. Taking for granted this relationship being the firm basis on which the science of logic is itself built upon, explaining the very same relationship in terms of logic would beg the question. This relationship could otherwise be conceived as the act of creation. It was seen earlier in the last verse to be effected by the Glory of God. We have just seen how the emanation of the world happens within the being of *Ātmā*. This *Ātmā* and the God conceived here being one and the same, the act of creation cannot be seen other than in God, other than as the God's Glory. Hence the words, "You are the creation."

You Are the Myriads of Created Things

The world (*prapañca*) is the effect. It emanates from God as a result of the act of creation that takes place within Itself because of Its own Glory. Where does this effect exist after its emanation? We get a clear answer in the analogy of the ocean's waves that we have already examined. Waves, as the effects, have no being apart from their cause water; ornaments have no existence other than in gold. Likewise, the world does not have being anywhere else than in God, other than as forms fleetingly assumed by God. Put otherwise, what appears as the world is God Itself. Therefore the words, "You are the myriads of created things."

The water of the ocean does not really remain without waves that arise on its surface; gold does not exist without having some form, none lasting, like ornaments, coins, nuggets or even dust. Such golden forms and the gold as substance, though understandable as separate, cannot really exist apart as separate objects, for the two always remain inseparable; it is impossible for one to exist without the other. Related likewise are the one *Ātmā* or God and the created forms. The two exist non-dually. Intuitively perceiving this non-duality is the crux of the Advaita Philosophy (the philosophy of non-dualism). God as the eternal Reality, as related to this context, is called *sat* (Existence or Reality) and the fleeting forms it assumes or the created things, *bhāva* (manifest forms) in the *Bhagavad-Gītā.* This basic book of Vedānta makes the above-said point poignantly clear as follows:

nāsato vidyate bhāvo
nābhāvo vidyate sataḥ ।
ubhayor api dṛṣṭo 'ntast-
anayos tattvadarśibhiḥ ॥ — II. 16

The unreal does not assume manifest forms; no absence of manifest forms is in the Real. The inner secret with regard to these two is perceived only by those endowed with a penetrating intuitive eye.

Narayana Guru also makes clear the very same point when he says,

cid eva nānad ābhāti
citaḥ param ato nahi ।
yacca nābhāti tad asad
yad asat tanna bhāti ca ॥ — *Darśana-Mālā* II

Consciousness (*cit*) alone and nothing else
Manifests as the world.
Nothing higher than Consciousness exists.
That which does not manifest
As the world is unreal;
That which is unreal cannot
Manifest as the world either.

In other words, an unreal God never assumes the form of the world, and no absence of the manifest form of the world is in God either. We have only to train ourselves to perceive God alone in the world we see, and the world in God.

Instantaneous Creation

We have come across a few theories of creation in our study. Likewise there are many other creation theories propounded by different schools of thought.

Though such various theories prevail even within Vedānta in regard to creation, the differences among them seem to vanish when we notice that God or *Ātmā* is pure and unconditioned Consciousness alone. Arriving at this perception is what the *Aitareya Upaniṣad* ends with. Its concluding words are *prajñānam brahma* (*Brahman* is Consciousness), which form one of the *mahāvākya*s (great dicta) of Vedānta. Narayana Guru also gives a topmost place to this aspect of the Absolute throughout his philosophical poems. Above all, the poem *Aṛivu* (Consciousness Examined) that is included in this volume is purely meant to reveal the essence of Vedānta from the point of view in which the ultimate Reality is *Aṛivu* or Consciousness alone. We have already seen in our comments on *Aṛivu,* particularly on verse 1, how everything is but Consciousness alone variously manifesting.

It is natural for Consciousness to function in terms of knowing, imagining and the like. It is the one unconditioned Consciousness that assumes the forms of fleeting ideas and imaginations one after another. Such manifest forms of Consciousness in Indian Philosophy are known as *bhāna*s. These *bhāna*s could take a gross or subtlest form. Assuming the subtle, causal and *turīya* forms are also possible as Guru describes in the *Bhāna-Darśana* (Vision by *bhāna*s) of his *Darśana-Mālā* (chapter V). Oneself being the knower is one such ideation, and the other being the known. How do such ideations appear even as gross material objects? Guru virtually says, "It is the gross ideation (*sthūla-saṅkalpanā*) of the Consciousness-Reality in its attempt to actualize and see all the potentials hiding within Itself. Of course, there is an element of mystery in this." In Vedānta, the *māyā*-theory was designed to admit this mystery.

All such theories are merely some kind of explanation we formulate with our thinking minds to make understandable the various phenomena we encounter or to explain certain scriptural passages. Even these theories are conditioned manifest forms of the one Consciousness. The prevalence of all such theories, including those of Vedānta, in no way affects the real and mysterious being of God or *Ātmā* and Its creative self-manifestation; It always remains one and unruffled.

We always yearn to know even this Reality by making use of our logically trained searching mind. This mind merely is a minute fragment of a conditioned form of the one unconditioned Consciousness. No wonder then that such a mind fails to comprehend the one Reality that manifests as everything. But on looking inwardly at our own being with an intuitively trained mind, we feel ourselves being filled with the being of God, necessitating no need to know God as an object. "I am God indeed" is the reality one then realizes. This is what the *mahā-vākya, aham brahma asmi* (I am *Brahman*) signifies. *Sarvam khalvidam brahma* (Everything here indeed is *Brahman*), yet another *mahā-vākya,* also reveals the same vision.

In short, the act of creation, the creator, the things created, and the Substance for creation are all thus different functional modes of one and the same Consciousness-Reality, which really is inconceivable and ineffable.

The next verse brings in the *māyā*-factor that causes Consciousness to emanate as everything subtle and gross, mental and physical.

Verse 6

nīyallo māyayum māyā-
viyum māyā-vinodanum ।
nīyallo māyaye nīkkis-
sāyujyam nalkum āryanum ॥

You indeed are *māyā,*
The maker of *māyā* too,
As also the enjoyer thereof.
You are even the noble one who
Removes the very same *māyā*
To grant us the state of Supreme Union.

You Indeed Are Māyā

We, in our comments on verse 4 above, have examined in detail, how *māyā* is inseparably one with God and how God is the maker of *māyā.*

As was noticed earlier, it is the primeval desire in God to unfold as everything that results in the creation of the world. How such a desire becomes materialized as the gross world is a mystery indeed. The necessity of explaining this mystery is why the seers postulated the idea of *māyā*. Thus it is a man-made theory. But the very theory involves the notion that *māyā* is God-made. The Reality that underlies the being of God, of the seers, of everything, is one and the same. So to say that God is the maker of *māyā* and that humans are the makers of *māyā* are equally true.

Let us see how *māyā* is of our own making from yet another point of view:

It is Sunday. I am sitting alone in the *āśrama*. A few children below 12 years, all smile and approach me. I can see from the badges they wear that they belong to the Sathya Sai Movement. I read from their faces that they want to ask me some questions.

I said: It seems you want to ask me something.

They: Yes Swāmījī. Have you seen Bhagavān Sathya Sai Baba?

I : No!

They: Then, which is the Bhagavān you have seen?

First I became a little bit confused. Then I asked, "Where does *Bhagavān* exist?"

A girl: Everywhere.

A boy: In our mind.

I : Then where should we look for *Bhagavān*? Is it enough to look within us? Would it not be *Bhagavān* that we see there? If *Bhagavān* exists everywhere as everything, is it not *Bhagavān* that we see around us?

They: Swāmījī, what you say is true. But we always forget it. Swāmījī, why is it so?

This forgetfulness in us is caused by *māyā*. Even when we constantly and directly see the modes of the one ultimate Reality alone everywhere, we think we are seeing the world. Then I think of myself as the perceiver of the world. I then develop some likes and dislikes in what I perceive. I like anything that gives me pleasure and dislike anything that obstructs my ability to have pleasure, as well as anything that gives me pain. This ultimately results in the feeling that I am lost in the *saṁsāra sāgara* or *bhavābdhi*, instead of seeing God alone in everything and in myself, and thus enjoying the Supreme Happiness of eternal union with God (*sāyujya*). Such a predicament in life is termed "embracing the demonic nature" in the *Bhagavad-Gītā* when it says,

> *na mām duṣkṛtino mūḍhāḥ prapadyante narādhamāḥ* ।
> *māyayāpahṛta-jñānā āsuram bhāvam āśritāḥ* ॥
>
> — VII. 15
>
> The evil-doers, the foolish, the lowest among men — they do not attain Me, for with wisdom taken away by *māyā*, they embrace the demonic nature.

The Nature of *Māyā*

The analogy traditionally used in Vedānta to clarify the nature of *māyā*, is of the rope and snake. Narayana Guru also uses it on many occasions in his various works. People become frightened on seeing a piece of rope at twilight, mistaking it for a snake. Likewise, on seeing Reality or God in Its various manifest forms, one thinks of It to be the world. When shedding some light upon the rope, it then appears to be the rope itself. Likewise, on bringing in the lamp of wisdom, the ultimate Reality or God appears as real. Whether seen as a rope or snake, what is real is the rope alone. Likewise, whether seen as God or the world, God always remains God.

When the wrong understanding of the Real gives place to the right understanding, our knowledge of the Real alone undergoes change; not the nature of the Real; It always remains the changeless Real. The very same Real, as Consciousness in essence, inheres of the potential to manifest either as the right kind of understanding or as the wrong kind of understanding of Itself. The former manifest form of Consciousness is known as *vidyā,* and the latter *avidyā.* That means, the potential to create the illusory vision of the world is also inherent in the one Reality or *Ātmā*. Narayana Guru, by way of clarifying this point, says in his *Ātmopadeśa Śatakam*:

> Seen from one side, activities go on;
> These seem to be real becouse of *avidyā.*
> Seen from the other, unconditioned
> Conscionsness alone exists,
> And this is the realm of *vidyā.*
> It is *māyā* that makes the Real
> Appear always two-sided.
> The enlightened awakening
> That transcends this duality
> Alone yields the *turīya* state. — v. 72

In short, *māyā's* function also is inherent in the Real or God. Hence the words, "You indeed are *māyā*."

The Maker of *Māyā* (*māyāvī*)

The original word (*māyāvī*) used by Guru here, as was noted earlier, means both "the maker of *māyā*" and "a magician." Comparing the creation of the world by *Ātmā* from Itself, as seen before, to a magician's performance was an idea very dear to Guru. In both cases, behind the creation could be seen a wilful imagination.

What does a magician do when he performs his skill? Nothing new is created by him. He simply imagines certain things. Such imaginations of his are simply illusorily seen by the spectators as if real. That means, they see nothing other than the imagination of the magician. Likewise, the skilful and wilful imagination of God is what we observe as the world and even as ourselves. Thus the subjective aspect, the objective aspect and even their mutual relation resulting in the experience of knowing, are all so. Because we are all part of that imagination materialized, we do not realize that it is but illusory visions that we are seeing and that these visions are really facets of God's manifest form.

Present in the magician's mind are certain wilful imaginations that form part of his innate or created traits (*vāsanās*). These traits are capable of creating the feeling in others that what they see is real, when truly it is the magician's imagination alone. Likewise is the wilful imagination of the Great Magician, God. This Latter Magician, in essential content, as we have clearly seen earlier in our commentaries on the other works in this volume, is pure and unconditioned Consciousness alone. The innate traits in this Consciousness are given expression to by Itself so as to look real. Such is the nature of the *māyā* of this Great *māyāvī*, God.

Each of us, and each entity in this world, is felt by us to have their own form as well as their own name. We have no idea of the forms of objects other than as we experience them, and no experience exists apart from consciousness. The names given to these forms are also creations of our own minds. Thus both forms and names have no existence other than as manifest forms of Consciousness, and this Consciousness is nothing other than God. As long as the nature of God's Mind, or rather God as Mind or Consciousness, remains unseen by us, we continue to think of this world of forms and names and ourselves who see it, to exist on their own. But on becoming enlightened of God's Nature, we see only God's wilful mind in everything. Clarifying this point, Guru says in his *Darśana-Mālā*,

> *vāsanā-mayam evādāv*
> *āsid idam athaḥ prabhuḥ* ।
> *asṛjan māyayā svasya*
> *māyāvīvākhilam jagat* ॥ — v.I.2

> The entire world in the beginning,
> Remained in the Lord
> As pure *vāsanā* in essence.
> He, then, by his power
> To create illusory visions (*māyā*)
> Brought it forth
> As does a magician.

The very same innate trait (*vāsanā*), having become self-activated and thus active in itself, is called *prakṛti* (Nature), which literally means "that which does actions properly." The emergence of the world from this *prakṛti* is also compared by Guru to the unworldly attainments or psychic powers (*siddhis*) of a *yogī*. Guru says again in the *Darśana-Mālā*,

> *āsīt prakṛtir evedam*
> *yathā 'dau yogavaibhavaḥ* ।
> *vyatanod atha yogīva*
> *siddhijālam jagat-patiḥ* ॥ — v.I.6

> As *prakṛti* indeed was this world
> Existing in the beginning,
> Comparable to the psychic powers
> Attained through *yoga*.
> The Lord of the changeful world,
> Thereafter, unfolded it from Himself,
> Like a *yogī* who unfolds his
> Multitudinous psychic powers.

The same *vāsanā* was seen in the first verse of *Advaita Dīpikā* as the dream of God. (see *Advaita Dīpikā* that forms part of this volume). The analogy of *māyāvī* (magician) thus occupies an important place in the method adopted by Guru to clarify the nuances implied in the *māyā*-concept.

The creative urge in God, the unconditioned Consciousness, is mysterious indeed. How does it become possible for the innate traits (*vāsanās*) to assume the form of the gross, visible world? Had it been possible to answer this question, it would not be necessary to compare it to a magician's performance. Such is the nature of the *māyā*-urge (*māyā-vaibhava*). And God's capability is like that of the unworldly attainments of a *yogī* (*yoga-vaibhava*). There is a story in the *Yoga-Vāsiṣṭha,* the famous text that teaches Vedānta in story form, which makes clear how inexplicable *māyā* is.

The King Lavaṇa, when seated on his throne in the royal court, happened to doze off for a few moments during which he saw a dream. In it he underwent a long chain of adventures that lasted many years, beginning with a hunting expedition. Upon awakening he was enthusiastic to verify those events. He sent his men out to discover whether anything like the dream events had really occurred in the forest. They reported back that the exact same chain of events actually had happened. How did a dream, that too one that lasted only a few moments, become materialized into the long chain of events that lasted a whole lifetime? The only answer is that such is the mystery of *māyā.*

You are the Enjoyer of *Māyā (māyā-vinodan)*

The word *māyā-vinodan* is interpretable both as "the one who enjoys the magic performance," and "He who enjoys his own *māyā.*" The spectators of an ordinary magic show witness but sit apart from the magician and his illusory shows. But it is not so with the magic of God. In it, the enjoyers also form part of the illusory projection and thus are not different in essense from God, because the creations of God do not exist apart from God as we have already seen.

Why does God actively project from Itself such illusory manifest forms? Consciousness in essence, God cannot remain otherwise, for Consciousness (*cit* or *caitanya*) is no Consciousness if not functional. The functioning of *caitanya* is known as *cetanā.* Put otherwise, *caitanya* never exists without *cetanā.* The animating principle in each individual is also known as *cetanā.* The above fact is a daily experience of our own consciousnesses. It never remains functionless. Functional modes appear in it incessantly one after another. Even in deep sleep, we unconsciously experience the soundness of sleep, about which we declare the next morning.

Why is it so? It is easier to answer from the viewpoint of our own individual consciousness as an example. When ideas, imaginations, emotions and other functions occur in our consciousness, one after another, we really are enjoying the actualization of the infinite potentials hiding within it. These experiences of enjoyment (*ānanda*) depend on nothing else except consciousness, though most of us remain totally unconscious of it. But such a happiness is consciously felt, for example, when we successfully complete some hard earned project. Even then we are ignorant that this happiness is really the experience of the very *ānanda* content of one's own self that is also *cit* or consciousness in content. But upon scrutiny it becomes quite clear that it is a happiness experience that depends on nothing else. The same is the case with the one unconditioned Consciousness or God also. God enjoys Its own *ānanda*-content through the creation of the world from and within Itself, with Its own *sat* (Existence) aspect for the Substance, by making use of the *māyā* inherent in Its own *cit* (Consciousness) aspect. God, in short, enjoys Its own *māyā*. This reality in Indian mythology is termed as the *līlā* (sport) of *Bhagavān*.

We earlier elaborated on other aspects of this enjoyment of God (see page 172 of the present volume).

You Grant Us the State of Supreme Union
(sāyujyam nalkum āryan)

All of us thus really exist in the wilful imagination (*saṅkalpa*) of God. In other words, the Substance in our being is God Itself. If we do not train ourselves to see God alone as existing, then we are under the spell of *māyā*. Be it humans, the Vedic gods of heaven, beings of other worlds, or even the three chief deities *trimūrti*s (Brahmā, Viṣṇu, and Śiva, the Creator, Sustainer and Destroyer respectively of the world), seeing many as real is caused by *māyā*. Narayana Guru, in his *Kāli Nāṭakam* (The Dance-Drama of the Black Goddess), where the one God is assumed to have the form of Kāli, says,

> Mahādeva (Śiva) and Brahmā too
> And all other gods, are trapped
> In your *māyā*, a mystery indeed!

As long as we are under the spell of *māyā*, we live ignorant of the one Reality in us; we are, so to speak, in a state of sleep in which we are yet to awaken. Only a person who has already awoken from this sleep, either through the Grace of God or through the contact with an enlightened *guru*, and who has seen the one Reality in themselves and everything, is capable of awakening us from our long sleep. Until such an awakening happens, we go on seeing dreams in our sleep, and remain in that state thinking that all such dreams are real.

The person who is thus capable of wakening us up realizes, what is Real in him or her is God. He or she thus sees God alone existing functionally in himself or herself and in everything. This is the sense in which the Upaniṣadic dictum says *brahmaveda brahma eva bhavati* (The knower of *Brahman* is *Brahman* indeed — *Muṇḍaka Upaniṣad,* 3.2.9). In other words, the person of God-Realization is God Itself, only that God in this case assumes the form of a human being. Such a person is known as a *guru.* Then, to say that it was a *guru* that awakened the person from his or her slumber or that it was done by God is to say the same.

God created us because of Its own mysterious power of *māyā.* The very same God also rescues us from this *māyā* and proffers us *sāyujya* (the state of Supreme Oneness with God), the union in which a *guru* always lives.

Verse 7

nī satyam jñānam ānandam
nī tanne vartamānavum ।
bhūtavum bhāviyum verall
otum moẓiyum orkil nī ॥

You are Existence, Consciousness and Value-Experience,
You are the present and the past;
And the future is no other than you.
Even these spoken words, well considered,
Are nothing but you.

You are Existence (*nī satyam*)

A traditionally acknowledged definition of *Brahman* in terms of what It is, as against what It is not, is *saccidānanda.* It is a compound word in which *sat, cit* and *ānanda* are combined together. *Sat* means

"Existence" or "that which ultimately exists," *cit* means "Consciousness," and *ānanda* "Value-Experience" or "Happiness." The scriptural support for this definition comes from the *Taittirīya Upaniṣad* in its words *satyam jñānam anantam brahma* (2.1.1) (*Brahman* is the Real, Knowledge, the Infinite). Adding *ānandam* to these three defining factors, the *Sarvopaniṣad* defines *Brahman* as *satyam jñānam anantam ānandam brahma* (*Brahman* is the Real, Knowledge, the Infinite and Happiness). The word *anantam* was later dropped, as *jñānam* or *cit* and *ānandam* together virtually connotes *anantam* also, and thus the definition was fixed as *sat-cit-ānanda* (*saccidānanda*). This revised definition of *Brahman* has found place in the *Vāsudeva Upaniṣad* (3), *Rāmottara-tāpanī Upaniṣad* (5), *Nṛsimha-pūrva-tāpanī Upaniṣad* (6), and such other later, minor Upaniṣads.

The great Śaṅkara insists that the three defining factors (*sat, cit* and *ānanda*) are not to be treated as the defining attributes of *Brahman,* but as the three together forming the essential content of *Brahman.* Narayaṇa Guru also is very fond of this definition as can be seen explicitly and implicitly in many of his longer philosophical poems. Guru, in his *Darśana-Mālā*, for instance, uses this compound word itself, thus,

sarvam hi saccidānandam
neha nānāsti kiñcana — II.10

Everything is *saccidānanda* indeed; the many here have no being at all.

It is also apparent that what the *Taittirīya Upaniṣad* means by *satyam* is no other than the *sat* of the later Upaniṣads. In the present prayer Guru therefore confidently replaces *sat* with *satyam* for metrical convenience. Let us now examine these three terms separately.

The Real or Existence (*satyam*)

Satyam is defined by Śaṅkara thus: *yad rūpeṇa yan niścitam tad rūpam na vyabhicarati tat satyam* (*Taittirīya Upaniṣad,* commentary 2.1.1). (That which never changes its intrinsic nature that is truly ascertained to be its own, is the Real). *Satyam,* in other words, is that which exists eternally, i.e., in the past, present and future, and everywhere with no spatial limitation and also with no entity-wise limitation. All that appear and disappear are not to be treated as Real. We the knowers also have no eternal existence. But this only means that our bodily being which constantly changes, along with our personal identity as so and so, as the son or daughter of so and so, does not exist for ever, and therefore is not Real. Still, this does not mean that I do not exist at all. I have the unbroken experience of existing despite all the bodily changes like growing old. These contradictory experiences only mean that the nature of my Real being is not what I think of myself as in day-to-day (transactional) life. It is something that transcends all such bodily changes and relativistic factors. Likewise, something beyond the appearance of everything exists in everything. That is the Real in them.

What then is the real and unchanging nature of the Real in us that we feel to exist unbroken? In order to discriminate the unreal apparent aspect from the Real content in us, let us take the example of a golden ornament. The real content in it is gold. An ornament is just a form the gold assumes. The ornament form, in this case, is the body aspect, and the gold substance the Real. The ornament form is alterable, but the gold-substance is unalterable and indestructible. Likewise, the body aspect of our being undergoes changes and is mortal, but the Real in it is changeless and immortal.

Gold becomes perceptible only by virtue of an assumed and destructible form. This form is really not of the gold, but is given by the goldsmith. Gold really has no form of its own, and thus is invisible. But it cannot exist without a visible form given either by us or by nature. Gold does not become non-existent just because it is invisible. Without the existence of gold no one can see a golden ornament. Where does that indestructible and invisible gold exist? We simply know that it exists. The whereabouts of its existence thus is in our knowledge, as knowledge.

This is the case of examining gold as separated out from everything else. Various such elements and their compounds constitute this world. Just as the substance of the element gold exists in our knowledge, all the other elements, their compounds and the world, their aggregate, have to exist in their pure state in our knowledge alone, in our consciousness alone.

We began this search with an enquiry about our own existence. This existence is not merely like that of gold which is but inert matter. Ours, on the other hand, is a living existence, a dynamic existence, a creatively enduring existence. A very subtle aspect called mind also functions in it. This mind is also as fleeting as the body aspect, and these two are of such a nature that one does not exist without the other in us. These two, in modern science and psychology, are termed mind and matter, the Sanskrit equivalents being *cit* and *jaḍa*. Of a perishing nature, both are considered to be part of the *śarīra* (body, literally "the perishable") aspect of existence, as explicitly stated in verses XIII.5 & 6 of the *Bhagavad-Gītā*. Then the real *sat* or what ultimately exists in our being is that invisible and unthinkable Reality that manifests grossly as the physical aspect of our existence and subtly as the mental aspect. The nature of this Reality was meditated on in verse 3 of the

Brahmavidyā Pañcakam and in our commentary earlier (see pages 38 to 48 above). The mind-matter duality is of no relevance in that one Reality. The same Reality (*sat*) is conceived as God in this prayer.

You are Consciousness (*nī jñānam*)

The Reality (*sat*) that is beyond the mind-matter duality, and that assumes the forms of both mind and matter in Its creative self-unfoldment, is pure and unconditioned Consciousness (*cit*) in essence, referred to as *jñānam* in this verse. How it is so has been made sufficiently clear earlier (see pages 44 and 127 to 134 of the present volume). Our search for the Reality in ourselves ends up in the conclusion that we are *cit* or *jñāna* in essence; and so too is everything else because all these are but various apparent phenomena just like us. The one all-underlying Consciousness is the God conceived here. Hence the words "You are Consciousness" (*nī jñānam*).

You are Value-Experience (*nī ānandam*)

The conviction I arrive at is that everything and myself are one unconditioned Consciousness (*cit*) in essence. All that appear and disappear are but that Reality's evanescent manifestations. This conviction fills my being with the contentment, "Nothing more remains to be known. I am not only Happy, but I am Happiness Itself." This Happiness is everlasting. It is not affected by the vagaries of actual life that cause pain and pleasure. This Happiness (*ānanda*) is felt nowhere else than in my own Consciousness content (*cit* that is *sat*). *Sat, cit* and *ānanda* thus not only become interchangeable terms, but merge together to make myself merge in It.

This *ānanda*-experience is not merely an effect caused by our knowledge of the Real. Realizing the Real or God in the way just stated, becomes transformed itself into the Happiness experience. This Happiness is not merely a Bliss. It helps us to perceive both pains and pleasures as the manifest forms of an opposite nature, of one and the same *ānanda*-content of God, or of ourselves. We thus inwardly experience the same Happiness when facing both painful and pleasurable situations of life. This explains why the word *ānanda* is rendered here as "Value-Experience." The *Bhagavad-Gītā* considers this experience in which happinesses and sufferings are treated equally, as that of a *yogī* of action (see verse II.38). Narayana Guru also in his *Svānubhava-Gīti* (Lyric of Ecstatic Self-Experience) says,

> The dance-drama no sooner is perceived
> Than one finds oneself
> Firmly and neutrally existing.
> He who exists thus
> For a long time uninterrupted
> Lives in Happiness. — v. 15

Admittedly everyone does not search for the Real that is experienced as unconditioned, eternal Happiness. Most seek after life's ordinary pleasures like being with one's husband or wife, having good children, owning wealth, having a comfortable life, being socially recognized in high positions, and enjoying entertainments. Possessing all such need not make them really content in life. At least some of them may even feel that something is lacking in them that would make life really and lastingly happy and meaningful. Sometimes this will bring on a feeling of disappointment with life. Such an uneasiness arises because they have a fundamentally wrong notion of happiness, which itself ensues from not knowing themselves. Not knowing oneself in the true sense is always accompanied by not possessing oneself. Possessing anything other than oneself does not ensure real and lasting happiness. On the other hand, possessing oneself by knowing oneself properly, yields full contentment in life and fills one with the feeling that one already possesses everything because one then sees oneself in everything. Such people enjoy the enduring Happiness-content of the Self, in spite of life's natural alternation between suffering and pleasure. The essential content of the Self and that of God, as we have already seen, is one and the same. Therefore it is said, "You are *ānanda*."

You are the Present, Past and Future

The one Reality, *saccidānanda,* is not something static and lifeless. Its existence is a living one, a dynamic one, one of constant progression. The infinite potentials in It incessantly find expression as urged by the *karma*-principle inherent in Itself. As a result, we came into being, everything came into being, old beings disappear, and new ones emerge. This process appears as the contiuned but changeful existence of the world. Actions (*karma*s) go on everywhere in the world because its being is simply a fragment of the ever active Real. These *karma*s find expression as events in nature, and we feel that such events take place in time and space.

Time (*kāla*)

Let us think of time first. Time is customarily divided into the past, present and future. We think, the events in the world pass through time which we even attempt to measure. Every event that has already happened is of the past, and every event yet to happen hides in the future. As I pen these words, every letter I have already scribbled has gone into the past and every letter yet to be written is part of the future. What was in the past extends backwards endlessly. Likewise, what hides in the future also stretches to the endless unknown. Then the present is simply a measurementless point or thin membrane where the unknown past and the unknown future meet as if from two sides. This present is, as it were, non-existent.

Let us look at time from the point of view of life-experience. We live in the present. Living either in the past or in the future is not possible. We can only remember the past events. This remembering also is a life experience of the present. Likewise, we habitually look forward with new hopes to the future. This looking forward also is an experience of the present. Thus, as a life-experience, neither the past nor the future has being, only the experience of the present continues endlessly. The present as a life experience, thus, is eternal. Such is the mutually exclusive nature of the past, present and future.

Time is called *kāla* in Sanskrit and Malayālam alike. The word literally means, "that which can be counted or reckoned," or "that which diffuses and mixes up things." Time, being a mysterious factor, could even be meditated on as the Absolute, as the *Bhagavad-Gītā* admits when it says, *kālaḥ kalayatam aham* (among those who diffuse and mix up things, I am time) (X.30). Mixing up things (*kalanā*) or changing one state of existence of things to another in which process their mixing up spontaneously happens, goes on incessantly in nature as part of its total system of existence. Unless this *kalanā* takes place, there would be no time-sense. *Kalanā* takes place only with something that exists, called *dravya* (basic material). Considering time also as one of such *dravya*s is admissible to the Nyāya Philosophy (Logic) of India. Such a time is so mysterious that it puzzles even the most modern theoretical scientists. What then is this time?

As we have just seen, the time-sense has relevance only when events of mixing up things happen. Let us imagine a nature where everything including minds stand still with no action or motion at all. Then there would be no experience of the passing of time either. Time too would then stand still.

Let us imagine that events do happen in nature, but no mind is present to observe it. Then also, the experience of time's passing is not possible because all experiences have to take place in some mind or consciousness. Time-sense, thus, is felt by a knowing mind that interlinks the events occurring one after another continuously. In other words, time is a way in which two or more events are interlinked in our minds. God then is the one Consciousness that interlinks all the events in nature so that it could have an overall flowing functional system. Therefore it could be said that time exists in God or that the universal Consciousness Itself is felt by us as time or *kāla*.

Space (*deśa*)

Another sense we have in our worldly experiences is that of space. This sense also is related to events. We measure the distance between two objects or places. The two objects or places existing separately are two events in nature. We try to relate these together in our understanding when we measure the distance between the two. That means, the space-sense is also related to events.

Then what is the difference between time and space, which undoubtedly are different? Our attempt to relate events vertically in our understanding creates the time-sense. Things related horizontally, on the other hand, create the space-sense in us.

Relating events thuswise is done by our own consciousness, and thus both time and space are creations of our consciousness or mind, and do not have existence of their own. This consciousness, in its universal dimension, is called God. Thus we easily understand how time and space have no existence apart from God. Hence the words, "You are the present and the past, and the future is no other than you."

Even These Spoken Words are but You (*otum moẓiyum orkil nī*)

Our attempt to understand God has finally ended upon realizing that whatever is knowable and unknowable, is nothing but God having assumed various forms. These speculations were penned by Guru by making use of words; I am commenting on those words again by doing the same. Where do these words well up from? From our own minds, from our own consciousnesses. Languages and words are devices created by human minds to give expression to what they feel within. These, thus, are rooted in human minds, and in essential content are human minds. Through these, human minds find expression as well. Not only in expressing ideas, but even in the formulation of ideas within, words play a major role. Unconsciously though, we give shape to our ideas with the help of the words of our mother tongue or some other language we are familiar with. One of the Peace Invocations of the Upaniṣads, therefore, says:

> *vāṅ me manasi pratiṣṭhitā*
> *mano me vāci pratiṣṭhitam*
>
> My words are well founded in the mind and the mind is well founded on words.

No word exists without a meaning and no meaning is a meaning without a word to signify it. The two always are thus inseparably one.

Just as everything phenomenal appears from one ultimate Reality, here called God, all the words of all the languages are also thought of as the various manifest forms of the one primeval Word of words that signifies God. This Word of words is symbolized linguistically by ॐ in India, pronounced *OṀ* (*AUṀ*). It is also known as *praṇava*. The *Yoga-Sūtras* of Patañjali, in recognition of this, says, *tasya vācakaḥ praṇavaḥ* (He — God — is denoted by *praṇava*) (I.27). The *Māṇḍūkya Upaniṣad* also begins with the words, *auṁ ity etad akṣaram idam sarvam* (*auṁ*, this imperishable syllable is all this). The Upaniṣad then goes on to say that whatever was in the past, whatever is in the present, whatever will be in future, all these are nothing but *auṁ*, and that which transcends the three tenses is also *auṁ*. We have already seen how all these are nothing but one Reality or God variously manifesting. St. John's Gospel in the Bible, likewise, begins with the statement, "In the beginning there was the word; the word was with God; the word was God." All these show that the oneness of God and words is universally recognized in all spiritual traditions.

The most sublime and unique gift of mankind is the ability to give expression to their feelings and ideas through words, written or spoken, through some language. A well recognized principle in Indian Philosophy is that the world-experience of humans is not simply confined to the realm of sense-perception. We directly perceive only forms or *rūpa*s. Along with such forms also come names or *nāma*s, because perceptual experiences find expression through words. Therefore it is thought, the world is comprised of *nāma*s and *rūpa*s (names or words, and forms). The world of perceptual forms, therefore, has a corresponding world of verbal expression. This latter world is known as *śabda-prapañca; śabda* meaning "words" and *prapañca*, "world."

All that constitutes the perceptual world, as we have already seen, are self-expressions of the creative urge in the one Reality or God. The same urge exists in everything thus created also, including human beings. Thus it is the creative urge of God that finds expression in humans as their creative urge. This urge within also assumes the form of the words that convey ideas and feelings. It is for this reason that by this urge of God humans find joy in expressing themselves through words and in creating a world of words. In other words, nothing other than God or the one unconditioned Consciousness expressing Itself creatively happens both in the creation of the perceptual world and the creation of the world of words. All is nothing more than a sportive self-display of the one Consciousness.

Verse 8

akavum puṟavum tiṅṅum
mahimāv ārnna nin padam ।
pukaẓtunnu ñaṅṅal aṅnu
bhagavāne jayikkuka ॥

Completely filling both within and without
Is the state of your grandeur,
That state we hail!
O God, sucecss be yours!

The knower and the known world are always differentiated in all our ordinary experience of knowledge. This in philosophy is known as the subject-object duality. The subject is felt to be a mind within us, and the object to be something existing outside. From the deliberations gone through so far in this commentary, it has already become evident that the real content in the subject is God alone, and the same is true with the object. That one Reality appears as both, is a basic stand of Vedānta. In the very first verse of the *Ātmopadeśa Śatakam*, Guru, by way of clarifying the main theme of the work of one hundred verses, says,

> . . . the core Reality that transcends all knowledge, that irradiates both as the apparent form of the knower and the objects external at the same time . . .

The object meditated on in this prayer admittedly is God. Thinking of God as an object, as we have noticed in our conments on verse 1, is more natural with prophetic religions, whereas meditating on God as the Reality in oneself is considered the proper way of spiritual discipline (*sādhanā*) in Vedānta. What is Real in one's own being doubtlessly is inside, and the God seated in the most high is felt to be external to us. The Real non-dual God is what assumes the forms of both at one and the same time. The *Īśa Upaniṣad*, in its *mantra* 17, recognizing this oneness, says, "Whosoever is that person (yonder) that also I am." The very same non-dual oneness of God is referred to in the present verse as "completely filling both within and without is the state of your grandeur."

Let us return to my conversation with the children who visited me at the *āśrama*, narrated as part of the comments on verse 5. To the question, "Where does *Bhagavān* exist?" one of the children answered, "In our minds," and another said, "Everywhere." Both were right. They also admit that this fact is always forgotten by them. What would happen if they did not forget this? They would see God's grandeur both within their minds and as existing everywhere. Each of them would see God alone in themselves and everything, and they would naturally love everything as they do themselves. Loving oneself is natural. This love becomes extended to everything upon seeing God alone in oneself and everything.

That State We Hail!

The more we think and the more we gain knowledge in the ordinary sense, the more we gain clarity. But this is not so with the knowledge of God, the Reality that fills both what is inside and what is outside. The more we think about It, the more obscure and mysterious It becomes. The person who has realized that Reality, in fact, remains totally silent with regard to Its real nature, because It is so vague and wondrous an experience that no word is capable of expressing It. For this reason, this kind of knowledge is considered to "transcend all knowledge" (see verse 1 of *Ātmopadeśa Śatakam*). The *Taittirīya Upaniṣad* says about this ineffable experience, "whence words return along with the mind, not attaining It" (2.4.1). In the case of a person who has not attained that state, but is aware of such a state, it is natural with him or her to praise that grandeur of God as done here.

O God, Success be Yours!

When praying to God or *Bhagavān*, the implicit yearning in the supplicant is to make the perfection of all the glorious qualities of God his or her own, namely, *jñāna* (wisdom), *śakti* (power), *aiśvarya* (controlling power), *bala* (strength), *vīrya* (vitality) and *tejas* (brightness), as we have already noticed in our comments on verse 1 above. But no such imparting of any quality from *Bhagavān* to *bhakta* is intended here, as *Bhagavān* alone is seen within him or her by the *bhakta*. In that case, God's attainment of success always becomes his or her success also. God's glory is thus felt here in actual life. In biblical terms, this would be the experience of the kingdom of heaven coming to the earth.

Verse 9

jayikkuka mahādevā
dīnāvana-parāyaṇā ।
jayikkuka cidānandā
dayā-sindho jayikkuka ॥

Success be yours, O Great Lord Divine,
Ever intent on saving those in mysery,
Success be yours, O the one

Consciousness and Value-experience in essence
O the ocean of mercy,
Succese be yours!

O Great Lord Divine (*mahā-deva)*

The word *deva* means "the bright one," and denotes a divine being. *Mahā* means, "the great." God, the greatest of all that is divine, as we have already seen, is pure Effulgence in essence, the effulgence of unconditioned Consciousness. All that apparently manifests here are nothing more than the modes that great Effulgence. Hence the epithet *mahā-deva* used here to address God.

God being such, Its success is itself the supplicants' success also, for their existence is not separate from God's

Ever Intent on Saving Those in Misery (*dīna-avana-parāyaṇa*)

Dīna means those in trouble," *avana,* "to save" and *parāyaṇa,* "always involved in." Thinking of God as always intent on giving salvation to those in miserable situations, is very common among the religious. In the usual course, people turn religious when facing troubles or when some seeking something that is difficult to acquire. It is then that they seek God's help. Such people are called *ārtās* (those who grieve). According to the *Bhagavad-Gītā* (VII.16), four kinds of people take refuge in God. They are *ārtās* (those who grieve), *jijñāsus* (seekers of wisdom), *arthārthīs* (those whose desire is for wealth), and *jñānins* (the enlightened).

The one who prays here evidently is not desirous of wealth. Even with regard to the daily needs like food and clothing, he or she simply admits that God already provides us with all such needs. Neither is seen any mention of miseries here — except that of being lost in the ocean of *saṁsāra* — in the prayer. Being salvaged from the above-said ocean becomes possible only with attaining wisdom; and this attainment has been maintained as the aim by the supplicant all through the present text. Thus this prayer could be treated as that of a seeker (*jijñāsu*).

Why should a *jñānin,* a person who has already realized God, also meditate on God? A *jñānin* really is the person who is well aware of the unknowability of God's Glory. This unknowability makes him or her an adorer of It, even while being one with It. Such is his or her way of meditating upon God.

Life is felt to be full of miseries only when one lives ignorant of the real meaning of life. On knowing that meaning, one realizes that what was till then thought of as miserable is merely the *māyā* of God finding expression. The ultimate salvation from all those miseries is felt when one becomes a *jñānin,* the only favour prayed for here. God, thus, wisdom Itself in essence, is the one who ultimately saves us from all miseries of life.

Consciousness and Value-Experience in Essence (*cidānanda*)

We have already seen in verse 7, the sense in which God is defined as *saccidānanda.* The success of such a God, from whom we do not exist separate, is naturally felt by us as our own success also. But, instead of addressing It as *saccidānanda,* God is simply referred to here as *cidānanda,* by dropping the word *sat* from it. Admittedly this is the context in which the success of God is prayed for. To be ever successful implies existence as well; and this must be the reason for doing so.

The Ocean of Mercy (*dayā-sindhu*)

To conceive God as full of mercy is very natural with those who take refuge in God, and God is the ocean of mercy in their perception. They, when doing so, mostly have a concept, of mercy that is only the mercy of humans, never the mercy of God. Do they, who take refuge in God alone, always feel the mercy of God? Don't they experience, at least sometimes, a merciless God also, particularly when they face disasters? Many have cursed the wrath of God, at least very occasionally.

As noticed in our comments on verse 1, the word *daivam* of this prayer signifies God, which in the original Sanskrit means, "fate" and "chance element." The chance element may cause anything in nature. Some of those events might be felt to be unfavourable or even disastrous, and thus be a curse of God, at least from the viewpoint of some. This feeling is guided by their personal interests alone, and not by any proper understanding of God. We have to train ourselves to look at the events in our own lives from the point of view of the one Consciouness that systematizes the existence of the total nature. Then alone we realize that it is the mercy of God itself that we sometimes feel to be unbearable events in life.

This peculiarity of God's mercy could be seen as forming the central theme of the famous epic poem *Rāmāyaṇa* of India. Rāma must leave his palace just at the moment fixed for his anointing as the crown-prince, only to live in the forest for twelve years, where Rāvaṇa abducted his wife Sītā. The pitiable lamentations of both Rāma and Sītā are all heart-rending scenes. All this finally results in Rāma killing Rāvaṇa, which by then was an imminent necessity in order to bring the world back to its righteous order. Seen thus, all the unfoldment of the otherwise miserable events were devised by nature for a good intention. In other words, it was the merciful mind of God that worked out all those pitiful events also. This may similarly happen with all of us. Our unenlightened eyes do not see the merciful mind of God. We need an enlightened eye to see it.

On seeing God's mercy throughout our life, we also naturally become merciful in life in the true sense.

Verse 10

āẓam eṛum nin mahassām
āẓiyil ñaṅṅaḷ ākave ।
āẓaṇam vāẓaṇam nityam
vāẓaṇam vāẓaṇam sukham ॥

In the deep ocean of your Glory
Let us all become immersed,
There to dwell, dwell forever
In Felicity Supreme!

The prayer ends with the supplicants expressing a final wish: may all of us become immersed in the ocean of God's Glory, to attain identity with It, and to experience Its eternal Happiness known in India as *sāyujya,* which we noticed earlier in verse 6.

As was stated earlier in our comments on verse 1, this prayer began with imploring God to protect us as if from the most high. But as it ends, the prayer is for all of us to become immersed in the ocean of the God's Glory and to live one with It in eternal Happiness. This ocean apparently is here and now. The Real being of God too, as was seen earlier, is to be discovered by the supplicants as the real Substance in their own being. This Substance, in Vedānta, is known as *sat* (Existence). It assumes the forms of the supplicants and of everything here, and of the most high heaven. The supplicant attaining oneness with this *sat* is known as *sad-gati, gati* meaning "reaching" or "attaining." This *sad-gati* is not an experience of going upwards to transcend everything here, but is an experience of becoming one with That, which exists here endlessly, extending both in width and depth. In the *Kaṭha Upaniṣad,* this experience is likened to a drop of pure water falling in the ocean of pure water. This transformation in the supplicant comes about by imbibing the wisdom clarified between the first and the last verses. Let us remember that in the first verse the supplicant prays to be liberated from the ocean of suffering, and in the last verse to become merged in the ocean of God's Glory.

The supplicant's intention at the beginning of the prayer was to be saved from the *bhavābdhi* they found themselves in. The very same *bhavābdhi* also underwent a transformation, again because of the wisdom that became revealed to them from verses 2 to 9. Now they find themselves in the ocean of God's Glory from which they do not wish to escape, but to become immersed in and live forever in Supreme Happiness. Really it was this ocean of God's Glory, that is *sat-cit-ānanda,* that was mistaken in the beginning for *bhavābdhi* or the ocean of sufferings. Now the supplicants see themselves to be like small ripples that emerge and merge back in the ocean of God's Glory. All the ups and downs of life, all the sufferings and experiences of happiness of each ripple-like and short-lived being, are now seen merely as part of the wave-like movement going on in the ocean, as a sportive self-display of God. Now they pray to never leave this ocean.

Mahas

The word *mahas*, rendered here as "Glory," has many meanings. Of these "brightness," "hugeness," and "water" fit well within this context. God, as we now know clearly, is pure brightness in essence. Being the one all-inclusive Reality, how immense is the dimension of God's Glory needs no mention. The ocean represents God's Glory here, and the substance in the ocean is water. Thus the meaning "water" also is significant here.

Forever (*nityam*)

Devotees, in the usual course, pray to God only for favours hardly of lasting value. But the prayer of the supplicants here is not of that order. Their wish is for something of eternal value. The only favour of that order is the ultimate Liberation, known as *mukti*, *mokṣa* or *sāyujya*, which one can attain while living here and now. The very same experience of Liberation is poetically portrayed here as the supplicant's immersion in the occan of God's Glory and dwelling in It forever in Felicity Supreme.

O God, Felicity Supreme!

This prayer began with addressing God with the word "*daivame*" (O God), and ends with the word "*sukham*" (Happiness or Felicity Supreme). This Happiness, as we have just seen, is none other than that of Final Liberation. This Liberation or *sāyujya* is not merely a sublime principle to be understood properly, but is the supplicants' direct experience of *ānanda*, value-content of God, as their own *ānanda* or Happiness. This *ānanda* signifies both absolute Value and absolute Happiness together. This experience is an event in Consciousness (*cit*) which is really the essential content (*sat*) of the supplicants' own being as well as of God's being. *Saccidānanda*, therefore, is considered the defining content-factors of both oneself (or the Self) and of God. To experience oneself as this *saccidānanda* in essence is what Final Liberation means. The attainment of this Liberation is the goal prayed for, concluding this text. Thus the first and the last words put together *daivame sukham* (O God, Supreme Felicity) gives the sum and substance of the overall nature of this text, as well as what is to be ideally prayed for. The state of final merger prayed for here is portrayed by Guru in the concluding verse of *Ātmopadeśa Śatakam* as follows:

Neither that nor this am I,
Nor the meaning content of existence;
But *sat-cit-amṛta* (Being-Consciousness-Immortal) am I —
Attaining this lucidity, emboldened,
With no attachment to being or non-being,
Let one gently, gently merge into *Aum sat*!

Auṁ Sat.
Auṁ Peace ! Peace ! Peace !

Glossary

Abhāva : Non-existence. The opposite of *bhāva*. Non-existence is of two sorts:

(1) The absence of one entity in another (*saṁsarga-abhāva),* which is of three kinds:

(a) Prior non-existence (*prāg-abhāva*)

(b) Annihilative non-existence (*pradhvaṁsa-abhāva*)

(c) Absolute non-existence (*atyanta-abhāva*).

(2) One object not being another (*anyonya-abhāva*) or reciprocal non-existence.

Abhinna-nimittopādāna-kāraṇa : A cause that is both a material cause (*upādāna-kāraṇa*) and an efficient cause (*nimitta-kāraṇa*) at the same time. *Brahman,* as the causal Substance, is the material cause of the world. Itself assuming the form of the ever-changing world, with no external efficient cause, because nothing external to It exists, *Brahman* is the efficient cause also of the world. Thus, as the cause of the world, *Brahman* is designated as the material-cum-efficient cause (*abhinna-nimitta-upādāna-kāraṇa*).

Adhikārī : One that is competent for something. In Vedānta, one competent for wisdom.

Adhyāsa : Superimposition; false attribution; illusion.

Adhyasta : That which appears to exist because of *adhyāsa* (see).

Adṛśya : Not perceivable; unknowable.

Advaita : Non-duality. The vision that one Reality alone has existence.

Āgāmī-karma : *Karma*s still to be done in life, in the future (see *karma).*

Agni : Fire, also called *tejas.*

Ahaṁkāra : The I-sense every individual has.

Ahaṁkṛti : Another word for *ahaṁkāra*.

Ahanta : I-sense denoting the subjective aspect of a knowledge situation.

Ajahal-lakṣaṇā : The indirect meaning of a sentence in which the literal sense is not forgone.

Ajāta-vāda : The theory that no creation ever takes place; what exists already merely becomes transformed into new forms.

Ajñāna : Ignorance. The mistaken notion concerning oneself and the world, that what appears manifestly is real, while completely oblivious of the one all-underlying Reality called *Brahman* or Ātman that is indestructible. The opposite of *jñāna.*

Ajñānin : The ignorant. The opposite of *jñānin.*

Ākāśa : Space. That which gives room for everything to exist. Also called *vyoman.*

Amṛtam : Immortality or the immortal Reality. Poetically imagined as the elixir within the golden pot that emerged from the Milk-Ocean when the *deva*s and the *asura*s churned it together.

Anādi : The beginningless. *Brahman* is beginningless and endless. *Māyā* and *avidyā* are also beginningless, but are not *ananta* (endless), because they cease to be when one attains *jñāna* (wisdom).

Ānanda : Bliss. To be understood in the context of the Good in Western Philosophy as the Supreme Value. *Sat, cit* and *ānanda* are terms conjointly used to describe the Absolute (*Brahman*) in Vedānta. Concerning an individual being, *ānanda* is to be understood as the value-consciousness that enables one to evaluate one's own experiences as either pleasant or unpleasant.

Ananta : The endless.

Anātmā (*Anātman*) : Non-self. That which appears to be real.

Aniṣṭa : The feeling of disliking something. One of three attitudes one can have towards any object (see *iṣṭa* and *udāsīna).*

Anṛta : The untrue. The opposite of *ṛta* (see).

*Antaḥkaraṇa*s : In Indian Psychology, the common name of the four mental faculties involved in the process of knowing, namely, *manas* (questioning and imagining), *buddhi* (reasoning), *citta* (memorizing and recalling) and *ahaṁkāra* (relating what is known to oneself in terms of value-experience).

Antaryāmin : Literally, that which controls from within. *Brahman* is the Substance in all the worlds, controlling them from within. *Brahman* thus is conceived of as *antaryāmin*.

Anyonya-abhāva : Reciprocal non-existence. One of four types of non-existence (*abhāva*). The condition in which the existence of one thing necessarily means the non-existence of another.

Atyanta-abhāva : Absolute non-existence. One of the four types of *abhāva* (non-existence). That which has no existence anywhere, at any time, e.g., the horns of a hare.

Aparā : Relativistic, conditional, the immanent here and now aspects of reality. (See *parā*.)

Aparokṣa-jñāna : Non-indirect knowledge, as against both direct perceptual knowledge (*pratyakṣa-jñāna*) and indirect knowledge (*parokṣa-jñāna*) (see). Self-knowledge alone is the example of *aparokṣa-jñāna*. Narayana Guru, by defining *pratyakṣa-jñāna* in a different way, equates it with *aparokṣa-jñāna*.

Aṛivu : A Malayalam word signifying consciousness *cit*. Often used as a synonym of the Self by Narayana Guru, in the sense of pure Consciousness, whose functional aspects are experienced as various mental faculties. As the Ultimate Reality, it is boundless.

Ārta : One afflicted with sufferings.

Asat : The unreal; the non-existent; that which is morally void.

Asti-bhāti-priya : Existence-functional modes of consciousness — experience of pleasure or pain. The essence of *sat-cit-ānanda* as experienced by an individual.

Ātmā (Ātman) : The Self (from the root *āt*, meaning "to pervade"). The invisible reality or stuff that pervades all visible forms. Often confused with *jīva*, the soul. Used in slightly altered senses according to the context. The simplest meaning of the word is "I" or "oneself." Also used sometimes to denote one's own body.

Ātma-māyā : The *māyā* (see) inherent in Ātmā (the Self) (see).

Āvaraṇa-śakti : One of the *śakti*s (powers) of *māyā* (see). One power of *māyā* veils the ultimate Reality, *Brahman*, from view. This specific power of *māyā* is called *āvaraṇa-śakti*. The other is *vikṣepa-śakti* (see).

Avidyā : Nescience or ignorance. The function of consciousness by which the unreal is taken as the real, and the real as the unreal. The root cause of illusions and sufferings.

Avyākṛta : Literally, that which is not specifically shaped. The gold-substance in an ornament has no specific form; then it is called *avyākṛta*. When given a specific shape it is called *vyākṛta*.

Avyakta : That which is not specific or definable. The opposite of *vyakta*.

Ayam-ātmā-brahma : One of the *mahā-vākyas* (see). It means, "This self is *Brahman*" (see).

Bhāga-tyāga-lakṣaṇā : One of the ways the indirect sense of a sentence is grasped. This way forgoes the literal sense partly. *Bhāga* = partly, *tyāga* = to give up; *lakṣaṇā* = indirect sense.

Bhagavān : The word denoting God, used in the context of devotion (*bhakti*). Literally, one in possession of brilliant qualities (*bhagas*).

Bhakta : A devotee. Literally, one who constantly meditates on what one adores.

Bhakti : Devotedness. Derived from the root *bhaj*, meaning "to meditate constantly on something." It can either be fully supported by wisdom (*jñāna*) or be in the form of full surrender to God with no understanding as such. The latter form is known as *prapatti*. A devotee is called *bhakta* (see).

Bhāna : Any apparent manifest form of consciousness. Literally, "lustrous appearance."

Bhāva : Any transient form that the eternal Reality (*sat*) assumes. Without *bhāva*, *sat* never exists, neither can *bhāvas* be without *sat* existing.

Bhavābdhi : Another word for *saṁsāra-sāgara*, the ocean of becoming or changes. *Bhava* = becoming, *abdhi* = *ocean.*

Bhava-sāgara : The same as *bhavābdhi*. *Bhava* = becoming, *sāgara* = ocean.

Bhrama : Confused or uncertain state of mind.

Bodha : Consciousness.

Brahman : The Absolute. Derived from the verb root *bṛh* meaning, "to grow constantly" Literally, "that which grows constantly."

Brahmavit : The knower of *Brahman*.

Buddhi : Understanding. Also denotes the reasoning faculty of mind. (see *antaḥkaraṇas*).

Caitanya : Another word for *cit*.

Cetanā : The life principle that animates beings. *Cit* in its functional state.

Chandas : Prosody. Regarded as one of the auxiliary disciplines of the Vedas. Vedic hymns. Vedic metres.

Cidākāśa : The consciousness-space (*cit* + *ākāśa*).

Cid-vastu : Consciousness considered as a substance. *Cit* = Consciousness; *vastu* = substance.

Cit : Literally, "Consciousness." The essesntial content of the imperishable Reality pervading all the perishable and visible forms, is pure Consciousness. Hence, *Brahman* is designated as *cit* in essence. See *sat* and *ānanda* also.

Cittam : The memorizing and recalling faculty of consciousness (see *antaḥkaraṇas*).

Daivam : The word denoting God in the Malayalam language, though originally a Sanskrit word. In the latter language it means, "fate, destiny, luck, fortune."

Dama : Checking and turning away the senses from distractions. One of the prerequisite mental preparations for attaining the wisdom of the Absolute.

Darśana : Literally, "vision." The Indian equivalent to "philosophy." Vision of Reality as seen from the point of view of a given system of philosophy. Nyāya, Vaiśeṣika, Sāṁkhya, Yoga, Pūrva-Mīmāṁsā and Uttara-Mīmāṁsā are the six such systems of what is called orthodox Indian schools of philosophy. Narayana Guru, in his *Darśanamālā*, uses this word to mean any particular point of view of the non-dual Reality. He presents ten such visions strung together systematically into a garland.

Devatā : A deity. A god as understood in the context of adoration or it worship. Every Vedic hymn has a deity it praises; *chandas*, the particular metre in which it is composed; and a *ṛṣi*, the seer who composed it.

Dhana : Wealth.

Dīpa : A lamp.

Dīpikā : A little lamp.

Dravya : Any substance that inheres qualities.

Dṛḍha-bodha : The conviction attained by an enlightened person. An enlightened one.

Dṛk : Eye. The viewing person, the knowing personal consciousness.

Dṛśya : The visible. That which is visible; the objective world; any object of knowledge.

Dvaita : Duality or dualism. The popular name of Madhva's philosophy. This name is given deridingly to the Madhva system by other schools. He calls his philosophy *tattva-vāda* (the doctrine of the ultimate principle).

Guṇas : Qualities or functional peculiarities inherent in nature *in toto* and in individual beings and things. These are three : *sattva, rajas* and *tamas.*

Guru : (From *gu,* "darkness," and *ru,* "to counteract".) The banisher of darkness or ignorance. A spiritual Master.

Guru-śiṣya-pārasparya : The intimate bipolar rapport between a *guru* and a disciple. No effective imparting of wisdom is possible in the absence of this rapport.

Guru-śuśrūṣā : Personal services a disciple willingly does for his *guru.*

Huta-vaha : An epithet of fire. Literally, the carrier (*vaha*) of oblation (*huta*). Fire is thus named because of the Vedic concept that fire carries all the oblations offered by humans to the gods in heaven for whom these are meant.

Indriyas : Sense organs. The five sense organs and the five organs of action (larynx, hands, feet, excretory organ, genitals) together.

Īśa : The Sanskrit equivalent to God. Literally, one who controls everything.

Iṣṭa : That which is favourable or liked; its opposite is *aniṣṭa.*

Iṣṭa-karma : Pious acts such as performing fire-sacrifices, worshipping deities, contrasted with *pūrtta karma*s which are pious acts meant for public benefits, such as digging public wells, building camp-sheds for travellers, planting shade trees.

Iṣṭāpūrtta-karma : The *Iṣṭa-karma*s (see) and *pūrta-karma*s (see) treated together.

Īśvara : The Sanskrit equivalent to God. *Īśa* + *vara*. *Īśa*, literally, the one who controls everything; *vara* means "the highest". A variant of the word *Īśa*.

Jaḍa : Inert matter.

Jagat : The world. Literally, that which is always on the move.

Jāgrat : (*Jāgarita*) The waking state of consciousness.

Jahal-lakṣaṇā : The indirect sense of a sentence, in which the literal sense is totally forgone.

Jahajahal-lakṣaṇā : The same as *bhāga-tyāga-lakṣaṇā* (see).

Jāti : Caste, kind.

Jijñāsā : The desire to know, inquisitiveness.

Jīva : The Sanskrit equivalent to "soul." Literally, a being that is sustained by breathing. Often confused with *ātmā,* the self.

Jñāna : Wisdom. In the Vedāntic context, the wisdom of non-difference between oneself and the universal Reality. The path of *jñāna* (*jñāna-mārga*) is contrasted with that of rituals or action (*karma-mārga*).

Jñāna-mārga : The path of wisdom. *Jñāna* = wisdom, *mārga* = path.

Jñānin : One who possesses *jñāna* (see).

Jñeya : That which is to be known; the object of knowledge.

Kalā : The minutest part of something; the part of the moon that grows by one day (these are sixteen). Also means "art."

Kāla : Time.

Kāraṇa : Cause. Gold is cause; ornament is effect. What really exists in ornaments is gold alone. Similarly, what really exists as the world is *Brahman* alone, which is its cause. This way of thinking is called *sat-kāraṇa-vāda* (theory giving primacy to cause). Indians distinguish two kinds of causes, viz., *upādāna-kāraṇa* (material cause), like clay for pots, and *nimitta-kāraṇa* (efficient cause), like the potter and his tools.

Kāraṇa-bhāna : Specially used by Narayana Guru to denote that specific mode of consciousness during deep-sleep in which one is ignorant of everything.

Kāraṇa-śarīra : The body with which happiness is unconsciously experienced in deep sleep.

Karma : All actions in general. Philosophically the creative urge inherent in the imperishable Reality, causing the emergence of all manifest forms from Itself. In the Vedic context, the ritual of burnt-sacrifice enjoined by the Vedas. As a religious belief of the Hindus, incipient memory factors or traits that cling to souls as a result of their past deeds. All are bound to enjoy or suffer the fruits of their *karma*s and will have to be reborn for this purpose. One might accumulate more *karma*s in the next birth. This vicious chain of action goes on until one attains final release. Such *karma*s are divided into three categories — *sañcita-karma* (the actions accumulated in all previous births), *āgāmī-karma*s (fresh actions yet to be done in the present lifespan), and *prārabdha karma*s (actions already initiated but eating of their fruits is not finished with).

Karma-mārga : The path of rituals or actions. *Karma* = actions or rituals; *mārga* = path.

Kartr̥tva-bodha : The sense of being the doer of actions.

Kārya : Effect. Clay is cause and pot an effect. Also means, "that which is to be done."

Krama-sr̥ṣṭi-vāda : The theory of creation through gradual evolution.

Lakṣaṇārtha : Indirect meaning as against the direct literal meaning (*vācyārtha*).

*Laukika-karma*s : Worldly actions (*laukika* = worldly).

Laya : Dissolution; final dissolution of the world; complete absorption of the mind.

Līlā : Sport. Play. The world is often thought of as a sportful self-expression (*līlā*) of what really exists, *Brahman* or God.

Loka : The world. Literally, that which is perceptible.

Madhyama-adhikārī : One competent of a middle order for acquiring wisdom.

Mahas : Glory.

Mahat : The great, the adorable. The second stage of evolution of *prakr̥ti* according to the Sāṁkhya system.

Mahā-deva : Literally, the great god or the greatest among those who are brightness in essence. An epithet of Śiva also.

*Mahā-vākya*s : Literally, "the great dicta." The conclusive formulae of Vedāntic wisdom, such as *tat tvam asi* (That thou art), *aham brahma* *asmi* (I am *Brahman*), *prajñānam brahma* (*Brahman* is Consciousness), *ayam ātmā brahma* (This self is *Brahman*), *aum tat sat* (*aum*, that is what is real), *sarvam khalvidam brahma* (everything here indeed is *Brahman*).

Manas : Mind. That which is constituted of *manas* is called *manomaya*. *Manas* consists of the questioning and imagining faculties of consciousness.

Manda-adhikārī : One of the lowest competence for wisdom.

Mantra : General name for the part of the Vedas that praises deities. Each stanza of such Vedic hymns or Upaniṣads. Literally, that which, on being cogitated upon, saves (*mananāt trāyate iti mantram*).

Matam : Literally, one's confirmed opinion. Also means "religion."

Mātrā : A measure. A unit of measure. In the *Māṇḍūkya Upaniṣad*, each letter of *AUṀ* is counted as a *mātrā* that stands for a *pāda* (quarter) of the function of consciousness.

Māyā : The mysterious urge inherent in the Absolute (*Brahman* or Ātman) to unfold itself as all the worlds and the phenomenon of life. The very appearance of the world thus ends up in becoming a sort of veil put over the Absolute, hiding its vision from our view, creating the illusory vision that the apparent world is real.

Māyā-vaibhava : The mysterious power of *māyā*.

Mukti (*Mokṣa*) : Final Liberation. Literally, freedom.

Mumukṣutā (*Mumukṣutvam*) : The state of being a restless aspirant for Liberation through wisdom.

Nāma : Name. *Nāma* along with *rūpa* (form) distinguishes every individual entity in this world.

Nimitta-kāraṇa : Efficient cause.

Nirvāṇa : Literally, burning out, as of fire. The Buddhist term for final extinction of the individual being. Narayana Guru uses the word in the *Darśanamālā* to cover all kinds of goals of spiritual enquiry.

Nirvedam : Another word for *vairāgya* (see).

Nitya-anitya-viveka : The ability to discriminate the eternal from transient.

Nityam : That which is eternal. The word is also used to mean "that which is related to our day-to-day life."

Parā : Beyond; pertaining to the ultimate or supreme, as opposed to the immanent here-and-now aspects of reality which is *aparā*. It could mean "the transcendental."

Pāramārthika : Relating to the ultimate metaphysical Reality (*paramārtha*) (*parama*, ultimate; and *artha*, the meaning-content). This is contrasted with *vyāvahārika* (see).

Parameśvara : The Supreme God (*parama* = supreme, *īśvara* = controller).

Pariṇāma-vāda : Theory of evolution. The theory that the world emerged as a result of gradual evolution. The same as *krama-sṛṣṭi-vāda* (see).

Pradhāna : That aspect of *māyā*, according to Narayana Guru, because of which the potential for the unfoldment of the world is contained in *Brahman*, just as a tree in a seed.

Pradhvaṁsa-abhāva : Annihilative non-existence. The non-existence of something after its external form is destroyed, e.g., the non-existence of pot in its shreds. One of the four kinds of *abhāva*s (see).

Prāg-abhāva : Anterior non-existence; the non-existence of some object in the form of potential in the causal substance before its formulation, e.g., the non-existence of pot in the clay.

Prajñā : Consciousness.

Prājña : Name of the functional consciousness during the deep sleep state.

Prajñānam brahma: One of the *mahā-vākya*s (great dicta) (see) of Vedānta. It means, "*Brahman* is Consciousness."

Prakṛti : Nature. Literally, that which is always in an active state. This activeness is inherent in the ultimate Reality or *Brahman*. *Brahman* in its active state is called *prakṛti*.

Pralaya : The Deluge. Literally, proper dissolution.

Pramā : Certitude arrived at through valid means of knowledge or *pramāṇas* (see).

Pramāṇa : Any valid means of certitude (*pramā*). Six of them are recognized by Vedāntins, and their validity is only in respect of worldly knowledge. They are *pratyakṣa* (perception), *anumāna* (inference), *upamāna* (analogy), *śabda* or *śruti* (scriptual testimony), *arthāpatti* (presumption), and *anupalabdhi* (non-apprehension).

Pramātṛ (*Pramātā*) : The knower. The Subject.

Prameya : That which is to be known definitely with the help of *pramāṇas* (see).

Prāṇa : The vital breath. The functions of vital breath are identified as five, namely *prāṇa* (going upward), *apāna* (going downward), *vyāna* (that which takes vitality to every part of the body), *samāna* (that which keeps the balance of the body), and *udāna* (that which leaves the body at death).

Praṇava : Another word for *auṁ*. Literally, the ever new.

Prārabdha-karma : See *karma*.

Prārthanā : Prayer, particularly the prayer of petition.

Pratibhā : Any idea that is formulated or shines in the mind.

Pratibhāsa : Phenomenal appearance.

Pratipat : Another word for *cit*.

Pratyag-ātmā : The most interior self-experience where subject becomes object, and their duality vanishes. *Pratyak* + *ātmā* : *pratyak* = the most interior or backward, *ātmā* = the self.

Pratyakṣa-jñāna : Perceptual knowledge.

Pūrta-karma : Any act of pious liberality, such as digging public wells, planting shade trees, building camp sheds for travellers. One of two kinds of meritorious deeds according to Vedism (see *iṣṭa-karma*).

Puruṣa : Literally, person. The word is used both in universal and particular senses. In the universal sense, He is the cosmic person who has the entire cosmos for His body. In this sense, He is often called *virāṭ puruṣa*. In the particular sense, the word denotes the individuated consciousness that possesses each body.

Rāga : The attachment one develops towards pleasurable objects.

Ṛṣi : A seer, an inspired sage, a singer of sacred hymns.

Ṛta : The eternal Reality unfolded as the world order, as well as the moral order of human life. Truth.

Rūpa : Form, along with *nāma* (name), distinguishes every individual entity in this world. Hence the world is often spoken of as constituted of *nāmas* and *rūpas*.

Saccidānanda : Existence-Consciousness-Value experiençe, the only positive definition of *Brahman*. (See *sat*, *cit* and *ānanda*.)

Sad-gati : The ultimate goal of life; also its attainment.

Sākṣātkāra : Realization.

Sākṣī-caitanya : The self or consciousness conceived as the witness (*sākṣī*) of all that is objective as well as subjective.

Śamādi-ṣaḍka: (*śamādi* = *śama*, etc.; *ṣaḍka* = six). The six self-disciplines a seeker has to undertake on his own to make him competent for acquiring wisdom. The six are, *śama*, restraining the mind; *dama*, restraining the sense organs; *uparati*, withdrawing oneself from depending on what is external; *titikṣā*, endurance; *śraddhā*, full faith in the words of the *guru* and of the scriptures; and *samādhāna*, to make the mind always oriented towards *Brahman*, the ultimate Reality.

Saṁhāra : Dissolution. The function of Śiva. It happens constantly as the reverse of *sambhūti*.

Saṁkalpa : Mind's wilful imagining.

Saṁsāra-sāgara : The ocean of phenomenal becoming. *Saṁsāra* = the phenomenal becoming or that which is always changing; *sāgara* = the ocean.

Saṁśayātmā : One who doubts the truthfulness of one's own *guru*'s teaching.

Saṁvit-sāgara : The ocean of consciousness. *Saṁvit* = consciousness; *sāgara* = ocean. The ultimate Reality is Consciousness in essence, and It is boundless like an ocean. Hence It is termed *saṁvit-sāgara*.

Sañcita-karma : See *karma*.

Sapta-jihvā : One of the epithets of fire; literally, the seven-tongued one: *kāli* (the black), *karāli* (the terrible), *manojavā* (swift-like-mind), *sulohitā* (the brightly red), *sudhūmravarṇā* (the copper-brownish), *sphuliṅginī* (the scintillating), and *viśvarucī* (the all-devouring) are the seven tongues according to the *Muṇḍaka Upaniṣad* (2.5.4).

Śarīra : Literally, that which perishes. The physical body or the visible and perishable aspect of existence.

Sarvam khalvidam brahma : Everything here indeed is *Brahman*. One of the *mahā-vākyas* (see).

Sarvāntaryāmin : That which controls everything from within (see) *antaryāmin*.

Sat : that which exists always. The subsisting Reality in all the transitory forms of the visible world, even as gold is the reality in all ornaments. *Brahman*, as this subsisting Reality, is designated as *sat*. See *ānanda* and *cit* also.

Sat-kāraṇa-vāda : The theory that cause alone is Real and all effects are superimpositions projected on to the cause, and thus unreal. This is the theory of Śaṅkara.

Sāyujya : Experiencing one's own merger in the Absolute.

Siddhi : Unworldly attainments; attainment of one's final goal.

Śraddhā : One of the prerequisites on the part of a seeker. Willingness to have full faith in the truthfulness of the words of the *guru* and of the scriptures. A necessary stepping stone to *manana.*

Sṛṣṭi : Creation of the world.

Sthiti : Sustenance of the world.

Sthūla-bhāna : The gross manifestation of Consciousness, the ultimate Reality, resulting in the experience of the gross (*sthūla*) world.

Sthūla-śarīra : The gross body with the help of which consciousness in its waking state becomes aware of the gross world.

Stotra : A hymn in praise of a deity.

Stuti : The same as *stotra* (see).

Sukṛta : Literally, that which is done well. In the Vedic context, the one who has performed the Vedic rituals properly, resulting in one's acquiring merits. In the Vedāntic context, the world is thought of as *sukṛta* because it emerged from, or emerges from, *Brahman* in the proper way.

Sūkṣma-bhāna : The functional mode of Consciousness because of which the subtle factors such as mind and sense organs, their objects and vital functions, emerge.

Sūkṣma-śarīra : The subtle body with the help of which consciousness creates and enjoys dreams.

Suṣupti : Deep sleep.

Svapna : Literally, the sleeping state. As a functional state of consciousness, it denotes the dreaming state.

Svarga : The Vedic heaven or Paradise, inhabited by *devas* (gods), whose chief is Indra.

Tamas : Dark and inert.

Taṁpurān : The Tamil and Malayalam word meaning "the Lord." Literally, one's own (*tam*) master (*pirān*).

Tapas : Austere self-discipline. Literally, heating up.

Tat-tvam-asi : "That thou art," one of the *mahā-vākya*s (see).

Titikṣā : Endurance of troubles incidental in life, without petulance or self-pity. One of the prerequisite qualities of a seeker.

*Triguṇa*s : The triple modalities of nature, conceived by Kapila in the *Sāṁkhya-Pravacana-Sūtras*: *sattva* (pure), *rajas* (active), and *tamas* (dark-inert).

Tripuṭi : The three factors involved in the event of knowing something, namely, the knower, the known and the act of knowing. Literally, the three-petalled one.

Turīya : Literally, the fourth. The transcendental state of consciousness in which the *tripuṭi* (see) merges in the all-engulfing self-radiance. Narayana Guru defines it as, "To know transparently that which is bottomless and topless, from top to bottom."

Turīya-bhāna: The mode of consciousness in which one is fully aware, "I am *Brahman* indeed."

Udāsīna : Indifference; the state in which no like or dislike persists.

Upādāna-kāraṇa : Material cause.

Upādhi : Conditioning factor that makes the indistinct Reality appear in distinct forms, or indistinct consciousness appears as distinct knowledges.

Upādhi-paricchinna : That which is limited by conditioning factors. *Upādhi* = conditioning factor; *paricchinna* = having become limited or divided.

Upamiti-jñāna : Knowledge acquired through inference.

Upaniṣad : When the chapter of *karma* or ritualistic action has been transcended by a religious student or *brahmacārin*, he is ready to receive the posterior philosophical teachings which constitute Vedānta (i.e. the end of the Vedas). The Vedānta is non-theological, being concerned with the Absolute or *Brahman*. The word is said to be derived from *upa*, "just below" and *niṣad*, "sitting near," so that it is a teaching received by a disciple when he is allowed to sit and listen to philosophical teachings near or by the side of the *guru*.

Uparati : The disposition of not being influenced by external matters and considerations when deciding what to do and how to do in the course of life.

Uttama : The best.

Uttama-adhikārī : The best among the competent for wisdom.

Vācyārtha : Literal sense of a word or sentence.

Vāda : Argument; theory put forward.

Vaidika-karmas : The rituals enjoined by the Vedas or any symbolic action. *Vaidika* = that which is related to the Vedas or that which is related to knowledge; *karma* = rituals, actions.

Vairāgya : Sense of detachment towards everything transient.

Vāsanā : Incipient memory factors or propensities that are inborn within individuals. Such unconscious factors decide to a great extent how one behaves in life.

Vedas : The earliest of the Indian scriptures, collected into four works, namely the *Ṛgveda, Yajurveda, Sāmaveda,* and *Atharvaveda.* These praise Indra, Varuna, Mitra and other phenomenal gods of nature. The word literally means "knowledge."

Vedānta : Literally, the end part of the Veda, as referring to the Upaniṣads. Also means the end of knowledge signifying the philosophy of the Upaniṣads, because the wisdom it teaches puts an end to one's quest for knowledge.

Vibhuḥ : The all-pervading.

Vibhūti : Specific manifest form.

Vidvān : A learned person.

Vidyā : Knowledge or science. That function of consciousness because of which one understands the Real as the real and the unreal as the unreal.

Vikṣepa-śakti : One of the powers of *māyā*. Besides obstructing the vision of the Real, *māyā* causes also seeing something unreal, the world, as if projected on (*vikṣepa*) the Real. This latter power of *māyā* is called *vikṣepa-śakti;* (see) *āvaraṇa-śakti* also.

Viṣaya : Any object of knowledge.

Vivarta-vāda : The theory that what seems to be creation is only the appearance of forms, effecting no intrinsic change in the causal Reality, the one pure Consciousness or *Brahman*. Thus creations are mere illusory appearances.

Viveka : Discrimination. The natural capability in one to discriminate the eternal from the transient in life, both existence-wise and value-wise.

Vyākṛta : Reality having assumed a specific form (see *avyākṛta*).

Vyāvahārika: That which is related to the day-to-day affairs of life, in contrast to *pāramārthika* (see).

Yajña : Sacrifice. The Vedic fire-sacrifice. It denotes offering what is considered as possessed by an individual, back to the universal *prakṛti* to which everything, including ourselves, really belongs.

Yoga : (from the root *yuj* meaning, "joining together") Each finding their inseparable oneness with the one causal Reality, just as an ornament finds its oneness with gold.

Different systems of *yoga* have been developed in India, each giving emphasis to some particular pair to be joined together. Patañjali's system is known as *Rāja-yoga*. The names such as *Haṭha-yoga, Karma-yoga, Jñāna-yoga,* and *Bhakti-yoga* are popular. Each of the eighteen chapters of the *Bhagavad-Gītā* is also named a *yoga*. The *Bhagavad-Gītā* claims itself to be a Yoga-śāstra (textbook on the science of *yoga*).

As a contemplative method of self-enquiry, the way of expressing an inexpressible reality by showing its two opposite expressible sides and leaving the unitive meaning to be intuitively perceived or understood by the reader or seeker on his own. For example, attaining immortality and crossing over death are two expressions that mean the same. But these two expressions are opposite in nature. They have in between them a meaning that cannot be expressed as it is.

Yoga-buddhi : The awareness attained by the method of *yoga* (see *yoga*).

Yogī (*Yogin*) : One who is an adept in *yoga*.

Yugapat-sṛṣṭi-vāda : The theory of instantaneous creation. The concept that the world is created instantaneously, as when the world appears upon waking up from deep sleep.

Index